Piracy Survival Guide

A cruisers guide to dealing with piracy

Captain Michael Pierce

Published by Capt Michael Pierce
dba: Celeste Publishing

Copyright © 2010 Capt Michael Pierce

Reproduction or publication of the content in any manner, without express permission of the author, is prohibited. No Liability is assumed with respect to the use of the information herein. Printed in the United States of America.

Library of Congress Cataloging in Publication Data

Capt Michael Pierce

   Piracy Survival Guide A cruisers guide to dealing with pirates

Includes index, Piracy Survival   2. Cruisers guide   3. Vessel Safety Management   4.   Distress Signals   5.   Open Water Survival   6.   Mariners Resources

Cover Photo: Released by the French Defense Ministry Licensed through Associated Press World Wide Photos

Questions regarding the content of this book should be addressed to:

Piracy Survival Guide

info@piracysurvivalguide.com

Copyright © 2010 CAPT MICHAEL PIERCE

All rights reserved.

ISN-0-615-36668-6
ISBN-13: 978-0-615-36668-5

Figure 1 My father kneeling and myself behind him on right.

Preparing for departure

DEDICATION

For: My Parents, Sam & Jean Pierce who taught me to go after your dreams, and that I could accomplish without limitations. And my daughter: Angelina Celeste Pierce who taught me of how much a person could love.

Contents

DEDICATION iii
HISTORY OF PIRACY 1
PIRATE ATTACKS 9
UNITED STATES 13
CARIBBEAN 15
CENTRAL AMERICA 21
COLUMBIA 29
VENEZUELA 41
BRAZIL 61
EUROPE 65
GULF OF ADEN 67
INDIANA OCEAN 93
SOUTH EAST ASIA 109
DANGEROUS REGIONS 119
DANGER AREAS 125
PIRATES 133
PORT OF CALL 141
PIRACY IN PORT 147
PIRACY 157
PIRATE TACTICS 165
COUNTERMEASURES 165
TECHNOLOGY 181
PLAYING THE GAME 187
DEVICES FOR 195
VESSEL SECURITY 203
GUNS ONBOARD 211
PASSAGE PLANNING 223
TAKING COMMAND 231
SLEEP OVER WITH 237
UNINVITED GUEST 237
RANSOM OR ESCAPE 249
AND EVASION 249
VESSEL SAFETY MANAGEMENT 253
SAFETY INSTRUCTIONS 255
INTERNATIONAL 257
DISTRESS SIGNALS 257
OPEN WATER SURVIVAL 259
MARINERS RESOURCES 264
ABOUT THE AUTHOR 279

Captain Michael Pierce

Disclaimer

I am not a lawyer and can not give advice on legal matters. I simply describe a situation one mariner too another, as to the problems that exist and possible solutions. Mariners deal with many emergencies and specialties that need studied to obtain proficiency at them. It is up to you as a mariner to study each specialty involved with our love for travel and the oceans. You must break down each situation too its specialty involved such as in self defense, weapons, hand to hand combat, survival and other topics involved in travel and safety. Research it yourself and practice to become proficient that you can depend on your capability in an emergency. Your life and your responsibility.
Best wishes!

ACKNOWLEDGMENTS

It is fitting to begin by acknowledging those who provided me with the use of information as well as those who provided the experiences needed for the writing of this book. Also those who work so diligently at providing information for those of use who love to sail, in order to make our travels safe.

I am a mariner, and like most of you; could say that English is a second language and American-ese my primary. So please forgive the mistakes, I feel the substance is of more importance than the opinions of the critics. Because of recent attacks on cruisers believe it is important to share this with those who need it without further delay.

I would also like to thank those at www.noonsite.com, www.icc.com; as well as the others for the use of records on pirate attacks against yacht owners and sailors. Without this it would not have been possible to provide the examples showing the importance of diligence on the subject of piracy. My hope is that those who read this book will utilize the information, and visit the sites that provide the information on pirate attacks; and while doing so support them, to insure the information continues to be available in the future.

I would like to thank my friends and crews members who traveled with me in the past; for the pleasure of their company. To my friends who have shared in this great adventure. May you all have good winds and calm seas; I hope that we can do it again. In addition, for my mother and my father, who state that their prayers are the only reason I am here today.

Thank you!

Capt Michael Pierce

The wise navigator uses all reliable aids available to him, and seeks to understand their uses and limitations. He learns to evaluate his various aids when he has means for checking their accuracy and reliability, so that he can adequately interpret their indications when his resources are limited. He stores in his mind the fundamental knowledge that; may be needed, in an emergency. Machines may reflect much of the science of navigation, but only a competent human can practice the art of navigation.

American Practical Navigator, 1962 ed.

PIRACY SURVIVAL GUIDE

A Cruiser Guide to Dealing with Pirates

By Captain Michael Pierce

Figure 2 History of Piracy

HISTORY OF PIRACY

When you try to pin point a date for the start of piracy, it is necessary that you go back, to a time when people first started using the waterways. Piracy has actually been around, as long as the technology that was developed for use upon the waters. The earliest reference to piracy, in the historical record, is that of the people who threatened the Aegean, and Mediterranean Seas, in the 13th century B.C. known as the *Sea People*.

The Greeks, recorded the period of the *Thracian Pirates,* who used the Island of Limnos, as their home port. The *Phoenicians,* resorted to piracy, in that they sometimes kidnapped children, selling them as slaves.

In addition, during the 1st century B.C., pirates, along the Anatolian coast, threatened the Roman Emperor. Julius Caesar, was kidnapped, by *Cilician Pirates,* and held prisoner, in the area of *Dodecanese*. The pirates, decided to demand a ransom of twenty talents of gold for Caesar, and he insisted that he was worth at least fifty. Which begs us to bring into question his intelligence?

The first time a government was to make policy for dealing with pirates, was in 67 B.C. The Senate invested Pompey, with powers to deal with the Pirates. It then took him, three months of naval warfare to suppress the threat.

The Goths, traveling as far as Crete, ravaged towns along the Black Sea coast, and the Sea of Marmara, as far back 258 A.D., they were able to seize enormous amounts of booty and enslave thousands.

Rome, established policy to deal with Frankish, and *Saxon Pirates*, who had been attacking the *Armorica,* and *Gaul Coastal* areas, in 286 A.D. Carausius, had been appointed commander of the *Classis Britannica*, which; had been given the responsibility of dealing with the threat of piracy. *Irish Pirates* enslaved Saint Patrick, after his capture in the *Roman province of Britannia.*

The pirates could arguably be the developers of the guerrilla tactic known as the hit-and-run, which was used by the *Pirates* in raiding the coastal areas, for taking slaves and booty. In the middle ages, this tactic perfected, by the *Vikings,* who looted areas from *Scandinavia*, all over Western Europe, including areas of the Black Sea, into the rivers of *Eastern Europe,* to *Persia.*

Muslim Pirates terrorized the *Mediterranean Sea*, and established havens along *Southern France* and *Northern Italy*. *Muslim Raiders* sacked Rome and the Vatican in 846 and controlled the entire *Mediterranean* from 824 to 961.

In the 5th and 6th centuries, the *Adriatic Sea* was so over run with Pirates that it was no longer safe for travel. During 827-82, the Narentines committed acts of p against the *Venetians.* They signed a treaty in *Venice* and baptized their leader into

Christianity. In 835, they broke the treaty and the *Neretva Pirates* were again raiding *Venetian traders.*

Irish Pirates joined with the *Scots* and *Vikings* in the *Welsh* invasion of *England* in 937. During this period, the *Scandinavian Vikings* pillaged *Europe.*

William Maurice convicted of Piracy in 1241 and was the first person recorded to have been hanged-drawn and quartered.

There were the Ushkuiniks or *Novgorodian Pirates,* who raided the *Volga* and *Kama Rivers* in the 14th century. The toughest populations in *Greece* the Maniots were pirates. During this period, piracy became the main source of income for the state, an occupation that circumstances forced on them, because of their state being so poor.

Even in American in its early history, there were people known as fierce warrior pirates and slave traders; the *Haida* and *Tlingit tribes* of *southern Alaska*, who raided *northern California*. Piracy is a worldwide occupation as well as a worldwide problem. As we look back in time, it is interesting that we consider it as being an occupation, and even justified on many occasion. Now, piracy is considered as outlaw behavior, which is a justified conclusion.

There is not a coast that at some period or another has been affected by piracy. You have the *Indian Coast* from the 14th century until modern times. *East Asia* recorded as far back as the 13th century, the *Wokou,* which based in *Japan* and spanned 300 years. The *Chinese Pirates* reaped havoc on area commerce and some of the most dangerous waters of our times are in these areas.

In the area of *Eastern Europe,* the *Cossacks* and *Uskoks committed acts of piracy* in the 16th through the 18th century targeting the inhabitants of the area. In *North Africa* the *Barbary Pirates* ruled the area until the early 19th century. In the *Caribbean,* you had a mixing pot, with pirates from every part of the world. The result of the wealth that is taken from the area, from 14th to the middle 18th century, many of which came after the end of the War of the Spanish Succession. Piracy also used as a method of attacking another country wealth without actually declaring war on them.

The period of 1620 through the early 1700 is considered the romantic age of piracy that we see glorified in the movies. The pirates during this period were groups of men who operated as a democracy with a contract they called "The Article". This covered everything from what being expected from the men in everyday life to how they would divide the proceeds. They even made allowances for those who lost limbs during raids.

At times, you can see that small governments have utilized Piracy as a means to raise funds for their government. Piracy; has also in the past been used as a method of depriving other nations of wealth and supplies needed for growth by competing nations. Piracy is Piracy no matter what name you attach to it, or how you justify the act, the nations who have used pirates usually end up creating a problem for themselves in the end.

During the romantic period of piracy, you find that they favored larger vessels with guns to make a good fight. In modern times, they prefer *small fast vessels*, making the approach of their target quickly and out of sight. This is particularly the case when shipping routes take the ships through narrow bodies of water.

Examples of these narrows found on maps when looking at the areas of the *Gulf of Aden* and the *Strait of Malacca*. Because of the ships size the features of the coast or the depth of the channel in these area's ships must reduce speed making them vulnerable to approach and boarding by these pirates in small fast boats.

Pirates operate in regions of developing or struggling countries with little of no navy or coastal police. Moreover, the possibility exists that the government in these areas are aware; and a part of the problem in some countries. Caution, must be taken when dealing with officials and individuals in these parts of the world.

They sometimes attack vessels in international waters and escape by entering waters controlled by governments that considered unfriendly to the people who may pursue them.

It is important for mariners to become familiar with the information available on the areas of danger as well as the methods and tactics of the pirates. The important websites that record this information maintain reports on pirate activity with records of attacks back to 1995. The information includes the particulars of the attack or tactics used by the pirates the time and other information. When preparing for an ocean trip those in charge, should research information on not only the countries they plan to visit, but also any that they will travel close too.

This information will affect your route and aid you in planning a safe passage. The information may not matter to you now, but this book will show you how important it should be when planning your passages.

In 2006, there were 239 attacks, 77 crewmembers kidnapped, 188 taken hostage with 15 attacks resulting in murder. In 2007 attacks rose by 10%; with 263 attacks with a 33% increase of attacks involving guns. Crewmembers injured were 64 in comparison to just 17 in 2006; this does not include hostages/kidnappings involving no injury.

You must also remember the authorities believe that fewer than 50% of attacks are reported and this number could be as low as 17%, this could be a result of many things including attack being filed with the wrong sources and not to the home country or possibly that, no one was left to report the attack. This unfortunately is just not, known!

ACTS OF PIRACY INCLUDE THE FOLLOWING ACTS:

- **KIDNAPPING OF PEOPLE FOR RANSOM**

- **ROBBERY**

- **MURDER**

- **SEIZURE OF ITEMS OF THE SHIP**

- **SABOTAGE RESULTING IN THE SHIP SINKING**

Pirates are increasing their use of modern technology to aid in their attacks; examples include Mobile phones, speedboats, assault rifles, shotguns, pistols, mounted machine guns, as well as propelled ammunitions like RPG's and grenade launchers. They also use radar, listen to radios for approaching traffic, and now jam radio signals when they attack vessels.

When planning, it is important to learn of the tactics used by the pirates on your route. Then plan your route using countermeasures to counter there methods used to locate vessels, and devise a plan to handle any attack that could occur while transiting the area. The study of the pirate attacks in the area will provide hints as to how they find and locate vessels in their hunting ground. Knowing there methods can give you the upper hand when trying to avoid them and their attacks. Possible actions to counter their intelligence gathering we will cover in a later chapter.

Recent changes in international law concerning piracy are helping to combat the problem. It is also providing changes to the information that they gather on the subject, which will aid you in your future travels.

International law

Piracy is of note in international law, as it is commonly held, to represent the earliest invocation of the concept of universal jurisdiction. The crime of piracy is considered a breach of _jus cogens_, a conventional peremptory international norm that states must uphold.

Those committing thefts on the high seas, inhibiting trade, and endangering maritime communication are considered by sovereign states to be *host is humani generis* (enemies of humanity).

In English admiralty law, piracy was, defined as petit treason during the medieval period, and offenders were accordingly liable to be drawn and quartered on conviction. Piracy was, redefined as a felony during the reign of Henry VIII.

In either case, piracy cases were cognizable in the courts of the Lord High Admiral. English admiralty vice-admiralty judges emphasized, "Neither Faith nor Oath is to be kept" with pirates; i.e. contracts with pirates and oaths sworn to them were not legally binding. Pirates were legally subject to summary execution by their captors if captured in battle. In practice, instances of summary justice and annulment of oaths and contracts involving pirates do not appear to have been common.

Since piracy often takes place outside the territorial waters of any state, the prosecution of pirates by sovereign states represents a complex legal situation. The prosecution of pirates on the high seas contravenes the conventional freedom of the high seas. However, because of universal jurisdiction, action can be, taken against pirates without objection from the flag state of the pirate vessel.

This represents an exception to the principle *extra territorium jus dicenti impune non paretur* (the judgment of one who is exceeding his territorial jurisdiction may be disobeyed with impunity).

In 2008 the British Foreign Office advised the Royal Navy not to detain pirates of certain nationalities as they might be able to claim asylum in Britain under British human rights legislation, if their national laws included execution, or mutilation as a judicial punishment for crimes committed as pirates.

UNCLOS Article 101: Definition

In the United Nations Convention on the Law of the Sea (UNCLOS) of 1982, "maritime piracy" consists of:

(a) Any illegal acts of violence or detention, or any act of depredation, committed for private ends by the crew or the passengers of a private ship or a private aircraft, and directed:

(i) On the high seas, against another ship or aircraft, or against persons or property on board such ship or aircraft;

(ii) Against a ship, aircraft, persons or property in a place outside the jurisdiction of any State;

(b) Any act of voluntary participation in the operation of a ship or of an aircraft with knowledge of facts making it a pirate ship or aircraft;

(c) Any act of inciting or of intentionally facilitating an act described in subparagraph (a) or (b).

IMB Definition

The International Maritime Bureau (IMB) defines piracy as:

The act of boarding any vessel with, intent to commit theft or any other crime; and with, an intent, or capacity, to use force, in furtherance, of that act.

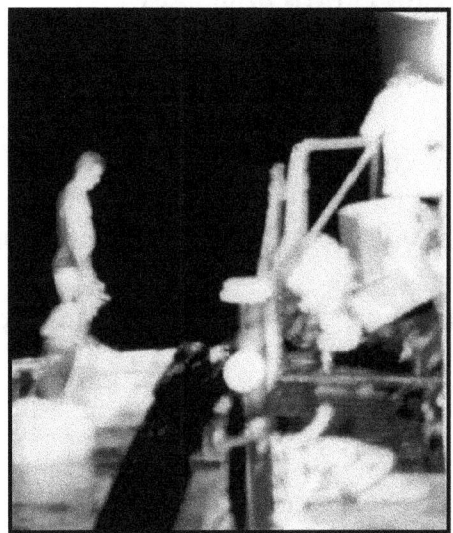
Figure 3 A fisherman caught trying to board

PIRATE ATTACKS
RECENT

When planning a trip to an area before you travel it is very important to check the resources for information on problems within and around the country, you are traveling too. Pay attention to political or religious unrest in the area as well as the attitude of the people towards those of other nationality or religious beliefs.

I cannot stress the importance of checking on the recent attacks and learn the tactics used to help prevent you from falling prey to these predators. In some cases, you may want to consider not displaying your country of origin when traveling to questionable areas. The resources that you should become familiar with are as follows:

http://travel.state.gov.

http://www.noonsite.com/

http://www.noonsite.com /General/Piracy

http://www.safetyandsecuritynet.com

http://www.icc-ccs.org/main/index.php

These are sites that you should become familiar with when planning a trip. You will find the information needed on the country, including the possible crimes committed against travelers and acts of piracy. You will also find information to help such as who to contact for help and information needed while visiting.

When looking for information that you need in order to plan your vessel's security protocol, you study the recent attacks in the area you are planning to travel too or near. Keep in mind that anything you read may be of use, do not ignore any portion of what you can find. The things that you want to take note of are as follows:

- The time of day the attack occurred (day or night, specific time late or early night, etc.)

- What was happening on the vessel at the time of or just before the attack? (Did it appear to the attackers that everyone was asleep or had just gone below and not been paying attention?)

- Did the vessel follow security procedures using lights on deck or in a lighted area like a marina?

- How many attackers were involved?

- What type of vessel and engine did the attackers use? (What is their potential speed in open water in various sea states?)

- The type of weapons, and equipment, used by the, attackers? (Did they have firearms what size or just machetes?)

- How violent were the attacks? (Should the area be by Passed by or avoided?)

- Suspicious activity, prior to the attacks, in port or underway?

- Was help available and when did it arrive?

- Location of the, attack?

- Make note of any information you can use no matter how insignificant.

- Was there any mention of religious beliefs during the attack?

With the information, you gather from these pirate report sources, you can start to plan for a safe trip, avoiding potential life threatening situations and high-risk areas. This includes any location that could submit your boat, crew to the chance of violent or deadly circumstances avoided, and the boat routed around the threat.

When in an area where you have no choice but to proceed, you will plan, using the data you gathered to avoid being located by, and contact with the pirates of the waters you are traveling. Night travel, and waiting for a weather system that can cover your passage as well as, many other tactics that you can use are covered in latter chapters. But before you can utilize these you must know, what you are challenged by; and then you can plan your countermeasure to avoid what you are challenged by.

Gather any available information before planning your trip. Not doing so would be to put your vessel at unnecessary risk. Many of the places you will read about are beautiful and the people very friendly; danger normally not of particular concern to travelers.

Please consider the reputation of the area, when reading the reports and use them as a warning to be used in order to prepare for the areas threats in the future. And not as a reason to avoid an area with very limited problems. You will also read of areas that need to be avoided at all cost. Each individual or vessel has limits and you as captain know your own capabilities. You will make your own decision on which to avoid, and what precautions need to be taken in others.

"The following pages are filled with actual reports of "pirate attacks" that have occurred throughout the world. These are just a few examples so do not consider this as the totality of information that you will need before planning your passage. This is just an example of the events that are taking place, many are a few years old, and when planning your travels you need the most current information to protect your vessel"

The following attack reports have been used by permission of http://www.noonsite.com, http://www.icc/imb.com as well as http://www.onpassage.com To find more attacks and to keep current on the latest situations making possible your safest passage, please visit these as well as the other sites that we have recommended. The following reports have had the names of the individuals and vessels removed.

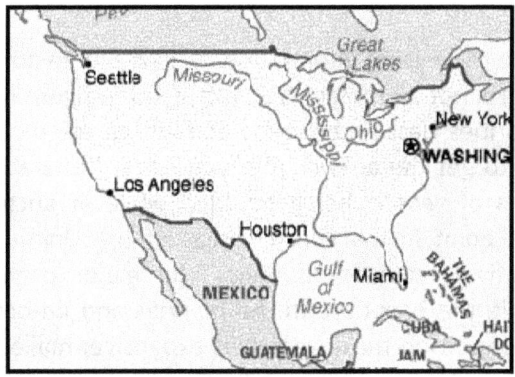

Figure 4 United States

UNITED STATES
Pirate Attacks

In the United States, the problem in getting any idea of the piracy problem is due to how these crimes are reported. Piracy does not have a category of its own and crimes-committed fall under the jurisdiction of the police departments in the area where the crime occurs. As a result, it falls into the regular categories in crime statistics under armed robbery, breaking and entering, or theft. But with the new definition of piracy, the actual numbers could come to the front in the future.

Do not be led into a false sense of security resulting from the lack of information, or the insufficient reporting on piracy in the US or any other country. The Coast Guard does not collect reports on crimes of this nature, and this is probably the same in many other countries as well. You can check with the local area crime statistics, for crimes in marinas on the waterfront to research the activity in any area. Nevertheless, most likely the best resource is word of mouth or reports from other mariners, as well as; travel websites for boaters.

Just because there is no information available in an area, does not mean there is not a problem. You just need to figure out how the local authorities classify the crime and where you would find these reports, to get the answer that you need. Generally there are not reports of vessels being boarded while at anchor and robbed at gun point in the coastal areas of the United States making it relatively safe for boating. The major problem in America is while the boats are in the marinas and un-occupied. Since the equipment on these vessels is expensive, make a good source of income for the local thief's and in many cases easy targets.

As poverty increases in each country, including the U.S., problems will increase gradually which leads to an increasing in boldness and brutality. Should the economy in any country continue to dive the crime rate will increase and those involved in crimes will seek out other opportunities in high priced items and cash, which eventually led to the waterfront, shipping and yachts.

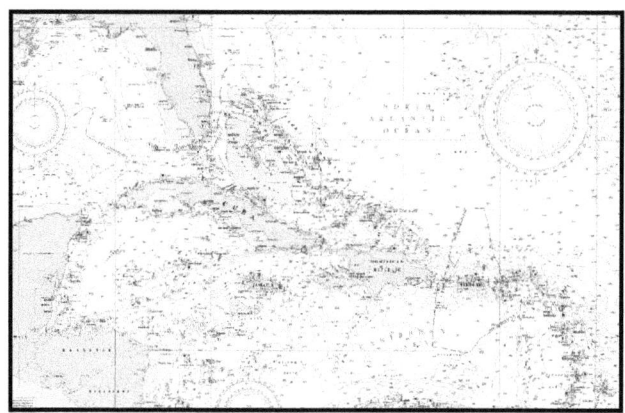
Figure 5 Caribbean

CARIBBEAN
Pirate Attacks

The Caribbean has had a continuous problem with pirates from the times of the Spanish through the age of the rumrunners and into the early days of drug runners. In the recent past, the concern with pirates had almost disappeared. With the economies of the world in trouble, the population increasing and the war on terror in full swing has caused many to slip further into poverty as a result some people have resorted to piracy to seek financial gain in these poor areas.

This along with the militant movement occurring in many places the world over, has made many areas a little less safe for cruisers to visit. No matter where you travel, you need to keep these things in mind and always lean towards safety when in port and at sea. Always maintain a watch or have systems in place to warn and equipment you need to chase off boarders when the situation arises.

Attack off St Vincent

Topic: Piracy Reports 2004

We were, attacked as we lay at anchor off the coast of St Vincent Easter 2004. We were, anchored in Chateau Bel Air on the west coast. Luckily, we all are alive, but they threatened my son with a knife! We would advise all cruising yachtsmen to avoid St Vincent altogether.

Attack at Cow/Bull Bay in St. Thomas Jamaica

Topic: Piracy Reports 2005
Countries: Jamaica

Anchored at Cow/Bull Bay in St. Thomas Jamaica (N 17 53.940 W 76 37.547), at 1:30am in the morning, December 16 2005, we were awoken by someone walking on our deck. Two men had boarded our vessel, one with an assault rifle. There was a third man in a canoe style fishing boat with an outboard motor. The men were interested in money, drugs, and guns. We directed them to our cash on board and they took in total about $4000 in money, electronics jewelry, and alcohol. There was gunfire from shore during this process, and they abruptly left our boat, telling us not to leave or we will be, killed.

We immediately prepared our guns that were, hidden, and started pulling up anchor when they returned (approx. 3 minutes after they left). This time there were five men, 3 with assault rifles on the canoe boat. Once the men started boarding our boat again without permission, I open fired with a handgun and cleared my boat. No shots were return fired, as the assailants were quite sure we were unarmed and this took them by surprise. I continued to pull up, anchor and head towards Kingston, while hailing on VHF channel 16. The Jamaican Coast Guard responded about 30 minutes after continuous hailing, and met us 1.5 hours after the incident.

Yacht Attacked Off Jamaican Coast

Topic: *Piracy Reports 2005*
Countries: *Jamaica*

At the end of May, we met in Port Antonio, Yacht of Spanish Registry, a single hander who was, attacked 4 miles off West point (the lighthouse), a few days before. He was coming from Guanaja, Honduras, with 2 crews, when he was boarded at 2 in the afternoon, by 7 armed men, held at gun point, while the men took money, electronics, his tool kit and several head sails.

He reported the incident at Montego Bay police headquarters, his crew flew straight home, traumatized, and after a short stay in Port Antonio, he has now sailed to Curacao.

I hope that by reporting the piracy to Noonsite, we can alert other cruising yachts to be prudent in this area (We plan to go to Guanaja, as soon as there is a window, and we plan to stay well offshore!)

Boarded and Robbed in Dominica.

Topic: *Piracy Reports 2008*
Countries: *Dominica*

It is with regret that I feel the need to inform your readers of our recent incident in Roseau, Dominica.

We arrived early in the afternoon of June 13, 2008 bare boat catamaran and proceeded to pick up a mooring ball in front. It is just north of the Anchorage Inn. Of course, this decision assisted by the prompt arrival of a local boat boy to make the mooring available, collect a fee, and points the way to customs and the bank, etc.

Having never been to Dominica, we decided to avail ourselves of a bit of local knowledge and comply. After clearing customs, we explored a bit of the south end of the island, had dinner, and returned to the boat around 10:30 pm. We were both quite exhausted and went to bed early.

Not being familiar with this boat and her "night sounds" we were aware of some noises but not alarmed enough to investigate them as we thought it was the mooring ball on the hulls. I had left my purse in the cabin and about 20 minutes after turning in, decided to switch cabins to enjoy the mist of an evening drizzle in another bunk (open hatch).

The night passed quietly and seemingly uneventful. The next day at breakfast, we went to pay the bill and discovered that all the cash been removed from the wallet on the boat while we were sleeping. Yes, I know, it should have been divided and hidden better but...hindsight. Good news is they left the passports and credit cards. There is no question as to when the money was, stolen, only "who had done it!" We certainly have our theories!

We checked around with other locals and the owner himself has a good name and reputation. He was quite upset about the incident. The incident was, reported to the Dominican Coast Guard and the board of Tourism as well. Most everyone on the island whom we met was very sad to hear of our misfortune and assured us that Dominica is usually a safe and trouble free place. These folks take a lot of pride in their beautiful island.

He himself also reported that there is apparently a "crack house" just across from the mooring ball where we were. Who knew? One more word of caution, the Dominican Coast Guard, while very respectful, likes to check you coming and going. It is understandable that they have a drug problem and want to maintain a strong presence. Do be advised. However, that they do not make a practice of putting out fenders when they come to check your vessel so be prepared.

Boarded in Roseau, Dominica

Topic: Piracy Reports 2008
Countries: Dominica

We spent two nights on a mooring in Roseau, and on the second night, August 12 2008, two men boarded the boat at 4:15 a.m. I have installed driveway alarms on both of my sugar scoops and the men set them off when they came onboard. The audible alarm scared them and one jumped off the boat while the other tried to hide in his small inflatable under my boat. When I spotted him, he rowed away to pick up his friend in the water. No one was hurt, and nothing was, taken.

Security Fears In St Lucia After Horrific Attack

Topic: Piracy Reports 2006
Countries: St Lucia

Yacht people reacted with horror and concern as the story circulated on Caribbean cruiser nets of a violent incident in St Lucia. The attack occurred on June 19 2006 in St. Lucia's Rodney Bay. Three men boarded a yacht anchored some 50 feet off the shore.

While the couple was sleeping, the man, a Dutch national. Beaten until he lost consciousness, and two of the three intruders raped his French wife.

Police subsequently arrested and charged three men on June 29, but the incident may have further repercussions as other reports have been made of an increase in attacks on tourists generally in St Lucia. It is, hoped that the Saint Lucia Air and Sea Ports Authority (SLAPSA) will soon have a boat with which to patrol waters and act as a deterrent to any similar attacks. The incidents in St Lucia did not appear to be at all isolated. A spate of robberies and attacks on yachts in the Grenadines was, reported in some magazines.

Captain Michael Pierce

Figure 6 Central America

CENTRAL AMERICA
Pirate Attacks

Costa Rica Pirates – Cruisers Be Aware

Topic: <u>Piracy Reports 2008</u>
Countries: <u>Costa Rica</u>

The cocaine from Colombia has been running up both coasts of Central America for years using various methods. The most common method currently appears to be 40 to 50 ft. speedboats with 2 to 3 200 HP engines. When these boats cannot rendezvous with their re-fuelers, they turn to any source, which lately has resulted in pirating small fishing boats at sea for their gasoline.

There have been a number of fishing boats that have mysteriously "gone missing," Anglers thrown into the water to swim ashore, high jacking, beatings, and even the boarding of a large day-sailing catamaran anchored in the crowded anchorage of Tamarindo Beach, Costa Rica.

These cocaine smugglers trying to make it to the next fuel stop; and are heavily armed. For the most part, all they are, wanting is more fuel, however we had been, advised by contacts in Costa Rica that "if you are overtaken by one of these boats, don't try to be a hero; they are probably Para-military, trained and ready to do anything. So let them have the fuel and send them off with a smile." So far, there have been no reports of cruisers being, approached for fuel, however play safe and be on guard. Local police are now using captured drug trafficking boats to patrol this coastline as incidents have increased in recent months.

Possible Piracy Problem – Nicaragua

Topic: Piracy Reports 2008
Countries: Nicaragua

I wanted to let cruisers know of a potential problem off the Mosquito Coast of Nicaragua.

On June 14, 2008, my husband and I were, approached by a 24-foot centre console boat with seven men on board. They hailed us in Spanish and asked if we spoke Spanish. I replied that we did not, and indicated that the other boat (that was accompanying us) had a person on board who could speak Spanish. He seemed to ask where we were, headed, and I told him. He gave me thumbs up signal and then headed for the other boat that was traveling alongside us.

When he approached them, my friend asked him who they were, and what they wanted (in Spanish). The three crew on had tazers, which the seven men saw when they approached. They did not answer and moved away.

They tailed us for a while, and we made up a game plan of what to do if they decided to come after us after dark. This incident happened at 1630. The boat had no flag, no VHF, no radar. It also had two large drums for fuel. Two of the men seemed to have uniforms on, but the other five did not.

I will never know if they were up to no good, but wanted to let other cruisers know about this incident. I had a satellite phone and called the U.S. Coast Guard, but they had no boats in the area to assist us. They later called me back and said it was probably a Nicaraguan Coast Guard boat, but the five of us have our doubts about that. Other than this one incident, we had no other problems traveling around Mexico, Belize, Honduras, and Nicaragua on our way to Panama.

Armed Boarding, and Theft, at Lake Izabal, Guatemala.

Topic: Piracy Reports 2008
Countries: Guatemala

We were sailing in the company of two other yachts, and, anchored just east of the village of El Estor. On our second night, April 2, 2008, four thieves boarded us at 2 a.m. armed with a pistol, machete, nightstick, bolt cutters to take our outboard. Waking in the night I entered the cockpit and was, confronted by the pistol bearing man and managed to disarm him but was beaten on the skull by one of the others and retreated to the cabin.

The engine was, taken and I went to the hospital for x-rays and stitches. The police and navy installation there did not respond to my spouse's calls for assistance. We reported the incident to the authorities that night, but they said there was little they could do.?

The Rio Dulce is safe from hurricanes but not ladrones.

Fatal Pirate Attack on the Boat in, Guatemala

Topic: Piracy Reports 2008
Countries: Guatemala

At approximately 10 p.m. on the night of Saturday 09 August, four men with machetes boarded an anchored vessel, with apparent intent to rob. When they were, met with resistance, it became a cruisers biggest nightmare.

They were, anchored off the small cove near Monkey Bay Marina and a house when the incident occurred. Details are still somewhat sketchy, but in resisting the robbers, husband was, killed and the wife, although seriously wounded, was able to use the VHF radio to summon help.

The stations and boaters that still had their radios on at that hour came to assist, and the wife was, transported to a private hospital in Morales, reportedly with a punctured lung. In a telephone interview from her hospital bed, the wife, 67, said, "They poked us and stabbed us with the machetes, and they were asking for money, specifically dollars."

The thieves were apparently unhappy with the take. "We had a few quetzals (Guatemala's currency), but we had no dollars with us on the boat," the wife recounted.

The couple, who is retired and live near Anchorage, Alaska, had bought the boat in February. They were equipping the vessel in preparation for a voyage into the Caribbean and eventually to the eastern coast of the United States. The wife said the four assailants may have reached the boat by swimming from shore and brandished long machetes that "seemed liked curved swords."

After assaulting the couple, the men demanded she hands over the keys to the vessel, which has an auxiliary motor. When she did not - she was unable to tell whether they wanted the keys to the boat, or a small dinghy the couple used to get to shore - the men left, also apparently by swimming.

She struggled over to the boat's radio and sent out a distress call. "I said we need help ... I said my husband was not moving," she recalled. She said she expects her children to arrive in Guatemala Monday and plans to be, transferred to the United States for medical care. Two suspects have now been, arrested.

According to information received from El Periodico in Guatemala City, They were, taken in custody after a search of their home resulted in the discovery of an ice pick, binoculars believed to have been, taken from the couples' sailboat, as well as a quantity of marijuana.

PANAMA

Pirate Attacks

Another Worrying Incident On Panama to Galapagos Route

Topic: Piracy Reports 2004

Following the attack on the yacht Yume Maru on April 5, 2004, in route to the Galapagos Islands from Panama (Yacht Attacked 400 Miles South West of Panama) Noonsite received the following report:

Information, and a word of caution; for cruisers sailing from; Panama, to the, Galapagos.

On July 14, 2004, we were, chased by a boat near the Isle De Malpelo at 3 deg 48.59 AND by 80 deg 21.6' W. The boat had a dark hull (probably black), small white cabin near the stern, 40 or 50 feet long, raised bow, rigging above the cabin and forward to the bow, the vessel was similar to many of the local, wooden boats we saw in the Galapagos. We first noticed the boat at about 10AM. It became apparent that he was on a collision course with us so we changed our course by 30 degrees. Shortly after we altered our course, he did the same and continued straight for us from the windward side.

We then turned on our diesel engines to increase our speed to 8 or 9 knots. The seas were very heavy and both boats were being knocked around, we were struggling to maintain speed. We are a 37, foot catamaran and seemed to have slightly better control than he did. We began to pull slowly away from him even though he followed our every turn. Eventually, we lost sight of him, and he disappeared from the radar when he was over 5 miles away. We then went to the opposite tack in an attempt to further, elude him. Roughly, two hours later we again spotted him coming directly at us from the windward side. As before, we did everything possible to increase our speed and were able to slowly, pull away from him. We maintained speed for the next 24 hours and never saw him again.

Yacht Attacked 400 Miles South West Of Panama

Topic: *Piracy Reports 2004*

On April 5, 2004 at approximately 15:00 local time, the sailing **yacht Yume** Maru, en-route to the Galapagos Islands from Panama.

Our boat was, rammed on the port side by a fishing-type vessel. The yacht's position at the time was reported as 03°20.0N AND 084°44.0'W, about 400 nm south-west of Panama. The two people on board the yacht report that there were seven or eight men on the fishing boat. Five of these men boarded the yacht armed with knives and handguns. The men who then removed electronics, charts and maps, navigation equipment, marine VHF and SSB equipment, GPS's, some personal jeweler and ransacked the vessel tied up the two people on the yacht.

The suspect vessel is, described as being a fishing-style boat, approximately 20m long. It was, painted with a black top, red bottom, and a white cabin. The victims also reported that the part of the fishing boat that struck their boat had blue paint under the red. After the suspect vessel left, the yacht's crew was able to free themselves and make their way back to Panama.

Yacht Pursued On Panama - Galapagos Route

Topic: *Piracy Reports 2005*

Australian yacht has had a narrow escape from possible pirates en route from Panama to the Galapagos Islands, closely echoing two incidents in 2004. , the Panama contact for the Scandinavian Ocean Cruising Association, forwarded the report to Noonsite.

The incident occurred on Friday February 11th 2005, at 02°13 N 86°22 W, about 300 miles from the Galapagos.

Account of the incident is as follows: "On route to the Galapagos at around 4:00am on my watch things were going as usual. Our watch system had become more and more lax as we were not seeing any vessels, and we were at great distance from any land. Something prompted me to get up and look around, and I saw two lights of a ship on our Starboard side. I was very confused as the brightness indicated a very close proximity, but I could not see the red or green navigation light that would indicate which side of the boat I was looking at. After a while, I woke my wife up to get a second opinion.

Over a period of about the next half hour, the lights continued to get brighter, and then I noticed a second set of lights on our port side getting brighter also. It was becoming obvious that it was not a container ship I was trying to identify but a number of small crafts closing in on us from both sides. After another 20 minutes or so, there appeared another boat coming towards us from another direction. At this point, we were in the middle of at least five boats coming in towards us.

I tried radio contact but none of the vessels responded. From a safety perspective, the situation was becoming more serious until I started to consider these vessels were trying to engage us. I immediately turned off our navigation lights to black out our boat. I noticed then the random direction the boats on our starboard side started to move. I started to head for the gaps to keep them as far away as possible. We managed to slip the net so to speak except for one boat the fastest and brightest of them all.

She clearly had us, on her radar, and; was pursuing, us on an intercept course regardless of the direction we took. With our engine in full power, we continued to keep her at a distance, but she was getting closer by the minute and it was approaching sunrise. As the sun began to rise, we could see the vessel clearly, and now they could see us not only on Radar but also with their own eyes. Their vessel appeared to be about 1/4 to 1/2 a knot faster than ours. We began to prepare, to be, boarded. I asked my wife to make her self less attractive by covering herself up as much as possible, and she got some money out, which would be high on their priority list.

When things were looking desperate, the wind picked up just a little enough to put out some sails, which increased our speed by about 1/2 to 3/4 of a knot. Over the next hour, we could put them over the horizon. I have since learned there was a piracy attack within 90 miles or so last April. A Japanese yacht attacked; and robbed on April 5, 2004 about 400 nm south-west of Panama, and yacht Sandpiper just managed to outrun another boat on July 14, 2004 in a very similar incident to that described above. See Noonsite reports for more details:

Figure 7 Columbia

COLUMBIA
Pirate Attacks

2002 Colombian Incident Should Be Seen in Perspective. An Eyewitness Account

Piracy Archive 2000-2002

As the recent incident at Punta Hermosa on the Colombian coast on September 29 2002, has attracted much interest within the sailing community we are pleased to publish here a report received from a sailing vessel. She was the second boat to be boarded but the crew managed to fend off an attempt to gain access to their cabin.

We are reporting a violent incident that occurred while en route from Aruba to Cartagena on 29 September 2002. After departing Ornamented, Aruba, at noon on 21 September, we made an overnight sail to Cabo de la Vela, where we joined two other boats,

From there we made another overnight sail to Bahia Guayraca in the Five Bays region of Colombia. Previous cruisers had reported that both Cabo de la Vela and Guayraca had appeared to be safe, and we found them to be also. We spent 3 nights in Guayraca waiting for the seas to come down, and then made a short sail around the corner to the anchorage at Rodadero.

This one was a very busy resort town and we were the objects of much curiosity from locals in pedal boats. To be able to cross the Rio Magdelena in morning hours, we wanted to leave Rodadero at about midnight and travel to Punta Hermosa to rest before making the last hop to Cartagena. While en route, one vessel began to have engine problems, which plagued them for the remainder of the day.

A large squall developed, on the approach to Punta Hermosa so we waited until it passed since an uncharted "breakwater" bound the anchorage area and can only, be entered, from the south. We arrived at 1430, anchored about 50 yards from each other (at 10 56.93 N, 75 01.89 W) and planned to depart very early the following morning.

The one vessel owner had worked on their engine, thought it OK, and was going to leave shortly before the other vessel. When we arose at 0300, the one vessel was still there having, experienced more engine problems. They worked on the engine all Sunday morning, were able to our plan for an early morning departure (between midnight and 0300).

The first the other couple knew, the boarders were coming down the ladder into their cabin. The five bandits, armed with three pistols and two shotguns, bound and gagged both of them and proceeded to tear apart the boat. They ripped cabinet doors off, dumped contents, and took virtually everything: sailing electronics; their clothes, passports, boat papers, credit cards, drivers' licenses; the dinghy and engine; kitchen appliances, laptops, and TV; food, etc. They emptied the refrigerator, pouring food over things and throwing eggs. They tormented and repeatedly threatened them, all the while drinking.

The bandits were waving their guns around and one of them discharged--whether by accident or on purpose, we do not know--lodging a bullet in the hinged top of the navigation station. They demanded money, but they wisely told them they only had. What was in their wallets--that otherwise they used credit cards--and the bandits did not find their hidden cash. In short, they completely TRASHED the boat. When we arrived, what few contents, were left was heaped on the cabin floor or on the counter tops. Broken eggshells and egg goop were everywhere. We made haste to help them clean up the mess enough to get underway. We gave them spare VHF and PFDs, broke up the raft shortly after midnight (Monday morning), and headed out for the last 50 miles to Cartagena.

We traveled under power (no wind) in close formation, maintaining no more than 1/4 mile between us all the way, and arrived in Cartagena at about 1030. During the clean-up process, we attempted to contact the Coast Guard on VHF 16. After many calls, we finally got a response from a very weak Spanish-speaking station who asked what the problem was.

We attempted to explain in our poor Spanish, but the signal was too weak to communicate. Eventually, the Baranquilla Port Control responded, in English, and asked about the situation. We explained where we were and what had happened, and that we would report to the Coast Guard when we arrived in Cartagena.

On the way in, we contacted friends already there, via SSB, to alert them to what had happened, and by the time we arrived, the wheels of response were already in motion. The reception we received upon arriving in Cartagena, from the Club de Pesca and Club Nautico marinas and the other cruisers, was marvelous.

The Coast Guard already had been there to get what preliminary information they could, and returned later in the day to talk to both boarded boats. The marina had contacted the check-in agent and informed her of the situation and the other boat had no check-in problems, despite their lack of official documents.

That afternoon, with the assistance of the agent, we made an official police report. We have all since been, re-visited by the senior officers of the Cartagena Coast Guard station who told us this incident is being, given very high priority, and they are intent on catching the perpetrators. In Cartagena itself, the Coast Guard patrols the harbor regularly.

In conclusion, we think it important to note that the increase in the number of boats taking the coastal route to Cartagena has doubtless created a concomitant increase in "targets of opportunity" for potential thievery. Dinghy thefts and petty thefts during stealthy cockpit visits are not, uncommon occurrences in cruising anchorages throughout the Caribbean.

While some boats coming to Cartagena have experienced these kinds of problems, many have made the trip without event. What we experienced, however, which we understand is unprecedented here, upped the ante from inconveniencing robbery to life-threatening piracy. In fact, we just learned that the incident has been, classified as an "act of piracy," which means that the Colombian Navy/Coast Guard will have a larger role, in concert with the National Police, in resolving the incident.

We are very impressed with the Colombian response and with their sincerity in wanting their coast to be safe for cruising yachts. The cruisers in Cartagena are working closely with the authorities to explore what can be, done to help ensure cruiser safety in the future. However, in the end, we cruisers must be alert, aware, and prepared to take care of ourselves, no matter where we are. Until there is some resolution, we would advise avoiding the Punta Hermosa anchorage.

Finally, and perhaps most importantly, we wanted to let everyone know how great Club Nautico and the staff at the Club de Pesca, here in Cartagena, have been to us and to the people on the other boat. In addition, the Coast Guard has been actively pursuing the incident and the local CG station commanders have proposed a meeting with cruisers here in Cartagena to pursue how cruising, the coast can be, made as safe as possible.

They have been extremely receptive to the ideas presented so far and have asked to have a follow-up meeting to discuss the issues further. Moreover, we think it is important to remember (and perhaps point out?) that these types of incidents are not unique to Colombia.

As you well know, shootings have occurred in Venezuela and Honduras in the past year or so; Trinidad was, plagued by armed robberies in at least one of the yards recently; and we just learned via the other boat's insurance agent that a cruiser in Venezuela was recently boarded and beaten (and still in the hospital). We believe it both unfair and untrue to suggest that Colombia is alone in having these kinds of problems (not that your statement did, but that it is important that we do not give that impression!).

We are so far enchanted with Cartagena and its incredibly friendly people. We feel quite comfortable here; and would not hesitate to recommend to other cruisers that they come. We are in fact, working with several friends in the ABCs to help them get here as soon as possible! We intend to be in Cartagena for some time and enjoy this beautiful city and its wonderfully friendly people.

Colombian Attack 2003: The Full Story

Topic: *Piracy Archive 2003*

We bought our boat, in Simonstown, Cape Town 5 years ago. The dream is to sail the seven seas, following the trade winds on our first circumnavigation. We left SOUTH AFRICA 4 years ago, doing the usual, ST HELENA, ASCENSION, FERNADO NORONHA, FORTELEAZA crossing.

On route to TRINIDAD / TOBAGO, we stopped over at DEVILS ISLAND, and stayed for 4 months on the main land, Kourou.

FRENCH, GUIANA.

We sailed up the island chain visiting CARRIACOU, PETIT MARTINIQUE, PETIT ST VINCENT , UNION, TOBAGO CAYS, CANNOUAN, MUSTIQUE, BEQUIA, ST VINCENT, ST LUCIA, MARTINIQUE, DOMINICIA, GUADELOUPE, MONSERRAT, ANTIGUA, NEVIS, ST KITTS to ST MAARTIN, come April the mass evacuation north or south, to be out of the hurricane belt by the official start of the season in June.

We hauled the boat in Trinidad and then left for PANAMA via the VENEZUELAN ISLANDS, TESTIGOS, MARGARITA, TORTUGA, LOS ROQUES, and DE AVES, onto the ABC, BONAIRE, CURACAO, and ARUBA.

The depth of sadness experienced when leaving a place varies according to the friendships acquired, and so it was with sad hearts that we said goodbye to ARUBA and once again set sail for PANAMA via CARTAGENA (a world heritage city). Seventy-two hours on passage, a medical emergency ensured a stop over at Pt Morro Hermosa, Puerto Velero, and Baranquilla, Colombia.

March 27, my brother's birthday, just after midnight, I was, wakened, by the sound of a boat wake hitting our steel hull; they had cut the motor earlier.

They, here I woke him, who is here? He asked,

The freaking welcoming party, I shouted.

He jumped up to close the hatch, and saw the first of six men armed with guns and knives board our vessel.

That night I knew, instinctively, as if I now know factually, that not all was well. I insisted that we lock the companionway, which can only be locked from outside, with a padlock, and so he climbed into the cabin through the hatch, which is left ajar, but secured.

Both hatches have bulletproof glass portholes, and so we could see them trying to smash the glass with the backs of their guns. They did not bring tools with them; they expected the companionway to be open. We are the fourth vessel attacked, in the same anchorage, in as many months. They only had, a little flashlight, and kept telling us to put the lights on. After ransacking the cockpit, they found a small brass porthole and a dive weight and tried unsuccessfully to break the lock open.

By this time, I was calling non-stop on the VHF channel 16 and SSB channel 2182, MAYDAY, MAYDAY. Using the dive weight as a hammer on the back of the knife, they started chopping around the lock. The wood is teak and hard, and it took them over 1 hour to gain entry. I called for help on the radios for the entire duration; the Colombian Coast Guard, who asked me to confirm my position as Pt Hermosa, Puerto Velero, answered me. Never to be heard from again, or ever seen.

The people's outside was getting frustrated, and so the two a side. They tried to lift the hatch up to open it, with enough prying they managed to lift it slightly. With that he could deploy a can of professional mace into 3 faces, he continued to hang on the inside of the hatch holding it down, and they were never able to work out that the hatch slides back to open, not up.

That is what saved us. Once the lock was free they could pull out the first and second splashboards, the third always sticks. With the hatch closed overhead, the entry was small and required crawling. It was safer for them to call us out one at a time, rather than they come inside, as they did not know what else we had to arm ourselves with for protection.

When it became evident that they were going to gain entry, the panic that had seized us earlier, evaporated. Calm overcame us and everything slowed down, it felt like my ears were blocked and my thoughts echoed in my head. I thought, we could die tonight, but that is o.k. I have had an excellent innings and this is as good a time as any…. With that, he took my hand and said when, the door opens, and we get out! Moreover, you get into the water, ASAP. Do not stop to chat, straight in the water, and I will follow.

They called us out, and he went first, three grabbed him, and they struggled around the table. He could maneuver himself to the back of the boat against the rail, the cockpit well is large and open, and so only one person had space to tie him up. He attempted to tie his hands together in front of him, he kept moving, and he was not able to tie a knot. They called for me, and I crawled out, still crouched down in front of the hatch, one person took my arm. One last look at him and I swung my elbow back as hard as I could and felt the crunch when I connected the gent holding my arm. He will not multiply anymore.

In one motion, I could pull myself forward into a dive, off the side of the boat. Hands brushed me in an attempt to catch me, but I was already in the water. He was using the distraction opened his hands and shoved the person back into the well, hitting his head. He was back-flipped into the water and dove down as deep as possible; I heard the splash behind me so turned around to see who was going to pop up. He did, right next, to me, "Swim woman. What are you waiting for" It was a dark moon that night, and we could not see their boat, thinking that it was tied up to our boat, and it would be only minutes before they come for us. We swam for our lives.

Once we were shallow enough to walk, I discovered that my little toe was broken, and he dragged me on the beach and runs to the cell phone, which was exhausting, and in the dark, we ran past friends house, ending up with some other fishermen, who sent a runner to phone the police. They arrived 2 hours later, in that time we heard, what we now know to be a large RED WOODEN FISHING BOAT return to fetch the six bandits and all our belongings. The fishing boat collided with MALAIKA hitting 1.5m above the waterline, bending the bull bar and stanchions on the starboard side, leaving red paint and wood chips behind.

03h00 we returned with 2 policemen, the other 8 stayed on the beach. We were given 10 minutes to assess the damage, and then against our will, we had to leave, to go and make a DENUNCIO, statement at the Baranquilla police station. 03h30 we left for the station. No one spoke English and so our statement was, made in limited Spanish, and many hand gestures.

06h00 we once again returned, this time to discover the actual magnitude of our loss. Our passports, boat papers, our navigation equipment, dinghy & two outboards, eight kites, and two sewing machines (for sail and kite repairs) been the biggest loss. Without passports, we cannot leave, and without kites, we cannot make money to replace our uninsured items.

10h00, we saw a large police presence on the beach, he swam ashore to speak to the police, re red paint, wood chips, balaclava, knife and pair of sandals found on the boat. Edgar, the owner of windsurfing school, arrived and knowing that we were unable to leave without a GPS offered to take us to Baranquilla. We left a cell number with the lieutenant on the motorbike, as a contact no, gave him the above mentioned items and headed to the city, in search of a GPS.

He was tremendous, in 8hrs, we managed to do the impossible, change travelers' checks without passports, buy a GPS, and establish that the one and only red wooden fishing boat has a permanent mooring at Las Florres. An old man on the jetty told us that it left for a fishing trip last night and has not yet returned. One last stop, before we can leave….

Contact the coast guard, office, to inquire as to why, no reaction, from them after their initial response on the SSB. In addition, to purchase a chart of Cartagena, as all our charts, over 500, were, taken as well. Zero help, Zero sympathy, in fact, one woman in the office called us GRINGOS, turned her back and slammed the door. Therefore, we left without an answer and without a chart.

18h00 March 27, we returned from Baranquilla with newly acquired GPS ready to set sail for Cartagena, only to discover the Major and two other policemen sitting in the cockpit, having boarded without permission. The major claimed that they had already arrested four men; he brought out a digital camera and asked us to identify them. Two could have possibly but it was very difficult to say from a photo. He proceeded to take photos of our vessel and us. When we requested to leave, we were, told we would hamper the investigation.

I expressed my fears about being on anchor for one more night, and was, assured by the MAJOR that he would place an armed guard on the boat with us for the night. Three other policemen and the dog arrived. The major made two more phone calls with those four more policemen with tools boarded. Our vessel was, subjected to a 5-hour strip and search, under false pretenses. We assisted the police in every way possible, he helped the two people inside, he elected to drill for them, and to strip what could come loose.

I entertained the rest outside, serving bottomless cups of coffee, and telling sailing stories, one of the police could speak a bit of English, and was constantly, asked to translate, especially the punch lines. I had them rolling around in laughter, except the major. One by one his officers reported to him, No my major, there are no drugs on this boat. By now, the MAJORS intentions were very clear to us.

In addition, I pointed out to him that if we were traffickers, we would have perhaps painted our boat navy gray and not PURPLE. In addition, that we would have owned a gun, with which we would have shot the bandits ourselves, or better still, as one of his own officers pointed out that I have a beautiful collection of Aloe Vera, Rosemary, and Basil, She is growing her own herbs my major, this is not a trafficking boat.

The fear of him planting something on our boat was very real. He had put a lot of effort into finding drugs on our boat, and we did not know how he would handle the disappointment. That fear had an odor, and I broke out in a cold sweat. At 23h30, the major stood up and said,"VAMOS" LETS GO! So this is how he is going to handle the disappointment, he is going to abandon us. I begged him to keep his word, and leave a guard with us.

He laughed and said that we are safe, as we have nothing left to steal. He told us not to leave, as an officer would return for him in the morning, to identify suspects. Therefore, he left us in the dark with no dinghy, no radios, and no way of locking the hatch. A new fear, one that completely dispels any fatigue, I was been suspects, feeling for lack of sleep in the last 50 hours, takes over.

My eyelids would not close, even afraid to blink, in case they never opened again.

08h00 March 28, a policeman returned for him, but he was not able to identify anyone. 14h00 we left for Cartagena. We found a safe haven in Club Nautico, with Chandelaria giving us free mooring, food and a sympatric ear. Thank you seems so inadequate.

The fight goes on, now it is the bureaucratic, red tape, war. 10 Days in Cartegena and we were not able to elicit a response from anyone, police, coast guard, port captain, even wrote to the President. The facts are we were the fourth boat to be attacked, in as many months in the same anchorage, by the same gang, with the same modis operandi, had the good luck of meeting the other pirated vessel, to confirm their story.

Three American boats traveling in convoy attacked. They managed to get to Presidential level, and the ADMIRAL OF THE NAVY, was, given carte blanche to sort this out afterwards. Well obviously, they did not...but worse, they said they did.... There has been no media coverage, the cruising guides, and even the Net on channel 8104 reports all is well in Colombia, otherwise we would definitely not have stopped...........

We made the front page of the Sunday newspaper at El Universal. The President visits Cartegena this week, and I am still trying for an audience with him. We have already been told that the retrieval of any of our goods would be wildly optimistic; the only success to hope for would be the arrest of the gang, and so this story is for any, and all our friends in our wake. BEWARE OF Colombia; IT IS LAWLESS...

Lastly, we would both like to say to the Residents of "one happy island" as the ARUBANS like to call it. GSST, AARGH, shoo chooby, dushi! When Armando and the occupants of de hutz heard about our experience, they did a beach collection and fed-ex us money the next morning. Enough money, to see, the light such unconditional giving....this is the very reason we are cruising, to meet people like the Arubans. THANK YOU ARUBA.

Captain Michael Pierce

Figure 8 Venezuela

VENEZUELA
Pirate Attacks

Crew Attacked in Venezuelan Waters

Piracy Archive 2000-2002

On 29 August 2002, five armed men in Careano, Venezuela, about 60nm west of Puerto la Cruz, boarded a Gulf star 47. The skipper was pistol whipped with a gun, had his face broken as well as three ribs. The other crew on board was tied up and a blanket thrown over him. The men stole the dinghy and outboard, and ransacked the boat.

The US Coast Guard was informed.

Pirates attack Swedish yacht in Venezuela.

Captain Michael Pierce

<u>Piracy Archive 2000-2002</u>

Trinidad 31 March 2001

Venezuelan pirates attack Swedish Cruiser.

Carnival time in Trinidad was over, all the planned boat work was, done, and we were ready for Los Roques Islands in Venezuela. On Margarita, we experienced very strong easterly winds, and we were no longer so eager to go west. The wind was roaring in the rigging 24 hours a day, and we were worrying about the trip back to Trinidad. We did not feel comfortable on the island and after discussing this, we decided to return to Trinidad, as soon as we could clear-out of Venezuela.

On March 19, 2001, we sailed from Margarita in an ENE wind, heading for the Venezuelan coast where the current is weaker as well as the wind. Next morning was beautiful, no wind, calm water with a slight swell, and we skipped the first anchorage and headed for the Bay. The engine was running at "vacation speed" and we were making about 5 knots with no vessels to be, seen. As we progressed east, I had noted that the land was very desolate, no villages, no roads, no smoke from burning fires in the hillsides. This must be the land's end was my thought.

At noon when I was serving lunch in the cockpit, we saw a pirogue coming from behind us. The pirogue was, filled with men; they came alongside and started asking for cigarettes in Spanish. My husband went outside the cockpit and told them we had no cigarettes. Then everything happened very fast. I heard a gunshot, my husband screaming "No" several times in anguish and he came back in the cockpit.

I saw, he was, hit, and pushed him down below, where he collapsed, on the floor. At the same time, four men with guns came on board and three of them entered the doghouse. They wanted jewelry and money. When I told them we had neither, they were very upset; they apparently did not believe me. My husband tried to talk and lifted his head; one of the men put his pistol to my husband's head.

PIRACY SURVIVAL GUIDE

I was screaming and this made them very nervous. They took a knife in the galley and threatened me with it; they wanted me to be quiet. Then two of the men started grabbing things, which were around like binoculars, sandals, sunglasses, chewing gum, flippers, snorkels, masks, a Sony Walkman, a portable GPS, handheld echo sounder, watches, a life vest, a small camera, etc. They demanded alcohol, and I gave them three bottles of rum and some beer. They found a purse with a few Bolivar's and our credit cards in a small plastic bag. When I begged for the cards, they threw them back. Locker doors were torn open and the contents thrown about.

Finally, I stopped screaming and said "finito - me marido muerte" and went towards them. They indicated that my husband's wound was nothing serious, and then they collected the stuff in a sleeping bag and went outside. I was told to sit down in the cockpit, when I stood up, one came back with his gun pointing at me. In the pirogue circling the boat, there were two men, one of them looking like an elderly fisherman. They jumped into the pirogue and sped away.

The pirogue was white with a green stripe, no name, and no number. It had a big grey outboard engine as well as a big black smudge on the starboard side at the rear end. I took the position, N10 44.6 W62 22.1 near Punta Toleta. My husband was conscious, complained of pain in the abdomen, and was bleeding from the wound on his back below the waist. After covering the wound and moving him outside, I started on the HF radio, frequency 2182. Very quiet, the two VHF sets had been ruined by the banditos, the cables were torn off.

My husband told me to activate the EPIRB, which I did. Handheld VHF was, used until the battery went flat. There was no talk on the HF-radio, and I was searching the frequencies. Finally, I thought I had to wait for Southbound II to come on at 2000 UT. At 1900 UT, I found people talking on the frequency 14000 MHz and could finally relay a Mayday message and get an answer. The people assisting me were very professional; I could even consult a doctor. My husband was still conscious, in pain and bleeding while lying in the cockpit.

He was very calm assisting me and not complaining. Sometimes my head went empty and simple routine things I had done hundreds of times were very difficult. I could not understand why the autopilot did not work until my husband told me that the transmitting was disturbing it. This is a daily problem and I often hand steer when my husband is on the radio. We headed for the Grand Boca and just before sunset, I spotted the vessel from the Trinidad & Tobago Coast Guard. Just 10 minutes earlier a Venezuelan Coast Guard vessel wanted me to come alongside. The heavy swell made such a maneuver very risky and when I realized that the vessel was from Venezuela, I turned again and headed for Boca Grande.

The Trinidad & Tobago Coast Guard put a big rubber dinghy in the water, two paramedics and two seamen came on board Lorna. What a relief to have professional assistance. Now we headed into the narrow channel on the north side of Chacachacare where we could go alongside, a Coast Guard vessel. My husband; was placed, on a stretcher; and transferred, to the boat. The two seamen stayed with me, took Lorna to the Coast Guard station where a car took me to the hospital, so I could see my husband and talk to the doctor.

After 5 hours of abdominal surgery, the bullet was, removed. The doctor told me that my husband is a fighter and his strong determination would help him through. I want to thank the Trinidad & Tobago Coast Guard for their assistance, the net controller, and everyone else helping on the radio. The SSB saved the day and with the help of the friendly people in Trinidad & Tobago and the cruisers, we will get over this and head for more, peaceful, waters.

Note....

This is the second; recent pirate incident reported by the Boca that involved a sailing vessel traveling along the north coast of Venezuela toward Trinidad. In each case, violence had erupted. (See Dutch Concrete Attacked - Boca January 2001). It is, suggested for sailing vessels transiting the desolate Venezuelan coast; travel in the company, of a friend's boat. In the last report prior to publication, St. Clair Medical listed, as satisfactory improving slowly.

Another Crew Attacked and Yacht Boarded in Venezuela
Topic: *Piracy Archive 2000-2002*

At about 2230 local times, on Sat 12 October 2002, the yacht Panacea was boarded at the island of Isle Coche just south of Margarita, Venezuela by five armed men wearing ski masks.

They tied the two onboard, took everything, ransacked the boat and as an afterthought while leaving shot the skipper in the knee. He is recovering in a Margarita hospital.

This is the fourth armed boarding in 8 weeks on the north coast of South America.

Yet, Another Fatal Attack on Yacht in Venezuela
Topic: *Piracy Reports 2004*

There have been several reports of piracy involving yachts on the Venezuelan coast in 2004, but the following has been the most serious. The captain of the French yacht was, found shot dead on his yacht, apparently coming out of the cabin. The single-hander was, anchored for several days at Ensenada Medina, Venezuela, in the company with another French boat. The second yacht left for Grenada early on June 17, with him intending to leave soon after for Los Testigos. The two yachts had VHF contact about 9 a.m.

After several days of no contact, the Venezuelan Coast Guard found him in a small cove apparently adrift, i.e. the anchor was on deck, the engine was not running, and the sails were, furled. The captain was, found with a gunshot to the head, and numerous valuables were, discovered missing.

The second boat was, contacted, via the Security Net and the French Net, and is returning to their homeport in Martinique to assist French authorities, who are cooperating with the Venezuelan authorities in the investigation.

The French net operates at 09.00am SSB 6945. The Caribbean Safety and Security Net: SSB 8104.0 at 1215 UTC, Primary Net Controller, Caribbean Cruising Association publishes detailed lists of all attacks on yachts in their region
www.safetyandsecuritynet.com/

Armed boarding, Punta Pargo, Venezuela
Topic: Piracy Reports 2004

Time: 2215 hours local time, February 28, 2004

This is a report concerning an armed robbery in Punta Pargo on my sailing yacht, a 40 feet aluminum sloop of French registry, and the murder attempt on the one person aboard, myself, traveling from Cumanà to Trinidad.

I was aware of the security situation on the Paria peninsula between Araya and Punta Mejillones. I thought of motor sailing, mostly at night, and avoiding the Puerto Santos area. I wrongly assumed the security better on the East side of the peninsula.

After stops on the way in Isla Lobos for the first night then in Carùpano for part of the next day, I motored overnight to Punta Pargo (10.43N 62.034W) and anchored there on Saturday February 28th at 09:15, planning to go the next day to Cabo San Francisco and leave early Monday for Trinidad.

I had various contacts with kids swimming to the boat to which I gave caps, with a fishing boat that was in need of fasteners – a few were, given to them. I strolled ashore; spoke with people, then went back onboard. I had a very good contact with a fishing vessel, anchored close by and the mate, who speaks good English. They invited me to share a lunch of grilled fish, rice, and arepas. They buy fish from the local fishermen and run it to Trinidad where it is processed.

Late in the evening, the bay started filling up with fishing boats coming in for the night, which gave me some misgivings. I was the only sailing yacht in the bay. I took the Bimini down over the transom, which makes boarding the cockpit from the sugar spoon area awkward and difficult. I settled to sleep in the cockpit at about 21:30, the dinghy tied up to the stern with a painter – a rigid bottom Bombard with rowing bench and oars. The outboard is stored on the transom railing.

At about, 22.15, I was, awakened by voices and noticed the presence of two or more men on the platform at the stern. I immediately started shouting loudly at them in Spanish to get away. There were voices and the flickering light of a torch (wood? gasoline-soaked rag?) coming from the starboard side, probably from the llanchita (small wooden dinghy with oars, no engine) they must have used to reach me. I realized that one of the men had a facemask and then assumed that the situation was the most dangerous.

I jumped through the companionway still shouting and started looking for flares. In the five, ten or fifteen following seconds, as I was rummaging for the flares, the intruders were trying to induce me to come out with soothing words: "Amigo, venga, venga". I perhaps poked my head out to see if they had come into the cockpit, went down again for the flares.

More or less at the same time, two things happened: a shot fired, and I triggered a flare holding it the wrong way and hurting my thumb. The intense pain prevented me from realizing that the shot was, directed, inside the cabin. Subsequently, I continued shouting at them to leave, begging them not to come on board and not to take the dinghy, screaming in the VHF a mayday that I knew nobody would respond to it.

I do not remember what they might have said at that time, I was struggling with the flares, and they perhaps thought I had a weapon. They were still trying to get me to come out. One of the men, the masked one I think, made some very clear death threats, I do not recall exactly if this was before or after the gunshot. I was still screaming, allowing silence to hear what they would say, or trying to find out about their movements. After a while, I could not hear anything coming from the stern, but could not know if the intruders were not standing still waiting for me, or if they had gone.

After a few moments of calm, I came out cautiously trying not to get, shot in the process and noticed no presence. I could see the dinghy rowed away with two men on board, barely visible along the cliff closing the bay on the East, towards the North, away from the beach. I started monitoring their progress with binoculars. The llanchita was not there. In the following minutes, the dinghy was, met by a motorized fishing llancha (roofless fishing boat).

The group was about 600 to 800 yards away apparently struggling to deflate the dinghy or take it aboard. The llancha pulled the dinghy further out and then West. It was impossible to determine whether the group was, headed for some place further down the coast to the West, (Ensenada Mejillones?) or if they stopped at the furthest fishing boat, perhaps before returning to the shore in Punta Pargo. I went back and explored the inside with a doused torch. I then noticed the tracks of the gunshot on the roof of the companionway damaging wood on the headliner and battens.

I also took stock of the fact that my head had been in the track of the gunshot a fraction of a second before it flew inside the boat.

I tried then to make plans for the rest of the night and decided it was impossible to stay alone on for the night – I would have felt insecure, and I realized I did not have the means to deal with another attempt. I summarily closed, went quietly into the water, swam to the fishing boat I was with earlier and woke them up. They had not heard a thing. I asked for shelter and spent the night there mostly not sleeping but looking at my boat barely visible in the dark a hundred and fifty yards away, seeing of course hordes of attackers boarding her from all sides.

At first light, I swam back and was happy to realize that she had not been, visited again. With daylight and freshly brewed tea, I could take stock of the damage – a quantity of wood shards littering the floor, big splinters of the overhead battens, one shot finding its way through the roof panel and inside the insulation - but overall mostly cosmetic, no navigation instrument, or other equipment damaged.

The men from the fishing boat came aboard and were very sympathetic, helping me to clean and comforting me. We then noticed half dozen holes in the forward bulkhead and a broken lamp. Later I realized these pellets continued to do damage on the other side of the panel, piercing aluminum tubes and paddles for a kayak, shortly after I left to complete my trip to Trinidad. In conclusion, the intruders probably approached in a small llanchita.

Two of them made off with the dinghy, the rest with the llanchita. They could not have swum to the boat, as the upper part of their body seemed dry. The one wearing a facemask seemed to me young –not over 30. An older man was present, not wearing a mask. I do not know who fired the shot but assume it was the masked intruder.

This man uttered some death threats in Spanish - something like "calla te o te mato" but much more expressive - not loudly (not to be overheard by the fishing boat anchored very close?) but in a voice with some unmistakable intentions in it. Are these men from Punta Pargo, or, from another settlement, or fishing village? Was this a pirate boat, or possibly a fishing boat or, a combination?

The Bimini made ingress difficult and awkward but also somewhat prevented me from seeing the major part of the intruder's bodies or someone has hidden underneath.

It seems the intruders, were not happy with the nearby presence of other fishing boats that might have become aware of what was going on. The nearest fishing boat clearly was aware of something but did not interfere – anyway it would not have done any good, they did not have a dinghy either, their engine had trouble starting and the prospective of being, fired at could not be more desirable on their side than on mine.

The firearm used is most probably a shotgun – one empty 12-gauge cartridge was left, behind, a few pellets were collected in a cushion or badly deformed by their track. Shotguns are a part of daily life in Venezuela, seen everyday and everywhere. They fire one shot at a time and need to be, reloaded for the next shot. The fact that one empty cartridge was left behind may mean that the shooter had reloaded. It may have been a homebrew firearm, common in Venezuela too. The cartridge is rusty.

Clearly, the intentions of the intruders were the worst that can be, imagined, and I realize how fortunate I am to be alive to tell this story, with no physical wounds and not in an utter state of terror. I am very happy – and lucky too – that the engineless dinghy was enough to satisfy them and that my boat was not, vandalized.

I was wrong in my assumption that anchorages east of Cabo Tres Puntos. However, remote from Puerto Santos, would be safe. If I had studied the recent events, I perhaps would have been in the opinion that there could be no absolutely, safe harbor except perhaps Carùpano where you can anchor a couple hundred yards from the Vigilancia. I could have continued straight to Trinidad on Friday, but was ahead on my schedule and wished to spend some time resting and cleaning the boat. I also wanted, ideally, to avoid the overtime tax in Trinidad, but ended up arriving Sunday anyway.

One will make his own recommendations to the light of this event, – whether to go or not to go, what precautions to take, how to behave or that sort of things. Things worked pretty well in my favor in this instance – but I have just been very lucky. It could have been much, much worse. In my mind are the ordeals that others have been through and the cruelty with which they have been, treated.

Firsthand Report of Pirate Boarding In Porlamar Venezuela

Topic: <u>Piracy Reports 2005</u>

We respectfully submit the following account of our recent pirate attack in Venezuela for posting.

On December 4, 2005 at about 10:45 PM, with some 85 boats in the anchorage, we were, robbed in Porlamar for the second time. Our circumnavigation was, started in September of 1996 and is almost complete. In all that time, we have only, been robbed twice.

This time by three to four pirates who all appeared to be in their 20's. The pirates were in our cockpit pounding on our companionway doors, screaming "Garda Costa" and shining a large spotlight in my eyes. Awakened out of a sound sleep and not thinking too clearly. I at first thought that it was a legitimate boarding by the authorities.

Two pirates with rusty automatic handguns forced their way below decks. Describing the guns to people who know guns they guessed them to have been either 22 or 32 calibers - not that it means much looking down their barrels. The first one below deck was drunk and barely in control of himself. He pointed his gun in my face and demanded drugs and money. I told my wife to go forward and close the forward cabin door. The second rather calm pirate came down and controlled me with his gun.

The first gunman went forward and started to kick down our forward cabin door. To calm the situation I told her to open the door. While she sat on the bunk in her underwear, the first gunman rifled our forward drawers and cabinets. My wife was amazingly calm and in control of herself. Given that we were dealing with an out of control gunman, I felt that calm and cooperation would be the best course of action.

I gave the second gunman all the money that I had in my wallet (about $65.00 U.S. in Bs.). He demanded more. I told him that it was all we had. I showed him an old out of date credit card that I keep for just such a purpose explaining that we used it to get money from cash machines when we needed it. We learned a long time ago to carry very little "show cash".

The pirates also stole the 12-volt power supply for our computer. They likely had no idea what it was, but they stole it anyway. They also stole our 35 MM "Minolta" camera.

The forward gunman started to remove our small forward TV when his friends outside screamed Policia and they all took off. I followed them outside as they fled in a dark hulled very high prow rather short penero with a very large outboard. They fired off one shot.

Luckily, the pirates were not very bright. There were many things exposed that they could have easily taken but missed. It could have been a lot worse for us.

As soon as the pirates were gone, we set off our alarm system and called for help on our VHF. German "Antonia", American "Piper" and French "Jotake" all offered assistance. There is a "Police Boat" stationed at the "Power Boat Marina" in Porlamar with three cops rotating duty 24 hours a day. Unable to raise the cop on duty on the VHF radio, we went to the "Power Boat Marina" to find him.

The cop had turned off his marine VHF radio; and his Police frequency portable radio, his cell phone and was asleep aboard a large powerboat. There was nothing the cops could do we were told. It had taken so long to find the cop and wake him up that the bad people had gotten away. The cop made us feel that we should apologize for having disturbed him.

The forward gunman had not worn gloves and had touched a number of plastic fastener envelopes as well as our small TV. His fingerprints were on our boat. The cop refused to visit our boat to, either file a report or to investigate.

We feel that we can identify one or both unmasked gunmen. From a pirate boarding a week or so earlier of another boat in Porlamar, we had a complete description as well as the registration number of the penero likely used by the pirates in our attack.

This was, presented to the Police the next morning when I filed a report at "Marina Juan". For a variety of lame reasons, the cops said there was nothing they could do.

We were not, prepared for a pirate attack in Porlamar. Had we been prepared, we would have handled the attack better. Having circumnavigated nearly around the globe, we pride ourselves on doing our homework. When we arrived in Porlamar, we specifically asked if there had ever been a pirate attack in the anchorage. We were, told there had been none. After our attack, a cruiser told us that there had been five in the last three years. We presented this information and repeated our question. This time instead of none, we were told that it might not have been as many, as five.

Nothing would likely change in Porlamar if a cruiser was knifed, machete, shot or even murdered. Things would likely change if the cruiser money went elsewhere.

Another Armed boarding in Porlamar, Isla Margarita, Venezuela

Topic: Piracy Reports 2005

There has been an armed boarding and robbery in the anchorage of Porlamar on the island of Isla Margarita, Venezuela. Our Sailing Vessel, anchored on the southern edge of the anchorage. Was boarded 10:45 at night on Sunday December 4, 2005 by three men holding firearms and yelling (in Spanish) "Venezuelan Coast Guard, this is a drug check?" After the boat owner opened the locked companionway, the pirates pointed a gun at the boat owner, demanded money, and took a 35mm camera.

The pirates were in their 30's. On leaving, the pirates fired a shot (I assume it was in the air). After talking to the Venezuelan police, they told the owner that there have been five armed pirate attacks in Porlamar in the past 3 years. This is in addition to the monthly outboards that are stolen, both from dinghies in the water and on the on davits.

This information was, heard over the local VHF cruiser's net in Porlamar, firsthand from the vessel. I thought it is important for cruisers to hear about any robberies here, especially armed, since they rarely get past official ears and are important to prepare safety precautions.

Cruisers anchoring in Porlamar should ALWAYS bring up their dinghies up, have an ALARMED lock for their dingy, and engine. VHF Channel 72 is, listened to at night for security and in the mornings at 8:00 for the net.

Another yacht assault in Venezuela

Topic: Piracy Reports 2005

The catamaran a Bahia 46, with owner and his wife on board, was, anchored in Carenero, Venezuela, a hundred yards or so from the Carenero Yacht Club.

On May 13 2005, at 2am, we were boarded, by two; young local people, there was probably a third one waiting in a small boat. They stole binoculars, shoes and some portable electronics. Bruno woke-up and fought with them, taking from them, a bat, and a hammer they were using as weapons. One of the two thieves wanted to kill him ("lo mato!") with a knife but the other said to leave. They jumped in the water and left, taking the gear and leaving their knife in the cockpit.

We then heard a shot and impact of a projectile in the water close to the boat. We called for help on CH16: after some time, some local "vigilance" relayed the call in better Spanish but no authority responded or showed up. Only the private guards of the nearby hotel called us and told us we could come and anchor a hundred yards closer to them. We later learned that the Guardia Nacional sent a patrol on shore, but had no boat to come close to us.

Despite numerous "mayday" calls between 2:10am and 6:00am no authority responded on CH16. Around 7am in the morning, the owner went to see the Guardia Nacional ashore: they finally made it to the boat at 10:15am, took our deposition and the evidence of armed robbery left by the thieves: a big knife and a 3ft bat. I later an officer from the "Capitania de Puerto Carenero" showed up who wrote a report of the incident.

To this hour, both have been very reluctant to give us any copy, even that of our own deposition. We invite you to broadcast this information as widely as possible in the hope to get more efficient reactions, from the, Venezuelan authorities.

Gunpoint Robbery in Venezuelan Anchorage

Topic: Piracy Reports 2006
Countries: Venezuela

On the night of November 11 a couple on the Icelandic yacht, was attacked by three gunmen who came aboard the boat and held them hostage for three hours while they ransacked the boat and stole everything of value. The owner and his wife were, anchored for the night just outside, the small village of Robledal (11°01,5N 64°22.7 W) on Isla Margarita, Venezuela, a spot where no security problems had been, previously reported.

Around midnight three men each armed with a gun approached in a small boat and boarded the yacht. Threatened with the guns, they were, tied up in the cockpit while the men proceeded to strip the boat of anything of value. The ordeal lasted some three hours before the men left.

The sailors proceeded to Porlamar where they reported the attack to the local authorities.

Attack in January, Isla De Margarita, Venezuela.
Topic: *Piracy Reports 2008*
Countries: *Venezuela*

A report from the International Maritime Bureau has detailed another Venezuelan attack on a yacht in Bahia De Robledal, Isla De Margarita, in January 2008.

Five armed men boarded the yacht, assaulting the crew and demanding all their property. One crewmember was shot and injured. The incident was, reported to local authorities.

There have been several attacks on yachts in Robledal Bay in the last few years and yachts wishing to visit Isla de Margarita are strongly, advised to stop at Porlamar only, which is more frequented by yachts. Yachts should be vigilant at all times, especially at night, and take extra precautions.

Recent Robberies at Porlamar, Margarita

Topic: Piracy Reports 2008
Countries: Venezuela

We were, anchored at Porlamar for one week (first week in July 2008). We had three robberies here in the anchorage and there was another at Pampatar. Luckily? We were not robbed, or boarded; however, other boats in the anchorage were not that lucky. Be aware.

Boarding by Pirates off NE Coast of Venezuela

Topic: Piracy Reports 2008
Countries: Venezuela

At approximately 1500hrs (local time) on Tuesday 1st July 2008, a sailing yacht was boarded by six heavily armed pirates NNE of Cacao off the northern coast of Venezuela (10 46.41N 62 16.80W).

None of the three crews aboard the yacht was physically, injured during the encounter. However, the yacht was, ransacked and everything of any value was, stolen. The pirates took cash, jewelry, computers, radios, satellite phone, cell phones, EPIRB, outboard motor, AC unit, food, clothing, bedding, and other items.

The boat was, approached from behind by a very fast pirogue-type open fishing boat. Although the boat was not far from a harbor, the attackers came alongside and asked for water. When the captain attempted to pass a water container to them, he was immediately facing six guns (5 x 9mm automatic pistols and 1 x semi automatic rifle).

The attackers made no effort to hide either their own identity or that of the attacking vessel. The attacking vessel was an open pirogue-type fishing boat with four Yamaha 75hp outboard motors. The hull was mostly dark green with a wide turquoise stripe over and a narrow red stripe separating the green from the turquoise. The boat displays the name "Amguna" on the stern and "Moss" on the bow.

Please make this information available to all cruisers so that they can make informed decisions about whether or not they cruise in this area. I for one will be giving the coast of Venezuela a very large offing in the future.

Attack on British Yacht 10 miles from Puerto Santos, Venezuela
Topic: Piracy Reports 2008
Countries: Venezuela

My parents were, attacked on their yacht after leaving Puerto Santos on 5 July 2008.

A pirogue with six men aboard approached the boat (whilst they were underway). One man was in military uniform. My husband proceeded to slam and try to sink the boat but shots were, fired.

The men boarded us, shooting and stabbing the family dog. They tied my husband on deck with a gun pointing at him, and went down, below and held a female with two guns pointing at her face.

They took US$300, laptop computer, tool boxes, the SSB radio, outboard motor, ripped the microphones from the VHF, ripped the compass out, tried to take the radar and forward looking sonar, but they were fixed too well, and left the boat a complete mess.

They also tried to take the wife's wedding ring, but she could not get it off and in the process cut her hand severely. After the attack, my parents had no means of communication at all, so we made the decision to get out of Venezuelan waters to Trinidad. The case is now in the hands of the authorities and the British Commission.

PEOPLE NEED TO BE AWARE.

Pirate Attack in Venezuelan Waters

Topic: Piracy Archive 2003

Noon site's Roving Editor sent us the following report:

On 10 January 2003, a little speedboat stopped a Spanish sailing boat 3 miles off the Venezuela coast at "Cabo Tres Puntas". The pirates were all masked, all armed with pistols and machetes and one even had a machine gun, which was, believed to be an "UZI".

People who know Venezuela better than us believe that these were organized pirates, who knew the procedure of yachts waiting behind "Cabo tres Puntas" before carrying on east through the night when the wind is light close to the coast.

Dinghy Theft in Porlamar, Venezuela
Topic: Piracy Reports 2008
Countries: Venezuela

On August 27, 2008 at 1830, my dinghy was stolen from the rum bar dock in Porlamar, Margarita Island. There were about 12 other dinghies tied to the dock as well. I had paid the dock attendant that day to "safeguard" my dinghy while I popped up to fetch the laundry (30 minutes only) but the thieves were too clever.

Note: He accidentally left the key to his dinghy and engine on the boat (hence, he asked the dock attendant to keep an eye on his dinghy). Noon site's recommendation is to always, padlock your dinghy and engine to the dock wherever in the world you are leaving your dinghy. April Brings New Spate of Attacks on Yachts in Venezuela

Topic: Piracy Reports 2006
Countries: Venezuela

As previously reported on Noonsite, the security situation for yachts in Venezuela remains of concern with the number of boarding's and attacks continuing. Details of the following incidents have been, recently sent to Noonsite:

Week of April 9 (exact date not known): At about midnight, a swimmer boarded the yacht anchored off Isla Cubagua. The captain shone a big spotlight on the boarder and fired off a flare. The boarder dove over the side and was, picked up by a penero.

April 26, 2006 at 03:30 AM: Belgian yacht, anchored in Pampatar, was boarded during the night, and robbed. A man and two boys, all armed with knives stole cash and some valuables. The captain resisted somewhat and received superficial cuts to his face and wrist, he felt that his resistance had kept his losses low.

April 28: Austrian circumnavigator survived an attack of five gunmen who boarded his yacht, which anchored off Isla Piritu, Venezuela. The attackers were, armed with one rifle and one revolver. They shot several times, one bullet hitting him in his chest. After they shot him, he tried to save himself in his dinghy, by making for the shore. However, was, pursued, by the attackers who beat him up asking for money. They eventually left him to die and fled, but fortunately some locals found him, and he was taken to a hospital. After two surgeries and the removal of one kidney, his condition is no longer life threatening.

Figure 9 Brazil

BRAZIL
Pirate Attacks

Armed robbery on yacht in Belem, Brazil, January 08

Topic: Piracy Reports 2008
Countries: Brazil

We want to report an armed robbery on 21 January in the Port of Belem, Brazil. Our boat was anchored about 200 meters from the ferry quay (01.27.43S 48.30.53W) in Belem as we could not reach the Belem Yacht club at that time due to low water. At about 01.00 hours, two men with pistols entered our boat and awakened me with two pistols to my head.

My hands were, tied with a rope and my wife was, awakened in the same way. In the dark, we were, asked to give all our money, mobile phones, and watches. After we had given these, they left. Belem is a very dangerous place around the harbors especially close to the ferries. Do not stay there and go only to the Marina about 1 hour further up to the river (01.28.59S 48.28.57) which is difficult to find and only with high water. We also found out that the cheap red diesel is very dirty and should not be, used.

Yacht Attacked At Sao Luis, North East Brazil

Topic: Piracy Reports 2007
Countries: Brazil

I want to report an attack in Sao Luis - Northeast - Brazil, at the end of November 2007. My wife and I were, anchored alone at the mooring just in front of the Sao Luis Yacht Club on our 42' sailboat. At 2.00 am, we were boarded and attacked by four armed men, three with knives, and one with a handgun. The boat was open. The man with the gun hurt me during 15 minutes, several head wounds that required stitching at the Sao Luis hospital emergency. They did not wound my wife, but they were very violent and aggressive. After 15 minutes, they disappeared with their rowing boat into the darkness.

They took money, two laptops, two cell phones, alcohol, cigarettes, and more. We spent 2 hours calling the authorities by VHF channel 16 before the police come, and we went to the hospital. Brazilian emergency is like a supermarket on Saturday!

If you do not need the Brazilian police, its better, they did not do anything, just wrote our names on a sheet of paper, and told me to take care the next time, which is it. The local yacht club, ship owners from the yacht club and even firefighters the same.

Therefore, the rule in Brazil is: Help yourself! We have been sailing for 1 year along Brazil's coast, and it is the same indifference everywhere, Brazilian people have so many problems, they do not care about you. Before this adventure, we planned to visit Venezuela, so this time we prefer to forget this dangerous country and forget this bad story for a while and sail in Caribbean islands and the USA.

So always the same advice; Never stay alone anchored; close the boat when sleeping, light on the deck by night, sail far from the coast.

And so on...

I have to report to, end of 2007. Another incident that seems an attack, but we are not sure. Because; we were sailing near Abrolhos, islands near Rio de Janeiro, 100 miles from the coast. When at 6.00 am a small fishing boat chased us with four men ready to jump on our boat. With a lot of wind, some big waves, and my engine running at the maximum rpm, we were able to make 9 knots speed and me calling for help on channel 16 while maneuvering. They thought it was too dangerous to board our boat, so nothing happened ... I do not think that 100 miles from the shore, they want to sell me fish or lobster!

Thanks to noonsite for helping us with all this very useful information and we hope our story will help others boats sailing in Brazil.

Captain Michael Pierce

Figure 10 Europe

EUROPE
Pirate Attacks

PIRATE ATTACKS IN AREAS CONSIDERED SAFE

When traveling by yacht do not assume any place safe. Each port will have its own concerns, but you should maintain vessel security with differing degrees of procedure depending on the concern for the safety of the vessel and the crew. There is now a growing concern with the developed countries, part of this is due to the definition of the term recognized as piracy.

In the United States, there is an unrecognized amount of piracy because it is considered, a domestic crime; or recorded as a burglary with the police instead of a marine authority. There fore the large number of thefts involving ships or yachts is recorded and not tallied towards piracy.

Armed Robbery of Super yacht in Corsica

Topic: Piracy Reports 2008
Countries: France

At approximately 2340 on Sunday 24 August 2008, a gang of four masked men boarded the 160-foot charter yacht from a motorized dinghy, and proceeded to rob its nine guests and ten crewmembers. The yacht was at anchor in Golfe de Porto Novo, Corsica (41°30'.3N 009°16'E).

It is the first time such a security breach has occurred in French waters, officials said.

The yacht had a charter party of German financiers aboard and although the thieves were only onboard for a few minutes, they managed to get away with 138,000 Euros ($204,000), according to reports.

The gang was, armed with handguns and rifles and easily overpowered the crew. The intruders ordered the captain to empty the yacht's safe and demanded that the nine guests onboard the hand over cash and valuables to them. The captain alerted the Coast Guard but the perpetrators have yet to be, arrested. The French Coast Guard purportedly stated that no shots were, fired during the robbery and no one was hurt. The boat was, reported to have been traveling from the Italian island of Sardinia and heading for a town near Porto-Vecchio. The yacht is, registered in the Cayman Islands.

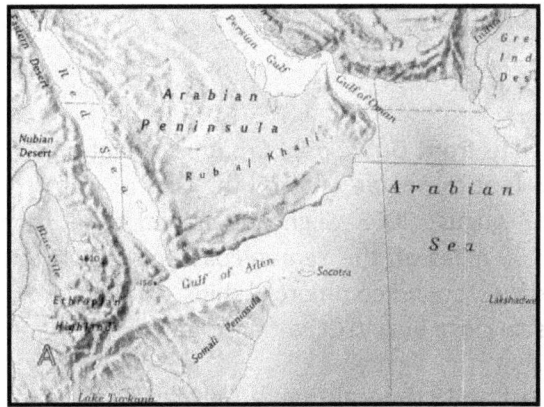

Figure 11 Gulf of Aden

GULF OF ADEN
Pirate Attacks

Yemen and Somalia have been the news capital of Africa in the recent years but all of Africa has problems with piracy and not a mild one. Whenever encountering pirates in or near Africa you can be sure, it will be a terrifying experience. Africa is a country with a huge poverty problem and few people have any steady source of income outside of scavenging or crime.

It is best to avoid most places that have a history in these waters but there are areas you can visit. Before you decide to travel to Africa check with the state dept for any travel advisories and do research on the country on piracy. If you can find other travelers who have been there ask them for any advice, they can give you. Most people will have traveled to South Africa; I have not found any that had travel to other areas in Africa on the water.

Pirate Attacks - Gulf of Aden

Topic: *Piracy Reports 2008*

19, 20, and 21 August 2008

On our voyage from Dubrovnik, Croatia to Kantang, Thailand aboard our 36-foot sloop, we entered the Gulf of Aden from the Red Sea on 17 August 2008. Slight winds and a full moon, we chose to keep 50 miles off the Yemen coast in the company with many east and westbound commercial ships. At night, we showed no lights and saw close by a VLCC with no lights.

On 19 August at 1915 local time a Mayday was broadcast on channel 16 from chemical tanker Bunga Milati at 012°45′.1 North, 047°57′.7 East, 120 miles Southwest of our position and only 25 miles from our previous nights track. The Filipino radio officer sounded terrified and broadcast his Mayday constantly as pirates boarded his vessel, until radio silence prevailed.

On 20 August, we heard another Mayday pirate attack on channel 16 but were too far away to know the details.

On 22 August, we entered the Port of Salalah where a French coalition warship was visiting and from an Omani naval officer we learned first hand that pirates boarded an Iranian oil tanker the following night.

He described how 2 pirate boats, usually Somali small fiberglass open boats, would be joined by a long rope across the path of the victim; as the ship's bow fouls the rope the 2 pirate boats are drawn alongside the victim and boarded.

On a lighter note, due to no wind and constant motoring, we had to put into Nishtun Yemen, for an emergency fuel stop. Where we found the local fishermen, friendly and who assisted us. Nishtun has no facilities for visiting yachtsmen, but we were able to buy 80 liters of diesel.

April 2008 Owned by French charter company was en route to the Mediterranean from the Seychelles when pirates boarded the vessel on April 4 2008. Le Ponant had a 30-strong crew on board of 22 French nationals, six Filipinos, a Ukrainian and a Cameroonian.

The three-mast, 32-cabin vessel, was, taken under the pirates control to Garacad, south of the port of Eyl in Somalia, where it spent a week while negotiations were under way between representatives of the pirates and CMA CGM and the French authorities. Local sources indicated that the Somali Marines, described as a highly organized group of pirates with warlord protection and a separate "business" structure for ransom negotiations, had probably seized it

On 11 April, it was reported that French special forces had detained six Somali pirates and recovered an alleged $1M in ransom money in an airborne raid after the pirates released the cruise ship Le Ponant. AFP quoted French defense minister saying that Somali authorities had authorized the operation.

Wide press coverage quoted French military leaders describing the helicopter raid on the pirates as they regrouped ashore after leaving the ship. The exercise said; to have been, timed so that the newly released hostage crew and officers of Le Ponant was safely aboard another French carrier before the raid.

Four helicopters were involved in the action to prevent the pirates getting away in a vehicle. Six of the pirates were taken into custody, while at least eight others got away, according to the UK's Independent newspaper. The commandos are also believed to have repossessed $1M in cash out of $2M in ransom that had been handed over to the pirates by French ship owner CMA CGM. The six detainees were, taken to France for trial.

French boat was, taken to Djibouti, where France has a major military base.

A French Catamaran skipper was, shot dead during an attack on Sunday 14 September, on board his yacht at anchor outside Marina de Caraballeda, situated on the Central Litoral coast between La Guaira and Cabo Codera, Venezuela.

Four robbers attacked the French yacht, using a pirogue to reach the yacht at anchor. In resisting the attack, Skipper, age 61, was, shot several times in the head. The second crewmember on board, remained captive until the robbers had finished their looting, taking an undisclosed quantity of money and equipment.

It appears that the pirogue driver was scared on hearing the shooting down below and fled, leaving the remaining robbers to swim ashore. The woman, onboard alerted police by firing a red flare when the robbers had left. It appears the couple did not hear the robber's board their yacht until they were down below.

This is not the first robbery or attack on a boat near Marina de Caraballeda, which frequently suffers petty theft and occasionally violence towards crews during robberies. However, it is the first with this sad outcome.

A Sailing Vessel, currently waiting for repairs to be finished to his yacht in Marina de Caraballeda, advises the following; "A note of caution to fellow sailors who visit our waters: Never, under any circumstances, anchor in the bay of Marina de Caraballeda for overnight stays. Please call VHF channel 16 to speak with the Marina Commodore or his assistant (they remain on duty during the daytime) and ask for help in anchoring. They will probably assign you a slip or even allow you to anchor inside the marina where they have security personnel".

Marina de Caraballeda is for public use and state owned and is officially, closed for repairs due to the damage suffered during the 1999 landslides. However, many boats remain in the marina waiting to finish their repairs.

Tuesday 3 September 2008

Couples from Tahiti were, seized aboard their 16m (50ft) yacht, on Tuesday 3 September, on their way from Australia to France. The pirates took the hostages to the Somali coast near Alula (written Caluula) at the tip of the Horn of Africa, from where part of the gang dragged them into a remote hideout in the Xaabo (pronounced: Hawo) mountains.

It is, thought; the heavily armed gunmen then took the yacht to sea again. While an attempt to sell the yacht at ports in the Gulf States cannot, be ruled out, it is, presumed that "Carre d'As" is at present being used to hunt for other ships. Warnings are that the vessel likely is, or will be, used to signal ships at sea as being under distress (simulating an engine failure or other emergency at sea), while hiding a small attack speedboat from view of any ships responding to the rescue.

The French couple spoke to their daughter, by satellite telephone shortly after they were kidnapped, and told her that they were fine.

Update 16 September 2008.

Two weeks, after their capture; the couple was, freed by the French army. The French president's office confirmed, "The two French nationals are safe and sound". One pirate was, killed and six others captured.

Sunday 24 August 2008

At approximately 2340, a gang of four masked men boarded the 160-foot charter yacht from a motorized dinghy, and proceeded to rob its nine guests and ten crewmembers. The yacht was at anchor in Golfe de Porto Novo, Corsica (41°30'.3N 009°16'E).

It is the first time such a security breach has occurred in French waters, officials said.

The yacht had a charter party of German financiers aboard and although the thieves were only onboard for a few minutes, they managed to get away with 138,000 Euros ($204,000), according to reports.

The gang was, armed with handguns and rifles and easily overpowered the crew. The intruders ordered the captain to empty the yacht's safe and demanded that the nine guests onboard the hand over cash and valuables to them.

The captain alerted the Coast Guard but the perpetrators have yet to be, arrested. The French Coast Guard purportedly stated that no shots were, fired during the robbery and no one was hurt. The boat was, reported to have been traveling from the Italian island of Sardinia and heading for a town near Porto-Vecchio. The yacht is, registered in the Cayman Islands.

British Yacht Attacked and Robbed Off Somalia

Topic: Piracy Archive 2000-2002

Report on the pirate boarding of British yacht off South Somalia coast. The attack took place at 10.30 on Friday 4th October 2002 at 04 40'N 48 34'E about 30 miles off the coast of Somalia, about 40 miles SSE of town of Obbia.

We were sailing at about 3 knots under main and spinnaker. Two open boats approached at speed. Each was about 8 meters long, white, with inboard engines and each carrying five men. On the side of one boat was, painted in large letters AL FIRUNAN. The boats also carried fishing nets and large cans of diesel. The men were quite young and wore colored tee shirts and trousers.

The first boat came close on our port side. The men waved, exchanged greetings, asked where we were from, and one said "no problems". We gave them packets of cigarettes, and they gave us a small bonito. When the second boat came close one said they were bad men.

The second boat came along our starboard side and three men immediately jumped on board, so two men came on board from the first boat. One man from the second boat spoke some English. He asked us what we were doing in Somali waters; we had problems, we had an engine.

He asked us to start it to show him. He acted, as an official but clearly was not. He said they wanted us to follow them to the coast or give them money. We gave them $50 we keep in a drawer. Then he asked about the radio and tried to use it to talk to a station in Somalia. I am not sure if he managed to, and I cannot remember the frequency he used.

Someone said they, had a kalashnikov in the fishing boat. We never saw one. Two men now had big fishing knives and indicated that we had to sit on the deck. Others went below and started bringing out stuff and taking it to one or other of the fishing boats which circled and came back. The second one particularly took no care and damaged our topsides and toe rail. The so-called official took me below and at knifepoint asked where our money was $630. It seemed a good idea to give it to him, it was, hidden, and he saw where I got it.

We had hoped that this would satisfy them; however, they wanted the radios and the cables were, cut with a knife. They said they would go after they took the radios but then wanted a solar panel and an outboard motor. They were not acting, unreasonable. They asked; what the radar was, and when told it was for navigation they left it and the installed GPS. I protested that we could not see at night without a torch, so they gave one back and one pair of binoculars in exchange for a solar panel. Someone was, prevented from taking all the tools.

All the men left except the two with knives. They were wearing two of our jackets. They wanted one of us to go with them. We now sat in the cockpit refusing to move. A man from the second boat who spoke a little English said they wanted more money. We said we did not have any. OK, he said 'I do not care I go.' He waved at the two men and shouted `Kill! Kill! Hack them to pieces!` We gave him the last of our money $300. They thought he had more, and he kept saying `you buy more dollars`. We protested we could not. We had nothing more and eventually after more repetitions of `Kill! Kill!` They left. They had been on board two hours.

We motored away at 7 knots. We were nearly 800 miles from the nearest available port Salalah, Oman, and it took 9 days to reach it early on Monday 14th October. We reported the incident to the police, as soon as we arrived. With no radios, we could not report before.

Money and equipment stolen from us:

Total value taken was between £4000 and $6000 Dollars. Which included Radio SSB Transceiver; VHF; 2 searchlights; torch; Camera; 2 Walkmans; Minidisk recorder; Piano accordion; Quatro (small guitar); Handheld VHF; TV; Video recorder; Solar panel; Music centre (Sony); Gamin GPS; BCG; 2 masks and snorkels; Shaver; Watch; Computer (Laptop); Briefcase; Outboard 2HP; clothing; Mattress and Sleeping bag; Batteries ; 12 cigarette lighters; 2 calculators; Gaff; tools; Box of floppy disks.

Yachts Pursued and Attacked In Gulf of Aden
Topic: Piracy Reports 2004

The following three incidents took place in the waters between Somalia and Yemen the night of 23 February 2004. US registered sailboat from Santa Cruz, California.

The first incident happened about 2000 hour's local times (GMT.

1600) in position 13 degrees 50 minutes North, 50 degrees 05 minute East, about 1 hour after the sunset, and 1 hour before moonset, We were traveling at about 4 knots under sail in 8 knots of wind on a course of 250 true. We were traveling with only a low powered all-around light due to the threat of piracy in the area. We saw a single white light slightly off the starboard bow. Radar indicated a small vessel at 2 miles, and we could see a bow wake as it headed towards us.

We responded by turning 40 degrees to port, and the other vessel changed course to intercept us. As the other vessel closed, we turned on the engine, turned on our running lights, turned further to port, and started to accelerate.

The other vessel closed to within 50 meters of our starboard quarter, and we could see what looked like a diesel powered boat, 8-10 meters in length, perhaps a ship's lifeboat, with 2-3 men on deck, coming toward the bow. They were clearly trying to approach our starboard quarter, with smoke coming from their diesel exhaust, but we accelerated away from them as our speed increased to 7 knots. They fell in behind us, and we broadcast a Mayday call on VHF channel 16, giving our position and the situation.

The Mayday call was, answered by a yacht 12 mile astern, and we advised them again of our situation and position. We extinguished all lights and varied course between 210 and 270 degrees. The other vessel receded behind us, and appeared to break off the chase after about 5 minutes. We came to a course of 210 degrees where the sails assisted our speed, and motor-sailed at 7 knots until the other vessel disappeared from the radar at about 5 miles. The ultimate intention of the other vessel remains unclear, as we could avoid contact closer than 50 meters, but it appeared that they are preparing to board us. No, weapons were seen or, heard.

The second incident took place about 2300 local time (1700 GMT) the same night, in position 13 degrees 39 minutes north, 49 degrees 49-minute east. While traveling without lights on a course of 250 degrees, we observed a single white light approximately on our port beam, which appeared on radar at 5 miles SSE of our position. By radar, it appeared to be heading on a course to intercept us, so we changed course to 300 degrees, accelerated to 7 knots while motor sailing, and tracked the other vessel. It continued to converge on us, and we estimated its speed to be over 8-9 knots.

After about 20 minutes, the other vessel was approximately 4 miles astern, so we made a course change to 240 degrees, and accelerated to our maximum speed of 7.5 knots. The other vessel responded by changing course to follow us. After 20 minutes, we repeatedly hailed it on VHF Channel 16, informing it that if it continued to follow us, we would broadcast a Mayday, but got no response. It closed to 3 miles behind us, and we broadcast a Mayday at 2340 with our position and situation on VHF channel 16 and HF 2182 KHz.

The only stations to respond to our Maydays were the group of four yachts 12-15 miles northeast of us. We requested one of the yachts, to use his satellite phone to call the authorities. He called Australian Marine Safety Authority (61 2 6230 6811), who told him that they would report the situation to the piracy control center in Kuala Lumpur (60 3 2031 0014), and told him to call back in 30 minutes. We fired two parachute flares during this time, which were reported seen by the group of following yachts.

After 20 minutes, the other vessel closed to 2 miles, but had swung in directly behind us, so we again altered course to 180 degrees, allowing us to reach across the wind, which had increased to 16 knots, bring our speed to 8.5 knots. The other vessel turned out its lights, making its location more difficult to track, but seem to be falling back slowly on radar. After another 30 minutes, we changed course to 140 degrees, slowing our progress to 7 knots, but heading into the waves and "hopefully" making it more uncomfortable and difficult to follow us.

The other vessel did not respond to this latest course change, and disappeared from the radar screen after another 10-15 minutes. We called the yachts following on the VHF and told them to report to the authorities that we no longer being closely pursued. We held the 140-degree course for another 30 minutes, and then changed course to 330 degrees to join the group of four yachts, which was following us. We made contact with them about 0130, and had no more incidents the rest of the night.

The second vessel never got close enough to get a visual description, but it was clearly more sophisticated than the first, with a speed of perhaps 9-10 knots, probably radar, and VHF radio. It had no problem tracking our radical course changes at a distance of 3-5 miles on a night with no moon. We believe that the combination of the flares, the VHF traffic with the other boats, and their small speed advantage discouraged them from chasing us for more than an hour.

The following morning a helicopter from the Coalition naval forces that had been, alerted by the other boat contacted us, and that afternoon, we got a visit from a Spanish warship. A boarding party came aboard to verify that we were not, being held hostages and took the details of the incidents. The Spanish warship provided a loose escort our group until we neared Aden. Words cannot express how grateful we were for the escort, as it was through a region where numerous yachts have been, attacked in recent years. We had arranged to convoy through this dangerous area, but our problems occurred about 80 miles east of the historical attacks.

Was the first boat innocent and just curious fishermen, and were we overreacting? Was the second vessel unable to understand English and trying to come to our aid after we set off the flares? We will never know for sure, but when a boat intercepts you at night in lonely waters 60 miles offshore in the Gulf of Aden, we believe it is wisest to assume the worst.

The third incident was the French Yacht. Who was, attacked, boarded, and robbed; by armed fishermen/pirates, on 27 February? At 13 degrees 30 minutes North and 47 degrees 51 minutes east. The yacht was approached at 1300 local time about 30 miles off the Yemen coast by a small fishing vessel with 5 men on board. The men had knives and automatic rifles, and took cash, cameras, binoculars, and other easily accessible valuables. The crew was shaken but unharmed, and proceeded to Aden. In this case, a Coalition warship heard the relayed distress message on VHF, asked commercial shipping to assist, and responded with a helicopter some 6 hours later.

Communications Both Sail mail and Winlink present challenges in connecting with distance transmitters here in the Red Sea. Winlink with transmitters in Italy and Qatar has been more users friendly. Winlink allows 30 minutes/day per station versus the 10 that Sailmail gives totally. You have more time to make several attempts at connection to Winlink. Transmitters for Sailmail are located in Belgium, Mozambique, and Brunei. Late evening connections to Brunei have given the best results on Sailmail.

Addendum to Official Report of Attack on the Sailing Yachts

Topic: <u>Piracy Reports 2005</u>

The attack, on two vessels, which occurred, on 8 March 2005, in the, Gulf of Aden, was perpetrated by pirates (?) or terrorists (?). They did not act like normal pirates (how do normal pirates act?). They were certainly trying to kill us from the outset. There is a very real possibility that it was an attempted hostage situation, especially if advance information was, sent from Salalah, Oman that four US boats had departed for Aden, Yemen. The two slower boats were 20-30 miles behind us at the time of the attack.

The real motivation for the attack will probably, never is, known. You would like to think that it is possible to transit the area at night, but the area of reported attacks is too large. You make your decisions based on circumstances at the time and live with them. We have had a lot of feedback concerning the attack from various sources. Most of it supportive, but also some from armchair pundits uttering stupid and ignorant comments and questions, "Walk in our shoes"! The whole episode was very traumatic, and we will not respond to any of those.

We have been in contact with Commander, USN at 5th Fleet Headquarters in Bahrain concerning the attack. He seems to think that a commitment to provide an escort for yachts grouping in Salalah, Oman and requesting an escort is possible, but there will have to be some pressure applied from higher sources ("political"?) or it probably will not happen. Let us not attempt to put all the pressure on the US Navy. There are yachts from numerous nations affected. The international yachting community has the capability of applying some pressure to their governments to follow up on this (please do so).

As far as we can determine at the time of the attack, the US Navy and the British Navy were patrolling the Arabian Sea and points north. The German, French, and possibly Italians were in the Gulf of Aden. One of the yachts with us was, stopped in the Arabian Sea, SE of Oman by the US Coast Guard for a "safety inspection". They asked the Coast Guard for emergency HF radio frequencies that the coalition forces, would be monitoring and were, supplied with two frequencies. We tried calling on these frequencies over the next several days. It turned out that they were fictitious, and no one was listening. One was actually a broadcast station. All of us tried contacting coalition vessels by VHF radio to clarify the frequencies but no one would ever respond.

At the time of the attack, we broadcast Mayday calls on all known VHF and HF radio frequencies. The only response was from a commercial vessel (see <u>Noonsite report</u>). This vessel sent out reports via satellite. The next morning a German warship was close by, and we could report the incident to them. This was 12 hours after the attack, and they had not heard anything about it.

When we arrived in Aden, we gave the Yemen Officials the report and had a long talk with the Yemeni Coast Guard commanders. They are just getting organized and do not presently have the capability to actually patrol the Yemen coast. They stated that many of the Yemen coastal areas are tribal and the central government does not have any control at all. They also warned us to be careful of retaliation by the families of the bad people.

We then contacted the authorities in Djibouti to voice our concerns about retaliation and requested that they keep an eye on us between Aden and the entrance to the Red Sea. They assured us that they would inform the naval authorities so that they could provide assistance. We did manage to contact a French warship outside of Aden when we left there. They had no information about our request for assistance, and if you can believe this, did not even know about the attack 8 days before in their patrol area! They did consent to watch over us until we made the entrance to the Red Sea, where we stayed on the west side going north. There is no sense, in tempting fate twice.

Bullets struck one boat about 14 times. The other boat was, struck three times. Fortunately, none penetrated the hulls and no one on either boat wounded. Thank Conclusion: Emergency HF radio frequencies, like 2182 MHz, no longer exist in most of the world. No one is listening. Any request for immediate assistance will probably come from a commercial vessel in the vicinity, but commercial vessels are not capable of effectively dealing with attacks of this type. At the most, they might scare the attackers off. These attacks happen so quickly that, unless you had an actual escort in the immediate vicinity getting help quickly will not happen.

The "Coalition Forces" out here is a myth. It appears that there is no central authority i.e. anyone in command. The right hand does not know what the left one is doing and most certainly, there is no communication between them. You are on your own out here, and you had better be prepared to stand on your own two feet. Thank goodness for steel boats!

USS Gonzalez wards off an attack on civilian mariners in Indian Ocean

Topic: Piracy Reports 2005
Countries: Somalia

2005-06-28

The U.S. Navy guided-missile destroyer USS Gonzalez (DDG 66), currently operating as part of Task Force 51 in the U.S. 5th Fleet area of responsibility, helped ward off an attack on motor vessel Tigris June 6 in the Indian Ocean off the coast of Somalia.

The guided-missile destroyer received word of the attack via a bridge-to-bridge radio report from Motor vessel. The crew of the motor vessel, who escaped uninjured, reported they were under attack and being, fired upon. "The master [of the vessel] sounded extremely scared and provided Gonzalez his position and requested immediate assistance," said Gonzalez's commanding officer.

USS Gonzalez, currently conducting maritime security operations (MSO) in the area, responded immediately and began moving toward the vessel at the best speed in order to render assistance. To let the attackers know of their presence, the crew of Gonzalez fired .50. Caliber machine guns, energized their searchlights, and fired flares in the direction of the attack in order to illuminate the area. "I believe that Gonzalez's very overt approach was likely observed by pirates, who then broke off contact on the vessel," said Griffin. "the vessel appears fortunate to have had a Coalition warship in the vicinity when the attack occurred, or she could have become a victim." USS Gonzalez continued with its MSO mission while concurrently monitoring the vessel's passage.

MSO sets the conditions for security and stability in the maritime environment and complements the counter-terrorism and security efforts of regional nations. MSO denies international terrorists use of the maritime environment as a venue for attack, or to transport, personnel weapons; or other material.

USS Gonzalez deployed from Norfolk, Va., March 25 as part of the USS Kearsarge (LHD 3) Expeditionary Strike Group, with the 26th Marine Expeditionary Unit (Special Operations Capable), based in Camp Lejune, N.C., and currently assigned to Commander, Task Force 51, operating in the U.S. Naval Forces Central Command area of responsibility.

Navy Ships Respond To Yacht's SOS off Yemen Coast

Topic: *Piracy Reports 2006*

Noonsite received an initial report that pirates attacked US-flagged yacht in the Gulf of Aden on Sunday April 16. Further reports then revealed that the yacht, with three people on board, had become, alarmed by the behavior of "fishing boats" in their vicinity and had sent out an SOS radio message.

The message was picked up by an Italian container ship and quickly relayed to the US Navy which sent two ships along with a Dutch navy ship to investigate the incident, which occurred about 25 miles off the Yemeni coast. At present, it would appear that the navy ships prevented an incident of piracy taking place. Noonsite will post any updates as received.

The vessel a 38' Choey Lee ketch and was heading up the Red Sea after having crossed the Indian Ocean via the Andaman and Maldives.

In another development, the Somali government claimed this week that an agreement has been, reached with the US to patrol Somali territorial waters in a bid to clamp down on the increasing numbers of pirates operating out of this area. However, US officials have denied that any such deal has been, made.

German Cruising Couple Still Being Held Hostage in Somalia

Topic: Piracy Reports 2008
Countries: Somalia

As reported by the Somali Press.

Seventeen days later, and the ordeal for the German sailors held hostage in Somalia is still not over.

For previous reports see:
Somali Pirates Double Ransom
Four Days Later and Pirated Demand US$1M
Sailing Family Seized by Pirates

The Somali Press has published an update of the hostage situation today, warning "it is very difficult to provide coverage of piracy in Somalia, and this has been very much the case with the "German Tourists" who were abducted last month from the Gulf of Aden. As we've said previously, news is sparse and unreliable, and often one false report is quoted for weeks."

However, what they can now confirm is that there are two sailors, a man (age 63) and his wife (age 51), who; abducted from their small yacht and dragged into the hills of Puntland, Somalia on Monday 23 June. They have been in contact with their families, the German Federal Police, and the German Embassy and told family members they were "well given the circumstances".

The hostages are currently being, held; in a remote area of the Badhan district of Sanaag. They were, moved due to soldiers capturing the Las Qorey district, where the hostages were previously, being kept.

An official with a Puntland-based human rights agency was, allowed to visit the Germans, and it was he, who confirmed their identity. "I spoke and stayed with the hostages for two days," the man told Radio Garowe. He went on to say that, the pirates are a group of "trained and well-armed men who are not easy to approach," saying they only allowed him to visit because it was for a "humanitarian purpose."

He found that the 63-year-old man "only (had) three days of (diabetic) medical supplies left." He was reportedly given additional medical supplies soon after. The 51-year-old woman "is in good health," but was roughed up during the initial kidnapping when she was reportedly "beaten lightly." According to the official, the hostages are well fed and have "their own cook." He added, "They (the Germans) are taken around each day, but the place is like Tora Bora (the mountains in Afghanistan where the Taliban hid)."

According to the Somali Press, there is still no solid news on the unconfirmed reports of a child and French captain who were reportedly, taken along with the German couple. They say little evidence has been, found that there are more than two hostages involved. However, one of their contacts in Somalia spoke with a clan elder yesterday, who reported again that there is, in fact, an eight-year-old boy. The elder stated that the child had been very ill with fever, but is well now. This information, however, is "completely unconfirmed".

The clan leader also stated that ransom negotiations were going well, and the pirates except the situation to be resolved soon.

Recent Developments,
However, in a recent development just reported by the Somali Press, it appears that Somali militants are now fighting each-other

to rescue the Germans. "We have surrounded the pirates," Gurey Osman Salah, the Somaliland commander in Las Qoray, told Reuters by telephone.

"We will not allow anyone near the area, and we will not hesitate to use force."

The move has angered the Puntland authorities, who withdrew their forces last week in order to avoid a clash with Somaliland troops, after local elders called for space to negotiate with the pirates and persuaded both sides to pull back.

International recognition has so far eluded both breakaway enclaves, and security experts say officials on both sides think rescuing the Germans would help their cause.

In Puntland's busy port city of Bosasso, residents said fighters were now preparing for redeployment, raising fears of a battle. Elders who tried to negotiate with the kidnappers were, said, to have withdrawn to Baran, south of Las Qoray.

"The troops have tested their weapons. We are preparing a force to be sent to Las Qoray," a senior Puntland police officer told Reuters. He declined to be, named.

Captured Yacht in use by Somalia Pirates
Topic: Piracy Reports 2008
Countries: Somalia, Yemen

BE ALERT WHEN YOU SEE THIS YACHT IN OR NEAR SOMALIAN WATERS.

The vessel captured by Somalia Pirates a week ago (see recent news item on noonsite), may be under use as a decoy vessel attacking other ships, warns the Seafarers Assistance Programme (SAP) in Kenya.

It appears that after the owners of *the vessel* were, taken ashore; the heavily armed gunmen took the yacht to sea again. While an attempt to sell the yacht at ports in the Gulf States can also, not be, ruled out, it is, presumed that it is at present being used to hunt for other ships.

The SAP warns that the vessel likely is, or will be, used to signal ships at sea as being under distress (simulating an engine failure or other emergency at sea), while hiding a small attack speedboat from view of any ships responding to the rescue.

A small attack vessel of the type that can hide behind the vessel usually carries 5-7 heavily armed attackers (equipped with bazookas, assault guns like AK47, G3, FAL, M16 plus RPG - rocket propelled grenade launchers, as well as hand-grenades and/or mines). Such attack-boats do deliver a swift and heavy assault."

The *vessel* is a 16-meter (53") ketch (two masts) with a doghouse-style dodger (fiberglass-enclosed cockpit). If you see this yacht, prepare for an attack and notify authorities immediately. For advice on what to do if, you see this yacht, or indeed suspect you are being, approached by pirates, please read article.

All vessels are advised to stay well off the Somalia coast (200nm at least, wherever possible), travel in convoys, and to keep a specific eye out for the *vessel*. The most dangerous area reported to be 12/14 degrees North and 046/053 degrees east. Coordinates from SAP of a suggested corridor through the Gulf of Aden are:
Waypoint: 12 15N 045E
Waypoint: 12 35N 045E
Waypoint: 13 35N 049E
Waypoint: 13 40N 049E
Waypoint: 14 10N 050E
Waypoint: 14 15N 050E
Waypoint: 14 35N 053E
Waypoint: 14 45N 053E

Find out more about being part of a convoy on noonsite, or contact: Net Controller, Maritime Mobile Net, SE Asia, and 14,323 MHz @ 0025hrs.Zulu daily and WX @ 0055hrs.Zulu daily.

Piracy report from UKMTO for Gulf of Aden
Topic: _Piracy Reports 2008_
Countries: _Somalia, Yemen_

There continues to be Piracy activity in the Gulf of Aden and once again on the East Coast of Somalia.

In the Gulf of Aden there appears to be targeting of vessels, being carried out around position 13 30N 050 04E. All vessels should be extra vigilant when transiting within a 10nm radius of this position. In recent attacks, Pirates have played music on Ch.16, to try to jam the channel and stop vessels contacting the coalition warships.

A Maritime Security Patrol Area (MSPA) has been, established to provide a route through the Gulf of Aden, which will be, patrolled by Combined Task Force (CTF) 150.

Whilst it cannot guarantee that attacks will not happen, it is, hoped that 150 assets will be able to respond faster to any attacks and the patrols will act as a deterrent.

Coordinates of the Security Corridor in the Gulf of Aden are as follows:

Waypoint: 12 15N 045E
Waypoint: 12 35N 045E
Waypoint: 13 35N 049E
Waypoint: 13 40N 049E
Waypoint: 14 10N 050E
Waypoint: 14 15N 050E
Waypoint: 14 35N 053E
Waypoint: 14 45N 053E

Since the inception of the MSPA, CTF 150 has helped deter more than a dozen attacks in the Gulf of Aden (per 22 Sep 08 reporting). However, criminals have still successfully targeted several vessels in the region.

The MSPA was, established on August 22, 2008 in support of the International Maritime Organization's (IMO) call for international assistance to discourage attacks on commercial vessels transiting the Gulf of Aden. The MSPA is a geographic area in the Gulf of Aden utilized by Combined Maritime Forces to focus their efforts against de-stabilizing activities. Coalition forces patrol the MSPA, which is not marked, or defined by visual navigational means, on a routine basis.

"Coalition maritime efforts will give the IMO time to work at international efforts that will ultimately lead to a long-term solution," said Vice Adm., Commander, and Combined Maritime Forces. "This is a problem that starts ashore and requires an international solution. We made this clear at the outset - our efforts cannot guarantee safety in the region. Our part in preventing some of these destabilizing activities is only one part of the solution to preventing further attacks."

All vessels off the coast of Somalia and transiting the Gulf of Aden are, advised to maintain a strict 24-hours anti-piracy visual watch and radar watch and should not hesitate to activate GMDSS, in addition to calling for assistance on VHF, if the vessel comes under threat. US Navy Exchanges Gunfire with Suspected Pirates

Topic: *Piracy Reports 2006*

News agencies reported at the weekend that two U.S. Navy ships exchanged gunfire with suspected pirates off the coast of Somalia on Saturday March 18, killing one and wounding five. The battle occurred at about 5:40 a.m. local time, about 25 nautical miles off the Somali coast in international waters.

At the time, the USS Cape St. George, a guided missile cruiser, and the USS Gonzalez, a guided missile destroyer, were conducting maritime security operations as part of a Dutch-led task force.

They observed a 30-foot fishing boat towing smaller skiffs and prepared to board and inspect the vessels. The naval boarding team noticed the men were, armed with what appeared to be rocket-propelled grenade launchers. The suspected pirates opened fire and the US warships returned fire with small arms. Several suspects were, taken into custody.

On March 15, the U.N. Security Council encouraged naval forces operating off Somalia to take action against suspected pirates as they have been targeting ships from the U.N. World Food Programme carrying relief to the millions of people affected by the drought in east Africa.

Yachts making the passage from Salalah to Djibouti or Aden have reported that US, and French airplanes have been conducting daily surveillance of the area, and the international forces are listening on VHF 16 and will respond to any calls.

Yacht Attacked by Pirates in Gulf of Aden

Topic: Piracy Archive 2003

Pirates while sailing through the Gulf of Aden attacked us. There was another attack on two yachts a week before only 20 miles from where we were, attacked. We were sailing in convoy with four other yachts. We had a couple of meetings to plan our contingency in case of the event of a piracy attack.

We would sail in a close formation not more than half a mile apart, at a minimum speed of four knots under sail and five knots if we were motoring. It is, believed that the pirates have access to, VHF radio. In addition; we would keep radio silence, on Channel 16, and not gives our position on any radio frequencies. We had a regular HF 2 MHz radio schedule every three hours.

At 0800 on the morning of March 9, while one lookout scanning the horizon and saw three small craft - they were coming in our direction. We called the others on the radio and told them. As the boats drew closer, we could clearly see the plastic tarps covering their hulls, and the heads of many people.

We immediately realized that these were people-smugglers and possibly the same boats that attacked the two yachts last week.

The attacking boats were about 20 meters long, wooden, and had plastic sheeting wrapped around their hulls. They were also loaded with terrified people, believed to be illegal Somali refugees en route to Yemen. We were later, told; that the refuges, are often, thrown; into the sea, on the coast or shores, of Yemen regardless, of whether or not, they can swim and left to their own devices. These people smugglers are ruthless.

We closed our ranks (a bit like a wagon train), turned on our engines, and went as fast as we could in a tight group. Our yacht was at the rear of the formation on the port side, which just happened to be in the vulnerable spot from an attack from this angle, just our luck. At least the other boat was on the inside of us and we were happy about that as they had children onboard.

Then, when they were about 200 meters from us, they started to shoot and, as I heard the first shot, I saw the captain in the cockpit duck on the floor. Immediately, we were on our radios, the Mayday calls were going out thick and fast, but with no reply at first. Then I heard the captain on the other boat speaking French (his mother tongue) to the French/German Coalition in Djibouti, but that was too far away.

They were sending an Orion plane that would arrive in about an hour. We could not wait for that long. Another boat was talking to the commercial ship that was also about an hour away, but would relay our message to the Piracy Center in Kuala Lumpur, Malaysia. That was great but offered no immediate help. Then I heard one boat speaking to the American Naval aircraft carrier that we had passed the day before with a warship practicing landing their jump jet Harriers. They could be at our position in three hours. "That is not good enough; we need help now," They said they would send assistance immediately, but we still believed it could not arrive soon enough.

In the meantime, I was calling Mayday on the HF international distress frequency 2182, with no response. Then we had a response from the Panamanian merchant ship ROYAL PASCADERAS, they were altering course to come to our assistance, and they were only about five minutes from visual contact! "Oh thank God," I prayed, all we had to do was keep the pirates at bay for a little while longer. The US Navy, in the meantime, was still talking on the VHF in a loud commanding voice. It increased my confidence, we would outrun these bastards, and we would live to see our children and grandchildren again.

After the gunshots, one person was lying in the companionway, steering the yacht by reaching his hand up and pressing the autopilot panel. He made me stay below in the cabin, the lower half of which is below the waterline, so I would not, be shot. I chanced a look through the cabin window (I have never been good at doing what I am told), and I could see the one boat that was still after us.

It was loaded, crammed with human cargo, like sardines. I also saw a man with a rifle on the bow. The other two boats were going behind us. I was not sure if they had given up the chase or were they going around behind to flank us. The main boat that was chasing us was slowly gaining. We realized this was it, they were going to board us, one of the other boats was their target, and we were the closest. We were surprisingly very calm. My husband put his arms around me and said, "We'll get through this, just give them anything they want, and they won't hurt us, they only want to rob us, so just let them have what they want."

He went up to check our course (so we would not run into the yacht in front of us) and he quickly jumped below again and grabbed the radio. He told everyone to look out the back, they had dropped back, the pirates had slowed down, and perhaps they had given up the chase. On the other hand, were they up to something else. No! It was our heroes, the ROYAL PASCADERAS had come over the horizon, and they were heading our way! Oh my God, thank heavens. We are, saved! We were safe, we had done it, and we were the first yachts to escape a pirate attack that I know of. We, had made it, yes, we had made it! Thank you, ROYAL PASCADERAS!

The three boats were quickly making their way towards Yemen; one was blowing a hell of a lot of smoke. Then, about 20-30 minutes after the pirates had left us; the Coalition Orion flew overhead and circled us a few times. We were on the deck waving and shouting like children. About an hour later, he returned from the opposite direction; he radioed to say he saw the numerous small local craft; none was coming in our direction or appeared to be a threat to us. Meanwhile, the ROYAL PASCADERAS sailed slowly beside us.

With the knowledge that we were safe, they bid us farewell and went back on their original course. We will never forget them, and hope that one day we will have the opportunity to thank them. Personally, I just want to give the captain a big hug and kiss.

About half an hour after the ROYAL PASCADERAS left us; a large US helicopter flew overhead and spoke to us on the radio.

Not long after this, the Coalition Taskforce 200 called and asked if we still needed assistance, they were on their way and would be with us in a few hours, but we told them the Orion aircraft said we were no longer under threat. Wow, every man and his dog were out to help us. No doubt, the problems and possible threat of invasion of Iraq had increased the navy presence in the area. Never before had a yacht under attack had so much assistance - we were indeed fortunate. Commercial vessels are notorious for not coming to the assistance of a yacht being, attacked by pirates, but not the ROYAL PASCADERAS!

That evening the Coalition Warship 992 contacted us by radio. They had come to assist us if necessary, and they stayed close by the whole night and again the next day. By then we were out of the danger zone, and we went our separate ways. We sailed on through the "Gates of Sorrow" with 25-30 knots of wind behind us and had a sleigh ride. We finally arrived in Port Assab, Eritrea; we were in the Red Sea off the north coast of Africa. The next things we heard, the American and allied forces were invading Iraq.

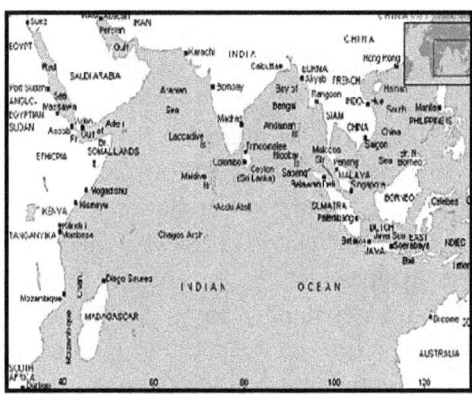

Figure 12 Indiana Ocean

INDIANA OCEAN
Pirate Attacks

Pirate attack in the Strait of Messina, Italy

Topic: Piracy Reports 2005

July 07 2005

British sailor has asked us to relay the following information.

He is presently cruising single-handed from Greece to Naples, on his Najad 390. As he was entering the Strait of Messina, he was met by a strong Northerly winds and decided to head for the port of Saline Joniche. This massive Industrial port, which is generally, described as unusable in the guidebooks.

An opening has, however, been created in the harbor wall, allowing vessels to enter and anchor in the basin. This harbor is especially important to smaller vessels, as it breaks up the circa 66 Mile long run from Rocella Ionica to Reggio di Calabria. So on

30.06.2005 he enters the harbor and anchors as the only yacht in the center of the basin.

At approximately 2200 hrs he notice's footsteps on deck, and as he climbs into the cockpit, is met by four young men. One of them holds a pistol to his head, and demands money. He hands him about 400€ in cash, which does not satisfy the pirates. As one of them holds him at gunpoint in the cockpit, the other three search his vessel, and, after finding some computer peripherals, demand his notebook. He did not bring it on the voyage. However, and they have to settle for his CD collection and other valuables. He presumes the worst as he notices them fumbling with a role of masking tape to bind him. In the confusion, he manages to jump overboard, dive, and swim to shore, where he hides among the rocks of the harbor wall.

The pirates obviously feel quite safe and start to search for him. When one of them is only about 10 Meters away, He leaps back into the water and swims to a small, open fishing boat. He slips inside, finds a fishing knife and a sturdy tiller, and waits. About 30 minutes later a fishing boat anchors in the harbor, and he swims over to them. Together they lock up his vessel and head to the Police station, where he spends the night before heading on to Reggio di Calabria in the morning.

We have since heard of several more incidents, in which yachts were, harassed in Saline Joniche. On 28,.06. 2005 and 05.07.2005 yachts had to fend off a small boat with 3 to 4 young males aboard. At times, they claimed to be the Harbor authority and demanded mooring fees, in the other incident; they simply demanded money in a very aggressive manner. Fortunately, both crews managed to chase them off either by alerting the police, or leaving the harbor as they were, approached late at night by the dinghy.

Vessels transiting the Strait of Messina should certainly avoid the port of Saline Joniche, or enter only in groups.

Possible Attempted Attack near Sri Lanka

Topic: Piracy Reports 2008
Countries: Sri Lanka

On 29.01.2008, we were underway, position 06:00.8N - 082:01.9E, 130nm East of Galle, Sri Lanka, when a red fishing boat with five men on board approached. Crew fired shots in the air, and they aborted the attempt. The boat attempted to close with us twice, at 0830 and 1100 UTC. Not clear if this was an attempted attack or not.

Chased by...near Sri Lanka - January 2008
Topic: Piracy Reports 2008
Countries: Sri Lanka, Thailand

On voyage to the Red Sea from Phuket/Thailand *on our Bowman 47*

We had been, warned from others in Thailand, so we took their advice to stay at least 60 NM off the Sri Lankan coast. To make sure and to be safe we sailed a distance of approx. 85 NM off the coast.

We entered the "Danger Zone" at sunset and opted for a "No Lights" sail. On the horizon, we spotted a boat about 4 miles away. Next to it were 2-3 smaller vessels, all not showing on the radar. As soon as they spotted us, they sent the smaller ones toward us. We started the engine, rolled the Genoa completely out and headed higher into the wind, which gave us a speed of nearly 11 knots.

This was just enough to keep the chasing vessel at bay. After 1 to 2 hours, they gave up, and we could resume on our course. During this chase, we heard them on the radio communicating with the mother ship and other vessels. Some of the words came in English, but it was clear that they were pissed off as we had escaped.

Later that night my partner was on watch, she saw strong lights heading in our direction. She woke me up just in time to play the same game again. We were lucky as the wind was a steady 18 knot from the NE and with pointing *our boat* higher up we had enough speed to stay ahead again. However, this time they did not give up so easy and chased us for more than one hour. The chasing vessel got as close as half a mile, and again we heard them on the radio. When they finally gave up, they screamed an "F...You" and some other stuff. I was almost tempted to tell them "catch me if you can", but stayed calm.

We sailed on our previous course again as morning came. There were some lights ahead of us, but we thought that we had passed the danger zone and stayed on course. The other boat did not see us for a while; but when the sun came up, they noticed, our presence. We really thought that they were honest fishermen, so we made no attempt to change our direction.

As soon as they saw us, they started the chase. At first we thought they had finished their work and, headed home. It looked like this, as they were not on an interception course, just heading towards Sri Lanka approx. 3 miles down from us. However, we were wrong, when on the same height, they changed course, heading straight for us.

There were three smaller vessels right behind them, which we had not noticed in the poor light and wave action, but it was clear now what they wanted. Two of them changed direction and by spreading out, they tried to cut us off further down. This was a real chase now, my engine was running on full throttle, all sails up, and we were, headed almost straight into the wind. The boats got closer and closer, we had to tack, changed course a few times, and when the mother vessel came from the portside, we thought that this time we would lose the game.

They were cutting our path but fortunately a good puff of wind came and only about 50 meters away from the pursuing vessel I steered hard to the side, and we passed in front of them. They made no attempt of slowing down, and they would have clearly hit us on the side, sinking our yacht. We could see their angry faces and throwing fists, but we escaped by an inch. The vessel kept chasing us from behind for another 20 minutes, and then finally gave up as we had enough speed to outrun them.

With shaking bodies, we continued our voyage but stayed alert until we reached the Maldives. No matter what other sailors say, we believe that this is organized piracy and those boats are just there to wait for any yachts that come by.

We were lucky but any slower boat would not have escaped them.

Piracy incident Majunga Madagascar SE Indian Ocean

Topic: Piracy Reports 2007
Countries: Madagascar

Sailmail Support for Southern Africa sent Noonsite the following report of an attack on French Canadian yacht off Majunga, Madagascar.

"The four pirates dropped in our boat at 2 o'clock in the morning on Friday the 19 of Oct. They came in through a hatch that was open for ventilation. I was, awakened by a suspicious noise and standing, trying to load my flares gun but the first punched me with a leg shot through the ribs and stepped over me while the second one was getting my friend and the third came to help the one that was trying to choke me.

This took not more than 15 seconds. As I caught in the dark, the hand of the second one, I realized that he has a knife that deeply cut my right thumb when he succeeded in sliding it out of my hold. He then went down and drove his knife through my left calf in order to neutralize me.

Immediately, I pushed my hand to his face, but he caught my thumb in his mouth biting it and holding it very fiercely. I realized at that moment that the one on my friend was about to kill her by strangulation; after shaking her legs, I heard her last whisper, and she fell unanimated. I stopped immediately fighting and asked many times for everybody to calm down, and that we were about to give them what they wanted.

They had already begun to shout like hell for the money (l'argent l'argent ou est l'argent...l'argent l'argent ...ou est ...) and they were so speedy and nervous that I felt this situation was extremely dangerous. It took a long moment to have a light calm down as they were shouting all together. By that time, they had tied roughly her who had started to come back to life by some long and noisy breathing. I had a very hard time to explain them that they had to free her because she was the one who could give them the little money we had onboard.

Their French was weak and English was totally misunderstood. "She was recovering from a deep trauma was completely lost in her head and about the situation; she was unable to figure where she had put the few Aviary's we had on board; after a while, always through their uninterrupted shouts, she found a bag in which there were a few euro's (44) and US $(26).

One of them rapidly put the money in his pocket and was very frustrated because he expected a lot more. They thought we were carrying the money for our whole around the world trip...!!! Therefore, they planned to attack her to get more. I was distracted with that perspective that they were discussing in Malgash. Until that moment, I was standing, untied under the menace of their knives, and I was from far the calmest of that whole gang.

Things were running very fast in my head, and I had to do something urgently: So I started to affirm, with all the conviction I could, that violence was a useless cause they HAD the money...they HAD the money and that this person has it in his pocket showing the one that took it from her. That was a good idea because, in the dark and the moving flashlight, nobody knew the amount of money he has put in his pocket, even me. I stirred up trouble in the group; they did not trust much each other and the thing started to improve for us. He even made the mistake to show a few bills asking her its value in Aviaries making the others more suspicious.

The moneyman came angry about how the situation had turned, as he was now the center of interest; so he came at me, pushing me a bit, and telling me to sit on the floor so that they could tie me. I gently accepted this, as a logical, proposition and declare, to them, that there was, nothing. I will try to prevent them from taking what they want. They charged the one that seemed to be the youngest one, to watch us. He tied my wrists and legs without conviction with innocent's knots and did not tie her who sat on the floor.

One of them came to me asking me to light the cabin lights. I oppose a firm "no way" repeating that I let them take what they want but I do not want to know their faces. So we stayed in the dark, otherwise, it could have been a sufficient reason to get rid of us before they left.

As we had been sitting on the floor for more than an hour with our security guard, we managed to have a conversation with him. It was hard at the beginning because he did not want to talk and asked us to shut-up, pointing us with his knife. However, after a while, as the others came many times asking us information about what they were finding, we succeeded in starting a very comprehensive conversation, avoiding any kind of blame.

We talked about their poverty, our nice contacts with the poor but proud people of St Marie Island, the gifts, we made to the extremely poor community of Mitsio, medication and other. The problem he has to live in Majunga...etc... Etc. and incredibly, I convinced him to give me back my laptop that I could hide from the three others. I in the same way hide under the map table, plenty of ropes that were on the floor in front of the door, ready to go out.

We start to feel better and at the end, as one was going out with my guitar, he asked me if I could play. As I said yes, he had a loud discussion, each pulling the guitar by both ends; he finally gave it back to me... with one more hour of conversation...? It is only many hours later that we realized how much we were, damaged; fractured ribs for both of us and many knife wounds that needed many stitches. Now we are slowly recovering from the pirate attack and everything is in a good way."

According to Justice Malanot, this is the first low-level armed robbery incident in Majunga in the nearly 10 years he has been hosting Sailmail in Africa. However, after posting the above report, contacted Noonsite to say:"Another sailboat was in Majunga two weeks before I went there, and they were boarded by pirates but their boat (French) is built like a tank, so they could not come inside and nothing happened. Another boat was, attacked and, stolen on the same, night. They send me an email to warn me, but it arrived 4 days too late."

Justice Malanot's assessment of the piracy risk in the region is as follows: Seychelles, Comoros, Chagos, and Coco Keeling areas: very low. East African Coast south of Somalia: piracy risk is very low-to-low, same for Madagascar. Somalia piracy risk is moderate to high. Justice advises: "Don't sail close to the Somali coast, sail in a group, do what it takes, have a backbone. It is a bad neighborhood in a great region, all cities the world over have one of those.

The precautions to take are that against petty criminals, and you avoid being a victim of a drive by shooting by giving the bad neighborhood a wide miss (80 miles plus). The mature assessment is that it is an acceptable risk."

Commercial shipping remains more at risk from pirates than yachts, suffering the majority of attacks around the world. Two dramatic incidents occurred in the past week off the Somali coast with the crew of a North Korean ship fighting off pirates and a Japanese tanker being, hijacked, in the Gulf of Aden and taken by pirates into Somali waters. In both cases, the US Navy intervened and efforts are being, made now to release the hijacked ship and its crew. The IMB Piracy Reporting Centre area assessment is as follows:

- The Gulf of Aden / Red Sea: A number of suspicious craft reports have been, received. These crafts either set a collision course, or pursue the ships. Mariners advised to be cautious. In the past, some of the vessels have been, fired, upon.

- Somalian waters: The IMB Piracy Reporting Centre has received 26 actual and attempted attacks so far this year. Many more attacks may have gone unreported. Some pirates are dangerous; and would fire their automatic weapons at ships to stop them. Occasionally, they would use their RPG (Rocket Propelled Grenade) launchers at ships. Pirates are, believed to be using "mother vessels" to launch attacks at very far distance from coast. These "mother vessels" are able to proceed to very far out to sea to launch smaller boats to attack and hijack passing ships. Eastern and Northeastern coasts are high-risk areas for attacks and hijackings. Vessels not making scheduled calls to ports in Somalia should keep as far away as possible from the Somali coast, ideally more than 200 nautical miles. Mariners are also, advised, to report any suspicious boats to the Centre.

IMB Piracy Reporting Centre, Kuala Lumpur, Malaysia, Tel + 60 3 2078 5763, Fax + 60 3 2078 5769, E-mail IMBKL@icc-ccs.org 24 Hours Anti Piracy HELPLINE Tel: ++ 60 3 2031 0014

Act of piracy in Kunniyakumari, Cape Comorin, India

Topic: Piracy Reports 2006

I would like to report on an act of piracy at Kanniyakumari (Cape Comorin, India's southernmost point) in the night of the 22nd of April 2006 and on how the local authorities handled the problem.

I attached a copy of the complaint, I made to the local police. After all, I must admit that the local authorities (i.e. the Customs Department) tried to stop me from making a complaint to the police and wanted me to leave immediately. They even supported the local media with wrong information, so that I found my crew and myself in the local newspaper the next day. The article gave wrong information on where we came from, where we intended to go and suggested a probable illegal immigration. Nothing about the robbery was, mentioned.

While speaking to the Sub Inspector of the local police, we were, told that "Kannyakumari is a very dangerous place", that "there are many thefts on boats", and that we should warn other yachts from calling into Kanniyakumari. The police have given me a receipt in which they refer to the incident as an "act of piracy". I regard the behavior of the local authorities as very unacceptable.

A copy of the complaint I made to the police:

Kanniyakumari, 23/04/2006

Subject: Complaint - Act of Piracy in Kanniyakumari (Cape Comorin, India)

Were on board of the, Sailing Vessel, on a coastal, cruise (as tourists), from, Cochin to Tuticorin. After having passed Cape Comorin, we were coming closer to shore looking for a possible anchorage on April 22, 2006. At about 10 o'clock p.m. we were, approached by a long tail powered fishing boat with 10+ people on it screaming and shouting.

We stopped to see what they wanted. They immediately boarded us and surrounded us in our cockpit. The captain had to block the entrance to the boat to stop the people getting inside of it. They were picking up ropes and winch handles, moving things around, and demanding Whiskey, Brandy, Beer, cigarettes, t-shirts, food, and money. They totally ignored all our requests to leave the boat.

During this confusion, there were two guys sitting on our well-tied life raft on the back of the boat and one guy wandering around with a torch we could hardly stop from picking up things and trying to hide them under his longer. One person even tried to take over the rudder while the other ones did not stop harassing us.

Eventually, they left the boat, and we decided not to visit Kanniyakumari but to set course for the East Cape. We sailed for approximately seven miles before we discovered that our life raft has been, stolen. We immediately turned. On our way back to

Kanniyakumari, we managed to inform the local police on the incident by mobile phone (via third party). We were unable to contact the Indian Coastguard.

Returning to Kanniyakumari, we were nervous when another small boat approached us. We were relieved as they identified themselves as police, so we invited them to come aboard our boat. A man identified himself as the Superintendent of Customs. I asked him if he was aware of what had happened to us and he said "yes". To make sure that there was no misunderstanding, he asked him if he had been, contacted by the local police but did not receive an answer.

As he informed him that we were in touch with a third party being (Reverend G.) who had contacted the Superintendent of Customs advised us not to contact the local police nor the church as they would try to protect the fishermen and assured us that the Customs would find our missing life raft.

Later, he asked if we would leave Kanniyakumari, as soon as we got our life raft back, and we replied that this would depend on the state our life raft would be in. Five minutes after we had dropped the Superintendent of Customs at the harbor, Customs returned the empty life raft-canister on our boat saying that we would get the rest of the life raft in the morning. We were still hoping to get it back undamaged / unused / not fired.

At 8:30 a.m. this morning, Customs collected us and brought us to their office to hand over the life raft. We found it inflated and with all the equipment missing.

This means:

• A life raft is only inflatable once and thereby of no use until it is, handed back, to the manufacturer for repacking.

• the survival pack is missing. We would like to inform you that it contains extremely dangerous high explosive rocket-flares, which still might be anywhere in your community.

We were then, asked to collect the life raft and to sign a document stating that he received his property back. This is absurd. We then went to the police. On arriving there, we were, told that the Customs Department had asked the police to forward any complaint; we would do to them, for investigation.

For us, this is very unacceptable. We make this complaint on the basis that the matter will be, investigated by the Police Department. We feel that piracy is a serious offense.

Violent Pirate Attack on Two Yachts off Yemen

Topic: _Piracy Reports 2005_

Here is a firsthand account of a pirate attack on two yachts. It took place only 30 miles off the coast of Yemen at 13°28' North 48°07' East on 8 March 5pm local.

This report has been, filed with the relevant authorities: the Yemen Coast Guard, Yemen Navy, Aden Port Control, US Coalition 5th Fleet, US Embassy and State Department.

Controller, Mobile Maritime Net, South East Asian Waters (14,323 MHz 0025 Z daily Wx @ 0055 Z daily)

On 8 March 2005, two sailing yachts were moving SW 30 miles off the coast of Yemen proceeding to the port of Aden from Salalah, Oman.

At about 0900 two outboard powered boats, about 25 feet long with 3 men in each one, passed off our stern moving south at about 25 knots. An hour or two later they returned, one coming quite close and looking us over carefully. The second boat passed our bows but quite a ways away. These boats were obviously not engaged in a normal activity such as fishing, etc. At that time we were south of Al Mukalla, Yemen. The area around Al Mukalla is well, documented as being a piracy problem area, and we started watching carefully for anything out of the ordinary.

At about 1600, we observed two different boats approaching us head on from the SW. These boats were 25-30 feet long, had higher freeboard and diesel powered. They were coming very fast directly at us. There were four men in each boat. The boats separated at about 200 yards, one boat ahead of the other, coming down one boats port side and firing into the cockpit. The other boat was firing an automatic weapon at both boat boats from ahead, more at the closest. These people were shooting, directly at, the cockpits; and obviously intended to kill us.

The first boat swung around behind our stern to come up and board us. At that point, we armed with a 12-gage shotgun loaded with 00 buckshot, started shooting into their boat. I forced them to keep their heads down so that they could not shoot at us. I am not sure I hit anyone at that point, although I could see the driver of the boat crouched down behind a steering console. After firing 3 shots at them their engine started to smoke, and I swung around to shoot at the boat ahead. At that point, I saw the other boat ram that boat amidships almost cutting it in two and turning it almost completely over.

I turned back around to shoot again at the boat behind us and that is when they turned away from, and were heading toward the stern of the other boat. They were beside us, about 100 feet away. The bow of the pirate's boat came right up against the others stern and two men stood up on the bow to board them. That was a serious and probably fateful error on their part. I shot both of them. That boat then veered away, and I shot the driver, although I am not sure of the outcome because they were farther away and I did not knock him down like the other two.

We kept going at full speed to put as much distance between the pirates and us as possible. As soon as we were out of rifle range, we looked back and both boats were drifting and appeared to be disabled.

If they had not had the presence of mind to veer over into one boat and ram it, the outcome of this attack would have been very different. All they needed to do was stand off a ways and shoot us to pieces with automatic weapons. We were extremely lucky. We broadcast Mayday calls on all VHF and HF radio frequencies, including two HF emergency frequencies supplied by the US Coast

Guard a few days before. The Coalition Forces in the area were supposed to be monitoring these frequencies.

There was no response except from a commercial ship in the area on VHF 16. Who approached and observed the disabled pirates for a bit, then sailed along side of us for 2-4 hours until dark to make sure we would be all right.

The pirates were well organized and well armed. There were at least 4 boats involved. They had set up a picket line out from the Yemen coast probably at least for 50-75 miles, so if you transited the area during the day they would not miss you. The two boats that attacked us appeared to have come from the south.

There has been speculation in the past that this ongoing piracy problem off the Yemen coast being, carried out by Somali pirates. Given the number, type of boats involved, and the direction the spotter boats came from, this does not appear to be correct in this case. This problem is getting worse and the pirate attacks are getting deadly. One could only expect that the Yemen Government will take more direct action. At the very least, allow yachts to group in Salalah, Oman and at some point on the NW Yemen coast to request an escort along the Yemen coast.

US Embassy Advice to US Citizens Traveling To Yemen

Topic: *Piracy*
Countries: *Yemen*

The following public announcement can be, found on the website of the US Embassy in Sana'a, Yemen. This Public Announcement is being, reissued to remind Americans of the continuing potential for terrorist actions against U.S. citizens in East Africa, particularly along the East African coast, and to note the dangers of maritime piracy near the Horn of Africa and the southern Red Sea near Yemen.

Supporters of Al-Qaida and other extremists are active in East Africa. Americans considering travel to the region and those already there should review their plans carefully, remain vigilant with regard to their personal security, and exercise caution. Terrorist actions may include suicide operations, bombings, kidnappings, or targeting maritime vessels.

Terrorists do not distinguish between official and civilian targets. Increased security at official U.S. facilities has led terrorists to seek softer targets such as residential areas, clubs, restaurants, American commercial interests, and western-oriented shopping centers, places of worship, hotels, schools, outdoor recreation events, resorts, and beaches. In particular, terrorists may target civil aviation and seaports.

Americans in remote areas or border regions where military or police authority is limited or non-existent could also become targets. Americans considering seaborne travel near the Horn of Africa or in the southern Red Sea should exercise extreme caution, as there have been several incidents of armed attacks and robberies at sea by unknown pirates in the last year. When transiting around the Horn of Africa or in the Red Sea near Yemen, it is strongly, recommended that vessels travel in convoys, and maintains good communications contact at all times.

US Government facilities worldwide remain at a heightened state of alert. They may temporarily close or suspend public services to review security. On occasion, the travel of U.S. Government personnel is restricted, and U.S. posts may recommend that private American citizens follow similar restrictions.

Consular services to American citizens could be, affected if employees' movements are restricted. In those instances, U.S. embassies and consulates will make every effort to provide emergency services to American citizens. American citizens in need of emergency assistance should telephone the nearest U.S. embassy or consulate before visiting there.

Americans living or traveling in East Africa are encouraged to register with the nearest U.S. Embassy or Consulate through the State Department's travel registration website, https://travelregistration.state.gov. Americans without Internet access may register directly with the nearest U.S. embassy or consulate. By registering, American citizens make it easier for the Embassy or Consulate to contact them in case of emergency.

US citizens planning to travel to East Africa should consult the Department of State's country-specific Public Announcements, Travel Warnings, Consular Information Sheets, the Worldwide Caution Public Announcement, and other information, available at http://travel.state.gov. Up-to-date information on security conditions can also be, obtained by calling 1-888-407-4747 in the U.S. and for callers outside the U.S. and Canada a regular toll line at 1-202-501-4444.

Figure 13 South East Asia & Far East

SOUTH EAST ASIA
& FAR EAST

Pirate Attacks

Worrying Incident Near Ayerabu Island, Indonesia

Topic: Piracy Reports 2005

20th May 2005

Report from: SAILING VESSELL

Route: Tioman Island to Port Bintulu. Destination: Kota, Kinabalu, Malaysia.

Our boat a 60ft Cutter Rigged Sloop, built in 1999 with a Perkins 135BHP Engine.

We left Tioman Island (Teluk Tekek) on Wednesday 4 May at Midday, traveled through the night, and sighted Ayerabu Island, Indonesia around 8.00am. 5th May 2005. We decided to take a short stop to check and make possible repairs to our Fuel Change over Pump. As we neared the Island a young man (early Thirties) came to the bow of the boat and was directing us to where he thought we should anchor, we kind of followed him into the bay and thought "Oh that's really nice" a friendly face; he had a long tail type boat with an outboard engine. This was at 10.30 am.

Whilst we were looking for a good place to set the anchor, another boat, which we did not see, or here came alongside us. The boat was around 4 meters in length, somewhat like a fishing boat, with an inboard engine. One male was waving a very large gun at us (looked like an AK47 machine gun) I would estimate that there were around 10-12 persons in this boat.

We stopped our boat and allowed them to board us, the male with the gun boarded us first followed by 8 others, and these were all young males in their thirties. The male with the gun was wearing jeans and a brown and white t-shirt with a marine motif on it, the rest was all dressed in shorts and t-shirts.

The male with the gun asked our Captain to go below decks with him, whom he did, this male could speak no English and the only word he uttered was passport, we produced all of our passports for him, he looked at one for a second and then proceeded to the Aft Cabin with the Captain. All he could say was dollars, dollars you have dollars.

We told him we did not have dollars, the captain offered to him cigarettes in the hope that they would leave; he took the cigarettes but still insisted on money. The male had been onboard now for some 20 minutes or so. The other eight, walked around on deck, or sat in the cockpit us.

The captain then gave him around 300.00 Riggits which was all we had close to hand, we did not want to open any cupboards or drawers, due to the fact that the male with the gun was following the Captain at all times. The male was still not satisfied with this amount and then showed it to the rest of the males onboard, they muttered something in Indonesian, and the male (with gun) came back below decks, the captain followed him this time, to see if it was possible to get him to leave.

We think that this agitated him or unnerved he because he proceeded to smash our saloon table with the butt of the gun, as he did this one of the other males immediately came below, and again they were muttering in Indonesian together. The male then spotted our hand phones, which he took, but they still wanted more money, I gave to them my handbag, I opened the purse and showed them all the money in it around 250.00Ringgits,

I gave it all to them and explained that was it, no more money, he could see the purse and all its contents on the table; he took the money and showed it to the others (some of it). They stayed onboard at least another half hour picking up sunglasses, cigars, cigarettes, lighters; etc. Anything that was on visible they took, but they did not take the fishing rods, outboard engine, or other big things that were above decks.

I did have a digital camera in the saloon, which they could see, but they did not take it or show any interest in. I have pictures of us arriving at the island. They had a few more looks below to see if we had anything else and then decided to leave. They shook hands with us all before they left, the male with the gun called back to the fishing type boat which came alongside, they all departed, happy and jolly as if it was just another day at the office. However, the first young male who directed us into the anchorage, followed us for about 1 mile before he turned back to the island.

The coordinates where the event took place are 02.46.064N and 106.12.285E.

We tried to contact the Asia Net to let him know, it was not possible to contact him, we tried for 3 days, on the 4th day we arrived at Port Bintulu where the Police made us very welcome and helped us moor the boat, we said that once we had everything.

Sorted with the boat we would come and see them for check in etc. We did go to see them twice, but were, informed that it was not necessary. Whilst at the anchorage in Brunei we were, informed that Asia net was trying to locate us, we managed to inform them of this incident on 18 May 2005.

We will wait until our arrival at Kota Kinabulu to report this incident to the Police.

Attack on Yacht near Lae Papua New Guinea

Topic: Piracy Reports 2004

In September 2004 whilst traveling from Ala-Tau to Madang after departing Australia from Cairns, on an 11m Australian Registered Yacht with a crew of two on board us were robbed and attacked at Cape Gerhard, Hamisch Harbor PNG.

We arrived at the harbor about 4.30pm after a day sail from Morobe and asked a local fishing boat for the best anchorage position for overnight. The group assisted cheerfully and on being, shown, the position another canoe with four males on board came out. We were, anchored about 50m from the shore. After anchoring, we gave boat vessels a gift of food and proceeded to eat and prepare for a good night's sleep. On retiring about 8pm, the boat was secured from the inside and a light placed in the cockpit for security.

My partner, in the meantime; attempted to close, a small hatch above the galley and was, chopped across her hand with a large bush knife. We placed a towel on the hand and attempted to contact other ships with a Mayday call. No response was, received. Threats to kill us were being, shouted, bush knives and a home made, gun were, being poked down the hatch, and a lot of bashing on the decks was going on. I shot a flare out the hatch among the robbers and immediately all went quiet except for a departing sound of a shot from the home made, gun.

After a few minutes of quiet, I armed myself with a knife and bolt cutters, cut the anchor chain, and motored away. No further sightings of anyone were seen and as my partner was bleeding, and we were not sure of the extent of the wound, we decided to motor to Lae (35 nm away) to get assistance. On arrival at Lae yacht club, we were, assisted, to a clinic and her injury was, stitched. This was a serious incident, more than robbery, and since then I have heard of more incidents in the area and around Madang.

I would advise any cruising yacht to be extremely cautious in the PNG area.

New Caledonian Yacht Attacked In Solomon Islands

Topic: Piracy
Countries: Solomon Islands

Several armed men boarded and ransacked a yacht with a family of two adults and two children on board the night of Saturday October 21. The catamaran anchored at Bita'ama in the north of the island of Malaita in the Solomon Islands. A group of men armed with a gun, knives and a club boarded the yacht around midnight. They stole about USD10, 000 and threatened skipper with a knife. Various other valuables stolen before the men eventually left. The yacht made its way to Honiara where the authorities were in for Somalia Pirates med.

The family, from New Caledonia, had already spent some three months, cruising; the Archipelago and had found it a welcoming place; now they have no intention of returning.

Following the reporting of the incident in local press in New Caledonia and the Solomon's, some tourists canceled holidays in Malaita, prompting fears among local businessmen that their fledgling tourist industry would suffer the consequences of this incident for some time to come.

Yacht boarded in Papua New Guinea.

Topic: Piracy Reports 2008

Countries: <u>Papua New Guinea</u>

I would like to share with Noonsite readers about an incident we were involved in about two weeks ago in Papua New Guinea.

We pulled into Wewak early in the morning on January 29 to check out with customs as our visas expired on January 31. We had Wewak recommended to us as being safer than Madang. While in port that day, many locals warned us that six months ago, an elderly couple was in Wewak, and one-night locals boarded them with weapons. Stories differed by the locals as to whether there were two couples or two boats, but they stole many valuable items including their GPS. Police were able to recover the GPS only, but I think it was more terrifying than anything was as the couple tied up while they were, robbed.

We had planned to keep a watch at night because of this. We are four young men aged 24-37 on a 45-foot Australian-flagged catamaran, so keeping watch in harbor is not a big deal for us. Around 10:45 we were watching a movie (no one was on watch yet) when I heard a noise outside. I disregarded it until about 10 minutes later when I heard voices. Then our skipper went outside to investigate with a flashlight and confronted 3 men who had boarded our board from both sides.

One had a gun, one had a machete, and one had a small axe. One of us shut the screen door upon realizing what was happening to regroup inside. They kicked open the door and forced our skipper back inside, but upon doing so hit the smoke alarm and set it off. This really irritated them but was enough of a distraction that two of us had gone to the galley to find any sort of weapon to defend ourselves. I was, forced to silence the alarm at gunpoint. At the time, the gun appeared to be from the 1800's. However, we later found out it was a homemade gun. That is only good at close range and shoots buckshot.

After the alarm was, silenced, the man with the gun went towards the galley to get the other two up into the saloon where they could watch us all. He pointed the gun at us but then looked behind at the Skipper and me, allowing us to push the gun aside and tackle the gunman. We proceeded to force them all outside where we managed to throw them down the steps on the transom. At this time, I was on channel 16 trying to raise anyone, but being a small port, there was no response. We had no local phone number for the police and our shouts went unnoticed.

Realizing we had the gun in our possession after the scuffle, we were worried they might return with friends, so we threw the dinghy in the water and chased after them. They had two canoes but we could see them swimming to shore. We managed to catch up with one of them and proceed to drag him back to the boat with the help of a couple of scary looking spear guns we use for fishing. This weapon terrified him. We got him back tied him up on the swim platform, and went looking for the others. Unable to find them, two of us went to the local yacht club and got some locals to come assist us. They contacted the police and came with us to the yacht to bring the captive back to shore.

The police in PNG are, known, for their own dealing of justice. If you have ever read about Port Moresby, you will know what I mean. We had to keep the locals from smashing this man's head in with our dinghy anchor and a piece of lumber. Once the police had him, they dealt with him by tying him to a tree and beating him while naked. We were, told. Had a particular officer been on duty that night this man would have been shot. Everyone asked why we brought this man to shore and did just tie his hands and feet and thrown him overboard, they were dead serious.

I do not know if this will change the mind of locals in Wewak for boarding yachts, or if they will just come more prepared. I had the feeling this man would not use the gun, and they were unprepared. However, this woke us up to the realization of being, boarded. We had talked about it, but when we left Australia, we were unable to buy flare guns or bear spray or anything offensive. As I have read before, the noise of an alarm seemed to be a major irritant to them. This may be the distraction, we needed to, stay safe. I was surprised at the usefulness of the spear gun. However - our captive cried out when we had it pointed at him or touching his skin, but barely made a noise, when being beaten by the police or locals.

This is very disappointing because I was in the process of writing many good things about cruising through PNG - friendly people, beautiful coral reefs, deserted islands, and good availability of supplies. It marred an otherwise excellent trip through PNG. So despite this story, I would still stay it is a great place to travel and recommend it to others.

In a separate incident, The Coastal Passage reported that yacht O'LGeta was boarded and ransacked by two men on Saturday 26th January 2008 at a village called Kaparoka, 40nm ESE of Port Moresby. At 2.30 am, the men boarded the yacht with a 2-foot bush knife and cut the anchor line.

Crewmember dived overboard and swam ashore; another came up from his sleeping berth at the bow and fell overboard when one of the men tried to attack him. He stayed under the boat's side until the men had ransacked the yacht. They took radio, food, 2 mobiles, and 40 liters of diesel. After they had left and climbed, back on board and motored quickly back toward Port Moresby. The police were, alerted' and traveled, too Kaparoka, where the two culprits were, apprehended. However, managed to, escape. It is, reported, that the village police will locate them and bring them back to Port Moresby.

The yacht arrived safely in Port Moresby where crewmember who jumped over could rejoin the yacht and after obtaining a new anchor and chain, they departed once again for Lae on Sunday 28th 2008.

Armed Robbery Warning – Tanimbar Islands, Eastern Moluccas, Indonesia

Topic: *Piracy Reports 2008*
Countries: *Indonesia*

In April 2008, we were cruising through the Tanimbar Islands on route from East Malaysia to Darwin.

In late April, we anchored in the early afternoon at Pulau Ungar on the western side of the Tanimbar Islands, position 07° 15'.5S, and 131° 23' .9E.

At 0030 the next day, two or three men armed with knives or machetes boarded us. They stole a number of items of deck gear and some items from our main cabin, before we awoke and disturbed them and chased them off the boat. They then paddled off in a canoe. We immediately lifted our anchor and moved (without lights) to another anchorage. We would recommend that any yachts visiting the Tanimbar Islands do not use the western island's anchorages, particularly at Pulau Ungar and the nearby anchorages at P. Vulmali and P. Yarngurral.

Care should be taken anywhere in the Tanimbar Islands.

Attack on Yacht in Madang, Papua New Guinea
Topic: *Piracy Reports 2007*
Countries: *Papua New Guinea*

After living in Madang for nearly 20 years and cruising in and around Madang without incident for the past year, we would have said that this was one of the few places in PNG where one could cruise in relative safety. That changed on 16 July when we were boarded, by three men; and assaulted, on our Yacht, while anchored in Madang harbor.

I was sleeping in the cockpit and my wife was sleeping below when at about 1 AM I awoke to find someone pressing a machete against my neck and telling me to stay still. Our plan in case of such an incident is for me to try to keep the assailants busy while she locks herself in the head and sounds like the portable air horn. Our assumption is that the best defense in case of attack, especially in a populated area, is to make as much commotion and noise as possible.

I called for her to sound the horn, unaware that someone was already below with her. When she tried to get up, he laid her forehead open with a club. By this time, I was grappling with one man in the cockpit while another covered me with a homemade shotgun. I could wrench the machete away from my assailant but not before receiving blows to the head and arms that would later require stitches. Apparently, the shotgun was not loaded because the third person's contribution to the attack was simply to hold it and attempt to look menacing.

By this time, she, in spite of being, dazed and blinded by the blood, had been able to get up, find the horn, and make her way to the head. She started blowing the horn and at that point, the assailants began going over the side. I could get one swipe with the machete at the person, who had hit me as he went over but unfortunately was not able to inflict much damage.

The last we saw of them, they were pushing their canoe back out into the harbor. The next morning, after receiving medical care, we filled out the appropriate police reports but the police are doing nothing. Their attitude seems to be, that since we were not, killed, what we are complaining about?

PNG is a wonderful place, and we would still recommend it as a cruising destination, but with the warning that if one stays around long enough, they will encounter security issues. For us, it took almost a year of cruising before it happened. Even so, this is our home, and we are going to continue to cruise here. We are definitely, going to rethink and upgrade our security arrangements. In addition, we would encourage anyone who is thinking of cruising here to be very security conscious.

Given the results of our incident, I would say that the best response to such an attack is to make as much noise and commotion as possible. These people are relying on darkness and stealth. Light and noise tended to put them off.

Madang, Papua New Guinea

Figure 14 On the Ocean again heading somewhere

DANGEROUS REGIONS

The areas considered high risk for pirate attacks in the world are many and growing. It is not isolated to one particular part of the world any longer. Though the risk is considerably higher in areas of government unrest and poverty, the problem of piracy is spreading to parts of the world that most consider safe. You will notice that the some of the official reporting sites on piracy are severely lacking in information on private vessels and cruisers. This is partly because most of these attacks are not reported unless the attacks are so violent that emergency services are involved and the trip comes to an end as a result.

Furthermore, many governments do not want the information publicized on the problem, which would possibly reduce the number of visitors. Many attacks are forgotten. Moreover, many are not reported by individuals because of the time that has passed, since the attack occurred. Another possibility is that these reporting agencies are supported by the commerce department and therefore only accepts report on commercial ships that have been attacked.

Having a reporting agency or source for yachters and cruisers has become a necessity. Cruisers need a tool that provides the information that they need so they can avoid the danger of sea travel. This reporting is needed for two different reasons first: the areas that they travel are different and not dictated by the commerce routes. Also, the ports used and visited are greater in number and they are not restricted to deep water ports. You will gain some information on the large ports that can help you. But you will need to check noonsite and other Cruiser sites to find the information on the areas and routes that you are concerned. For your safety become familiar with these sites and the information, they provide.

Keep in mind that these organizations operate on donations; please show them your appreciation by contributing for their service to insure their continued reporting for your protection. The following information is from the IMB Piracy Report, this is necessary read for anyone that will be traveling across commercial shipping route of risk. Keep in mind that this is a report dealing with commercial shipping and not the full story for those of us who love to travel by sea.

The IMB defines Piracy as ;

"An act of boarding, or attempting to board, any ship, with the apparent intent to commit theft of any other crime and with the apparent intent or capability, to use force in the furtherance of that act."

IMB was pleased to record that the International Maritime Organization (IMO) at its 74th meeting addressed this and drafted a Code of practive for the Investigation of Crimes of Piracy and Armed Robbery against Ships (NSC.Curc,984) article (2.2) (The Code of Practice).

This Code defines Piracy and Armed Robbery against Ships as the following:

- Piracy means unlawful acts as defined in article 101 of the 1982 United Nations Convention on the Law of the Sea (UNCLOS):

ARTICLE 101

Definition of Piracy consists of any of the following acts:

A) Any illegal acts of violence or detention, or any act of depredation, committed for private ends by the crew or the passengers of a private ship or a private aircraft, and directed-

(i) On the high seas, against another ship or aircraft, or against persons or property on board such ship or aircraft;

(ii) Against a ship, aircraft, persons or property in a place outside the jurisdiction of any State;

(b) Any act of voluntary participation in the operation of a ship or of an aircraft with knowledge of facts making it a pirate ship *or aircraft;*

© *Any act of inciting or of intentionally facilitating an act described in subparagraph (a) or (b).*

"Armed Robbery against Ships means any unlawful act of violence or detention or any act of depredation, or threat thereof, other than an act of "piracy", directed against a ship or against persons or property on board such ship, within a State's jurisdiction over such offences"

This now defines attacks on ships, whether the attack is actual or attempted, and; a ship being at anchor, docked or underway.

With this new definition, you can hope now to have information that will help you to form an actual map of danger areas in the future. The areas that a mariner should be concerned with at the time this book was written are listed in the following pages. You also need to keep in mind, that during and since the time this book was written; the information has constantly changed, with attacks occurring more frequently in some areas, and spreading too new areas of concern. While also the severity of attacks changed in many areas with problems. I hope this book will give you an idea of what you should be concerned with while traveling. There are many more reports available at the websites we have listed. Please visit them and become familiar with the sites and how you can use them.

Also; I am not trying to be a total one stop source of information that you can relied on for planning your passage. My intent is to give you some precautions and tactics or a basic understanding of the problem mariner's face, that can be used to build on for the protection of yourself and your boat. In addition, to inform you of the sources of information that you can use for the planning and preparation of your travels which will enable you to prevent or avoid these violent acts.

When planning a trip, check for recent attacks along your planned route and mark them on your charts, avoid danger areas if possible. Do not tempt fait! Just because you have taken the proper precautions and hope to make an attack more difficult does not guarantee the outcome to be favorable. Use the information that you gain from this book as a guide for thought, that you must improve on in order to plan a course of action. Plan according to your capabilities, and do not take chances with the lives of the people you are responsible for. Moreover, remember that just because a country is not on a list does not mean that you are safe from pirate attacks.

It is important that you not rely on just one information source because of the lack of reporting on yachts and small non-commercial vessels of the past. Although there are, a few sites that are putting a great effort forth on the matter, and are becoming a one stop source of information for the cruiser. Please work with these groups in reporting to them any information that you gather on piracy. Also, refer them to people you meet that have been attacked, this will save lives and help others in the future. There is a major concern that with as little as 20% of all attacks being reported there is much that we do not know concerning the survival rate and the total number of attacks on private vessels.

Figure 15 Fisherman along the coast

DANGER AREAS

Countries of known Piracy Danger

AFRICA

It is hard to separate the trouble spots in Africa, with each coast having so many problems. There are areas that are less dangerous than others that can be visited. The United Nations Security Council and international maritime safety organizations have urged the Southern African Development Community (SADC) to take drastic action against the gangs of heavily armed pirates.

According to their report, between January and November 2006, 48 ships were, attacked around Africa by gangs of pirates armed with an assortment of weapons - including surface-to-surface missiles, rocket propelled grenades, armed helicopters and heavy caliber machine-guns such as anti-aircraft guns.

The report also uncovered that some of the pirates operate phantom ships disguised as vessels in distress. In addition, that the pirates had speedboats, heavy machine guns and radio systems to coordinate their attacks and regularly left dead and wounded - Pretoria News reported that Ruthless pirates plunder hundreds of ships each year off the coast of Africa are moving south, threatening South African waters. The pirates did not content themselves with just floating targets: they also used their speedboats to launch lightning raids on banks in towns along the coast.

Clearly, pirates are moving their operations further south as they discover there are few, if any, navies operating in southern African waters, especially around countries like Mozambique, Madagascar, Seychelles, Comoros, and Namibia.

"This means pirates will continue to move south, coming closer to South Africa where yachts, fishing ships and cargo vessels will be attacked. The two countries of the greatest concern are Nigeria and Somalia, they account for over 70 attacks in 2007. The attacks in these areas are normally violent usually end up with hostages and many people are injured in these regions pursuant to the boldness of the pirates and their willingness to use weapons in their attacks.

Any time you plan to travel to any country, ensure you research the recent attacks, and plan your trip accordingly. When traveling near an area on this coast take the appropriate measures to ensure you can do so with out encountering these pirates.

Countries to be concerned with currently are as follows: **Angola, Cameroon, Congo, Dem. Congo Republic, Egypt, Equatorial Guinea, Eritrea, Ghana, Guinea, Gulf of Aden, Ivory Coast, Johannesburg, Kenya, Liberia, Madagascar, Mauritania, Morocco, Mozambique, Nigeria, Senegal, Sierra Leone, Somalia, Tanzania, Togo,**

In the Gulf of Aden around the Indian Ocean and the east coast of Africa it is wise to check in with the local authorities, Military units and private escort groups in the area before attempting passage. You can find information on these groups at http://www.noonsite.com where you will also find a form that you should fill out if attempting a passage in this area. My recommendation on this area is not to attempt it alone, and avoid it if possible.

AMERICA'S

Piracy has been increasing in the America's with growing concern in the areas that normally hosts many cruisers to their regions. The things that had grabbed my attention in recent years and while writing this book were the reports in the Caribbean Islands that were considered, safe until recent? I had known of the problems in South America but as poverty is increasing in many places people are driven to provide for themselves in any way possible. So with this in mind you should be concerned in the future with the areas that were normally perceived as safe cruising areas.

This is an overview of the reported crime incidents against yachts from 2005 through June 2008, as reported to the Caribbean Safety and Security Net (CSSN). This analysis simply counts the reported incidents for all Caribbean Islands from the Virgin Islands to Central America. Only incidents that were, reported are included here.

Countries reported as areas of concern are: **Antigua & Barbuda, Aruba, Barbados, Bonaire, British Virgin Islands, Curacao, Dominica, Grenada, Guadeloupe, Honduras, Martinique, Panama, St. Marten, St Kitts & Nevis, St Lucia, St Vincent & the Grenadines, Trinidad & Tobago, US Virgin Islands, Venezuela**

Other areas that you need to check on not in this list are:

Brazil, Columbia, Ecuador, Guyana, Haiti, Jamaica, Peru,

VENEZUELA has turned out to be the major piracy concern in this part of the world. I have had several problems there and had two boarding's while in this country. Keep in mind that if you decide to travel too this location. At least a couple of times a year that we know of, attacks result in the murder of those onboard.

In the past, the problem was that the FARK Military from Columbia would kidnap tourist on the border with Venezuela and many of the group's members would travel for relaxation to Venezuela, at least this is what I was, told by friends in Venezuela. The government has organized to fight the problem, and they have a web site where you can check a map for areas of concern.

The name of the organization is "The Venezuelan National Rescue and Maritime Safety Organization" There site is

http://www.onsa.org.ve/enidex.shtml#

You will find information on reporting piracy and info to help avoid areas of concern. Take caution when planning to travel by boat to the coast areas and be sure to avoid the areas where the attacks have resulted in serious harm.

The CSSN is a Short Wave SSB Net for cruisers in the Caribbean. This net operates on frequency 8104 at 8:15 Monday through Saturday.

The Yacht Services Association of Trinidad and Tobago (YSATT) is a good source for that area, you can get information on the YSATT website http://www.ysatt.org/ as well as the Caribbean Marine Association http:www.caribbeanmarineassociation.com/ these websites. – Implemented; September 2006, for the safety, of cruisers, visiting the area.

In addition, check with the Northwest Caribbean Radio Net there you can get information on recent attacks and security issues as well as weather, bureaucracy matters, and they have a bulletin board.

SOUTH EAST ASIA

South East Asia is a very dangerous area, pirate attacks in this area are deadly, and particular attention needs to be given to the details of the attacks when planning a passage of this area. Until the recent past when piracy was spoken of, this is the area where most thought the problem existed. It is an area with the most history involving merchant ships being attacked until recent years. It is hard to get a lot of information on private or small vessels attacked in this area. It is a popular occupation in this area because of the lack of jobs and poverty. Some also go so far as to blame over fishing and lack of food on part of the problem.

Most piracy involved the perpetrators being armed who threatened and often kidnapped injured or killed the members of the crew. The pirates are often fishermen, common criminals, and Asian mafia, in some cases members of the maritime security forces. It was reported that most attacks occur with the ship in port or anchored, this area is known for the pirates boarding moving ships and killing or stranding the crew on life rafts. The problem in this area to present has been the lack of cooperation between organizations and countries to battle piracy in this region.

Ships have been advised to use caution in all ports in **Indonesia, Gelasa Strait, Bangka Strait, Berhala Strait, Sunda Strait, Bangkor Bar, Manila Bay, Singapore Strait, Phillip Channel, Sprately Island, Chittagong Roads, Mongla Anchorage, Chennai Anchorage, Tuticorin Roads, Kandla.**

Other countries and areas that you should take notice of at the current time are: Malacca Straits, Malaysia, Myanmar (Burma), Philippines, Singapore Straits,

THAILAND/GULF OF THAILAND

To gather information on this region check: ICC Commercial Crime Services at:

www.iccwbo.org/ccs/imb_piracy/weekly_piracy_report.aspwww.iccwbo.org/ccs/imb_piracy/weekly_piracy_report.asp.

FAR EAST

The Far East is an area not traveled by foreigners very often and not easy to get information on besides that gathered by the organizations gathering reports on commercial shipping. Again, a good source is ICC Commercial Crime Services and their website is:

www.iccwbo.org/ccs/imb_piracy/weekly_piracy_report.asp

China, Hong Kong, Macau, Papua, New Guinea, South China Sea, Vietnam

INDIAN SUB CONTINENT

INDIAN SUB CONTINENT, which includes Sri Lanka, is of special interest; it seems that there are groups of militants. Who oppose the government in this, area? Each claims that the other is involved in piracy. The Maritime Rescuing Coordinating Centre in Falmouth UK received a message from a vessel that it had been boarded by armed pirates at 03:30 on Saturday the 23 of December, they quickly began to pillage the cargo. The message was, forwarded to the Sri Lanka Navy, shortly afterwards a message was, received from the Liberation Tigers of Tamil Eelam (LTTE) who stated that they noticed the ship drifting into their waters and noticed the suspicious activity of the Sri Lanka Navy, so they rescued the crew. In some areas, it is hard to know who to trust, in cases such as these, both should be, avoided.

Sources of information for the area are again the ICC Commercial Crime Services and their website is:

www.iccwbo.org/ccs/imb_piracy/weekly_piracy_report.asp

Other countries in the area that should be of interest are: Bangladesh & India. Traveling to this area one should do some research on the particular area that you plan to visit to find current attacks to base your strategy on before you start.

There are other areas in the world where pirate attacks have occurred, and you should be aware of and they are as follows:

Arabian Sea, Belgium, France, Iran, Iraq, Oman, Pacific Ocean, Seychelles, UAE, and United Kingdom.

Check each country on your route with the State Department for recent travel alerts. Then check this against the reports on http://www.noonsite.com and http://www.onpassage.com, which will also give you an idea of the local requirement for your visit.

Once you have the information on piracy you can plan with the normal materials used for navigation and passage making. This information will give you an idea of the areas that would require special precautions or further research for planning your passage.

Figure 16 Armed Guard after a bad attack

PIRATES
Recognizing a threat

Pirates will not raise a jolly roger as they approach you in order to create the feeling of fear in those on board your vessel. They dress as anyone else in the area you are visiting, they may be fishing on a small fishing vessel along the coast, or repairing a net on the shore. They may be working on the dock where you are tied up while traveling. My point is that they go about their lives as a spider waiting for some signal that easy prey is near there location.

They are looking for an opportunity, should it presents its self. To protect yourself, you need to understand how they operate and how to recognize this potential threat, once you understand this, you will gain an advantage in countering these dangerous situations.

In the previous chapters, you read a few actual pirate attacks. While doing so you possibly made mental notes on how others were able to prevent attacks from being successful or at least recognize the security measurers that could have been in place to help prevent their success. Pirates change their style of attack over time, with each success; they develop their tactics and become bolder going after more challenging vessels.

You will notice that the attacks differ from one location to the next. Because of this, you cannot rely on general knowledge. You need to know the type of attacks for each location on your route. You need to check for the most recent information at the websites and only by doing this can you be prepared for that possibility and then be able to protect your vessel, family and friends. This is your responsibility and it would be neglect as a captain not to keep current with the information that you can gather that can aid you in an emergency. Just as it would be, neglect not to keep up with the "notice to mariners", the "light list"; and other aids when planning a trip.

To stay safe in these situations and to avoid most pirate attacks will depend on your situational awareness, your ability to anticipate danger signs in people, and in situations that are taking place in your proximity. Being able to read body language associated with acts of violence and behavior of those who plan to take action against you can be one of the greatest tools you can utilize when on your own in a strange place. Nevertheless, again it is useless without the proper research needed to understand the threat that you are dealing with and being prepared for them.

Knowing what to look for and being able to anticipate a threat will in the best cases, allow you the time to disengage the situation or evacuate the area before they have the opportunity to organize their plans against you. In addition, in the worst case it will provide you enough time to activate your plan for protecting those you are responsible for, and your vessel. Always remember that the lives of those on board are more important than the vessel, and the valuables on board it, these can be replaced, should you have to sacrifice them for your survival.

You need to evaluate every situation and look for suspicious behavior that can give warning of the danger. You will learn from researching the attacks what the type of vessel the pirates were attacking from will be important. This will provide a clue as to what you are looking for at the areas of risk, keeping in mind that any vessel can be utilized, and in some cases they have swum to the boat they attack. Pirates will use small fishing boats, which to us would be, considered large double-ended fishing boats, these vessels usually hang close to shore while dropping their nets. While they are fishing, they are looking for opportunities. Be aware of these boats when they remain in your area for more than a few settings of their nets. Or if they just set near by without their nets in the water. These same vessels will go miles off shore when a possible opportunity presents itself as in a vessel anchored or traversing the coast. They will watch from a distance and should they not see any activity on your boat, they will move closer and watch until they can slip onboard without being seen.

The pirate attacks that have occurred well offshore have involved small speedboats, open fishing boats, and larger fishing boats. Some pirates in busy areas will pick a time during the day or night that they have had success in the past and head out to see what they can find. When researching you can see a routine develop in some areas, as to the time of the day, and the days of the week that attacks mostly occur this information will aid you in planning your passage.

On some occasions, pirates use information gathered by contacts in other locations near by which inform them when a vessel will be in the area. They then can motor to the location near where they suspect you will pass, and wait, or lay a trap. Knowing how far offshore the attacks have occurred is important in planning your travel also. When traveling past an area well offshore beware of anything that seems out of place. A speedboat traveling well offshore on open water, which would not normally be use in the waters you are transiting. Vessels traveling on an intersecting course would also be a good bet. I would not think that there would be many people out for a casual day at sea in those high-risk areas and this would be a situation in which you should use caution.

A vessel with no females or fishing gear on board would also be something to watch for. Attacks further from shore are more often a bolder type of attack, with possibly a increased risk of violence. There may be an overwhelming force of men involved or at least enough to control the people on the vessel they wish to attack. You may see one large vessel or a couple of speedboats approaching you, or possibly only a couple of people on the boat that would require several to operate. You just never know how the threat will present itself and should always use caution.

This is where a good set of binoculars come in to play. The further you can see the more time you have to prepare. Distance is time. They have also used vessels they have captured during previous attacks, in order to deceive other vessels. To know which style vessels have been taken will give you a heads-up on danger.

You will learn more from studying the attacks than from my generalization of possibilities. Pirates can use any vessel and the pirates themselves can look like anyone. You need to be aware of the possibilities while you watch for the signs that warn of an attack well before it happens. During these times it is important to know the body language as well as voice signals that can warn you of a threat as well as what to watch for in vessels that could pose a threat. Recognizing a close threat to your safety is a good place to start in order to gain the knowledge that you need.

We all have heard several sayings in our childhood that we did not make since of until we were older; one of those is the saying that "the eyes are the window to the soul". I remember hearing this many time, and imagined a supernatural process in which you could see a persons past life in his eyes, but as I got older I started to see that a persons life weights heavy on themselves, and you can see the hardness and the lack of concern or empathy for others in their eyes. Furthermore, by watching persons eyes you can see signs of what is going on in their head. This will make more since later in this chapter.

While in the Marine Corps, we used the eyes to judge the situation that we were in. The "_thousand yard stare_" is one that most people are familiar with; it is as though they are "day dreaming" while you are talking to them. Like they are looking right through you, and they probably are, most likely, they are thinking of going through you to their objective. Another possibility is that they are scouting out the situation using their peripheral vision and at this point are in a different world. This is one thing, which you need to be aware. Moreover, when noticed you need to start putting distance between you and them before things can escalate.

Another giveaway is a "_glance_" it is also known as a "*target glance*" I do not like to call it "target glance" because it does not describe the things that you can tell by watching a persons glance. A person may throw a glance at or in a direction to see if the path is clear, the police use this in case someone decides to run. Before they do so, they will throw a glance in the direction they plan to go.

An individual may throw a glance at a part of your body that they plan to attack, or at an objective in a conflict before it starts. They may throw a glance at your chin looking for the button before they swing at you, or to, crouch; or, shift stance, before they kick you. You need to watch and anticipate their actions to protect the others onboard. At this point, you need to step backwards a few steps and find a way if not too late to leave the area.

There is the "_target stare_" or when a person looks intensely at you and their eyes narrow. The narrowing of the eyes enhances the depth perception that is, needed; when planning to attack or to "reach out and touch someone". At this point, you have already engaged someone, they have locked onto a target, you should immediately step back to create distance; he has shown that he is hostile, and you need to get away as quickly as possible.

It is always better to try to escape a situation in doing so you can always defend yourself, but remember your objective is not to fight, but to avoid it and escape. Nevertheless, you must be ready to stand when the situation gets to that point where there is no other way. Now you have no time for looking for something to aid in your protection. This is why it is important not to allow others to have the opportunity to get close to you and your boat without a challenge, this prevents this close proximity confrontation.

Remember that the survival of those with you onboard is directly tied; to you being successful, should a fight break out. When you engage a group of people in a fight, the safety of all on board your boat decreases greatly. Should you lose the fight; the attitude of the attackers is, escalated, to something that in combat is, known; as bloodlust. You do not want to fight if there is any possibility that you may not win, you must fight on your terms when you have things in your favor, and you will win or cause the attacker to break off the attack. You have to have a plan for all situations. Should you encounter pirates that prefer to come in with guns firing your choices are limited, you fight, or you give up. It is important that you research the attacks in the areas where you plan to travel; the area where this type of attack is a possibility needs to be, avoided.

Remember hearing about the "fight or fight response" it occurs when a person perceives a risk or danger. It not only affects the person that is being, attacked; but also manifests itself in the body of the attackers. Leading up to an attack the adrenaline starts to flow providing signs; that, if you know what they are, can be use as a warning that something is getting ready to happen. When the body knows something dangerous is about to take place the heart begins to race and the body requires more oxygen.

This results in rapid breathing and panting. Look for these signs, the rapid breathing as though they have been performing strenuous labor, and perspiring when there is no evidence of hard work. In addition, you may be able to notice a rapid heart beat in the veins in the neck, or head. A another sign resulting from these are the skin color changes in which a person becomes red when aroused or angry or even growing pale or scared before an attack. These all can be, used, as signs that warn of a possible attack.

In some people, the effect of fear or danger causes tremors; this is another side effect of adrenaline. They usually occur in the non-dominant hand almost immediately followed by the dominant hand and then the legs at the knees. Some people this occurs before a fight. This can help in you in several ways. It not only shows that there is something about to happen, but it shows which hand a person will often lead with. It also shows that they are as afraid of you as you are of them.

Remember this does not work all the time some people have diseases that cause these tremors such as Parkinson has or low sugar. This should always cause caution and give a reason to distance, yourself until, sure of the situation.

The expressions of the face and body gestures also give warning of an aggressor switching to fight mode. People that are emotionally upset are not aware of the expressions that they make with their face. The clinching of the jaws, grinding of the teeth are possible signs to watch for when a person tightens up the lips is another. A person may use "stress breathing" or "combat breathing" in which they take in a breath and hold it then let it out slowly. This is, used; when you have started to take in too much oxygen before the strenuous activity has started and need to restore normal levels before the fight starts.

When a person maneuvers his body into what is known as the "fighter's stance" a stance that is best to take and give punches. When your body is about 45% to that of the person, you plan to fight. It is also, known as the "front stance" in Martial arts and the "shooters stance to shooters. In this position, you are, balanced to take an impact in any direction. Therefore, if you notice the person in front of you take a step back with one leg placing him in this position, and you see his hands clench into the fist or slightly open raise to a level between the waist and shoulders; you are going to fight.

You need to look for movements that have no meaning other than nervous behavior, a person who is pacing back and fourth, at a dock, or; who bounces up and down, on the ball of the foot. In addition, will be the clinching and unclenching of the fist, these signs show arousal and anticipation of physical violence.

When you notice these things you need to create the most important asset you have at the time, and that is distance. By creating distance, you defuse a volatile situation you also create time that can be, used to take action. Buying time also creates confusion in the attacker allows time to activate your plan and in most cases will delay or overt an attack, giving you time to leave the area.

Remember; these are cues, to behavior, that occur before a possible attack, or; in situation involving deception. In addition, should be, studied, and practiced when observing people in day-to-day life in this way you can prepare for a situation in which you may need the skill while at sea cursing. The reading body language, can be, used over great distances, and should be something you watch for when observing other vessels through your binoculars. You can still make out actions of deception and danger, which could give you the upper hand before an attack occurs. For more study on this topic

I recommend that you visit web sites where they specialize in body language that you could utilize in reading situations as they develop. Most of the information in this book comes from old training manuals and notes that I had taken during training. It is important that you utilize other sources for your training for these emergencies. There are several sites and groups that offer training in self-defense tactics and other specialties you will need. It is a matter of breaking down the different parts of situations that are involved in an attack, and seeking out the sources for that specialty.

Figure 17 Approaching the sea buoy

PORT OF CALL

ARRIVAL AND DEPARTURE

Traveling by sea offers a great opportunity to meet and mingle with people of different backgrounds and cultures. With this comes the added danger of those who profit from crime. Most countries do not have the resources available to counter crime and piracy so you must be prepared to handle all of your own safety and security.

When you leave your home country, you must change your attitude concerning many things we take for granted. You may leave items on deck and the hatches unlocked for brief excursions into town. But when you leave familiar waters, you leave that security behind. Therefore, you must leave your lax nature about your security behind, as well.

When approaching a port you must put in place the security measures before you come near the port that you plan to visit. If you do not act on this until you are in the port it will be too late, and you would have given information on what you have on your vessel that may be of interest to those who may wish to take it.

Therefore, you need to prepare your vessel before prying eyes have a chance to scope out your vessel and those onboard.

Another thing that you need to keep in mind is, when entering a port; you need to observe the people as you arrive for possible warning signs. You must watch for those who are watching you. Should you enter a port with women on deck in bikinis you will have many people gawking at you? To ensure you are not misreading their interest, you should ask the ladies to either remain below for a time during and after entering port or have them dress in an unattractive way, and remain on deck to help watch for those who show a more than casual interest in your arrival.

You do not want to give reasons to watch your boat when you are trying to read the surroundings. This precaution will only be needed in areas of risk, but a good precaution to take. Pirates have also been known to rape or even take the females from the boat on occasion. You do not want to create additional benefits' for those who may want to attack your boat.

While traveling it is not practical to write security procedures every time you move to another location. For this reason you should have established security protocols that can be followed with minor adjustment. I have found it best to establish before hand three different security protocols each having their own precautions and procedure that must be followed. The first or level one would be the precautions and security that I normally use in my homeport. The second would be for ports that are questionable and the third for ports with high risk of piracy or robbery.

For example, at home I leave things on deck and leave hatches open. I do not worry about people standing on the dock and coming along side my boat. Whereas, I would take additional precautions when entering a port at which there is a possibility, and a slight risk of piracy because of the poverty in the area. In addition, and different still would be entering a port where acts of piracy have occurred regularly and people injured. When writing your security protocols always remember the basic security for all things that is; Lighting, Locking, Looking.

Example of my security protocols:

Security protocol level one, this should be the least security you have utilized on your boat. Using your homeport as a starting point, you can list the precautions you normally take for security underway, in port. What measures, are, taken, when going to town and when securing your vessel at night?

Security protocol level two, you try to anchor or dock in a well lighted area with other boats. Secure your valuables and items that can be stolen from deck. Lock hatches when leaving the boat.

Security protocol level three, at this level you will be operating, more like a military unit with the requirements and watches that are required. At this level before entering port you remove anything that can be removed from the deck and place it below deck. This includes any navigation or communication equipment; which can be, disconnected, and moved, below deck. Before entering port, everyone changes clothes to working clothes. Ladies remain below deck or dress un-attractively and remain on deck to help watch for suspicious persons.

All the precautions of level two are included, but you need to ensure that you have someone on deck and on watch at all times, and possibly two people at night. A list of items that need to be accomplished during the daytime in preparation for night such as ensuring batteries are charged and lights are in working order. Radios must be in working condition, pepper spray at strategic location or provided too everyone. Those onboard should know what they are to do should pirates try to board the vessel, and any equipment made ready.

Having established procedures will help ensure that everyone understand and know what has to be done. Ensure that all on your vessel learn each level and the duties that need be performed, not only in preparing for the different levels but also in fending off possible attacks. When each person knows what is expected of them, and all are working towards the objective, your safety and security will counter many attacks before they occur. In an emergency, actions of those on your vessel should be automatic, this will make it possible to overwhelm and stay ahead of the attackers while working together.

Example: You have three security protocols and can adjust each as needed. You are entering an area where pirates have boarded vessels during the night with the owners. In past attacks, they have taken (dingy, outboard motors, life rafts, and valuables, etc.). You do not consider the pirates to be more than thief's and therefore, put, in effect, security protocol two before entering the port.

To meet the requirement for this, everyone must ensure that all valuables are placed in a secure location, and the outboard motor is stored inside the boat, and the dingy secured on deck. All items on deck that can be removed are placed below deck, and all hatches are closed or screens in place, no display of wealth jewelry or expensive items lying about, and a security watch is established. Someone is to be onboard the boat at all times. This is your security level two, and level three will build on this.

The things you need to include for level three would be the following. All equipment that can be removed from the deck and placed below is stored. All hatches not used are locked and screens are only used in areas that are occupied. Clothing is to be changed, before entering port (everyone wears clothing that they can work in) you want to look like you do not have a great deal of wealth and ladies dress accordingly.

When entering the port, everyone is, assigned areas to watch for suspicious people. You make sure you can exit the port or area you are entering at night should you need to do so, for safety reasons. Ensure lights are charged and any equipment to fend off and attack is at hand. A watch schedule is adhered too with the strongest and most experienced on watch when an attack will most likely occur, etc.

When researching the attacks in the areas you plan to visit you should have made notes on the items that the thieves had most often looked for, within the area. This should be paid particular attention to while outlining your procedures for that port and any special precaution taken to counter the attacks that are prevalent in the area.

ARRIVAL TIME IN QUESTIONABLE PORTS

When traveling to a port that has the problem of piracy you need to select your arrival time as to avoid any dangers that exist. While researching the area take notice of the types of attacks and the times that they occur. List the attacks offshore and the attacks near shore separately.

When arriving at a potential danger area, your arrival time should make the best use of the time of day, to avoid the potential danger in the area. If traveling to a port where the pirate attacks recorded have occurred during the late night, early morning hours from 0100 to 0400 you should plan your arrival time for just after sunrise. At this time, most of your marauders are asleep, and you run little risk of attack. You also have the added benefit of being able to avoid their eyes, limiting the number of people that know of your arrival and location.

Should you not plan on staying and are able to leave after a few hours. You can again avoid any danger by leaving before the late afternoon. Therefore, being well out of their reach by the time they are out scouting for their next victim. Route your course to avoid areas of concern, and establish a lookout at the highest point of your vessel. You must see them before they see you too avoid the danger.

If the port you are sailing too has a problem with piracy offshore, you will plan to arrive at the area of danger about sunrise and possibly make it to the dock before late morning avoiding both dangers. Most pirates are not operating at their best at early morning hours, and you will find it to be a good and safe time to travel. When planning your approach, while having to plan for potential offshore as well as the coastal attack.

Plan each portion (Travel and Arrival) separately. Schedule the time of your arrival offshore and in the port in such a way as to minimize the risk of attack. You may have to accept a short time of added danger but should be able to avoid the majority of the time frame that is most problematic. Remember that time is also a tool for your use in combating this problem. Plan your time and route accordingly to best avoid possible attacks.

Figure 18 Fisherman getting too close in port

PIRACY IN PORT

ANCHOR OR DOCK SIDE

You may have noticed that most of the Piracy Reports only detail the actual attack. They do not mention much if anything about suspicious activity leading up to the event. This one thing; should be changed in the reporting of pirate attacks. This would provide mariner's information on what to watch for to enable the anticipation of problems before they occur and give the ability to counter any attempts. If you have been attacked in the past or know of someone who has been; inform them that they need to file a report that includes anything that was suspicious leading up too and including the attack itself.

Overall traveling and exploring new places can be a lot of fun and for that reason; I do not recommend visiting places where you know there is a high likelihood of having a problem. Ensuring your safety and security can suck the fun out of a trip very quick as it takes up all your time, making it impossible to leave the boat for any period. Regardless there are things you can do too protect yourselves from the possibility of pirate attacks.

When you plan your travels, the number of people you have on board should to be a consideration while planning your route. This in its self will dictate weather or not you stop in some places where safety and security are of concern. Traveling with other boaters or several people on your boat is an added level of protection. There are times when you will not have a choice; the need to seek refuge from a storm; or make repairs are a couple of possibilities. There are many hurricane holes that you can duck into for this reason, some are safe, others are not as safe as you would like.

Most pirate attacks are "Attacks of Opportunity", in which the people of the local area observe a stranger entering their domain. In their eyes, you are wealthy and have many things that could make their life easier, or provide them with a means to take several days off their regular routine. Should you be naive and un-observant the opportunity exists that they can rob you without being seen?

Unfortunately, this is what happens in the majority of the acts of piracy against cruisers. These attacks can be prevented by merely stowing the gear and locking everything inside the vessel. In addition, ensuring that the most important security measures of having a well lighted area and a watch schedule are in place.

Many people who decide to cruise the oceans are not mentally prepared for these possibilities and therefore, do not plan for them. Most are not aware that they need to make the psychological change from operating in an environment of safety, too the mentality of being on guard protecting your boat and crew at all times. Here (in the United States) as well many other countries around the world. We generally do not worry about individuals or vessels in close proximity to our own.

Our marinas are busy places in which there are people standing on the dock sometimes leaning against your boat and/or small boats, motor or row along side you; without much notice. You must change your attitude concerning this zone around your vessel as soon as you leave your home waters.

Again, if you are sailing by yourself or with a mate, it is recommended that you stay away from places that require a watch. Traveling thru questionable areas can be enjoyable if you have others that can share the responsibility of security. Only then can you relax and let your guard down to some degree. It is possible to stop in a questionable place for a few hours make repairs or rest, if you leave while you have time to get safely out to sea. Or, you may decide to stop in a port to rest before entering an area of danger.

These are all things you need to consider when planning a passage or planning your way out of an emergency situation. You should always be on the look out for others traveling to the same destinations or along the route you are following, this could be an opportunity to travel together especially through dangerous regions for added security.

After you arrive in a country where piracy is a concern, be aware of those people who are watching and testing your limits. Doing so, can prevent the losses of equipment and items from the boat, most important, it can save your life. Watching for danger will allow time for you too turn the odds in your favor. I have been to many places where the marinas and anchorages felt as secure as those at home. This will be the case in most places. You must be able to recognize the dangers and be prepared to handle it when it manifests itself.

You can continue to be friendly and cordial as usual. This is what makes, the lifestyle, so great. Hopefully, after reading this you will be a better judge of this danger and know when you need to shift to a more secure mode of operation or when to depart from a location to ensure your safety.

Attacks at anchor or at dockside are more common for the mere reason of being close and accessible to those who would commit such acts. The further from shore you are, the fewer people that have the ability to reach you. In an area that warrants the precaution it is wise to anchor your boat out of range of most swimmers.

There are several reports in which the attackers gained access to the vessel while at anchor by swimming. Joshua Slokem, had an occurrence while sleeping, someone had swim to his vessel and climbed to the deck. He had taken the precaution before retiring of dumping tacks on the deck after noticing he was being watched closely. And he was awoken by a scream, when that person climbed to his deck and stepped on the tacks. By the time he got up on deck, the boarder was gone.

When you are arriving at a port that has a history of attacks on boaters, it is usually best to stay at a marina. You want to select a marina that caters too cruisers. They will have made the preparations needed to provide security to prevent these crimes. In best cases you need to be sure they have a gate limiting access to the boats and slips.

Once at the marina talk to the office about security and ask for any recommendations they may have. Regardless you do not want to let your guard down; you still need to ensure the safety of your vessel and those onboard. Take whatever precautions necessary to ensure your safety during the night.

After your arrival at the dock, while working at securing sails cleaning and other chores watch for those that hang around and watch your boat. If you notice anyone acting suspiciously, with more than casual interest in your arrival and boat, spending a lot of time in proximity of your location. This in itself is behavior that should be recognized as a danger signal. They may move in and around your vessel in order to see what items and equipment you have onboard. Or they could just stand around talking and scanning in your location. Make a mental note of the individual and watch for them and their activities, throughout the day.

Make sure they are aware that you notice them. Do not be afraid to confront and individual by saying something to them. If they ask you questions, do not be forthcoming with information. You need to probe them and not allow the opposite; this can stop a problem before it starts. It is OK to be direct and ask someone what they are up to. Do not be timid; if you act in such a way you will be stereotyped as someone who will be an easy target and this will embolden the attackers. Do not be so forceful in your approach as to pick a fight with the individual. There is a fine line between the two that must not be crossed. You can confront someone and remain friendly but forceful.

You must be mindful of the possibility that someone is gathering information that could be useful in planning an attack against your vessel or stealing items from it. The statement below from the IMB is a warning concerning information being, passed, to pirates on movement of vessels by individuals up the coast, for attacks. Always be on guard for such possibilities in which individuals are asking about your plans and destination for your travels.

Sailors Suspect Pirates Informed Of Yacht Movements

Topic: Piracy Archive 2003

There had been strong suggestions from several sources that at places like Salalah, Oman and Al Mukalla, Yemen, information on yacht movements might be, passed to people engaged in piracy on the coast. The statement mirrors a concern held by a number of yachts an, is, based, on documented reports of previous incidents. The pattern is that several of these attacks followed a visit to one of the above ports. Whether there is substance to this or not, several skippers decided that, it would be beneficial to remain unseen and take the necessary precautions.

Measures taken by some national authorities to discourage piracy have been effective in some areas, particularly the Malaysian Malacca coast and among the islands between Langkawi and Phuket, Thailand. Yemen, has implemented, a counter piracy program, but it remains to be, seen how, effective it is. There has been some criticism directed by cruising sailors at the IMB Piracy Reporting Centre in Kuala Lumpur, Malaysia as well as the 24 Hours Anti Piracy Helpline, whose main activity appears to be limited to the compilation of daily and weekly reports on piracy incidents.

While approaching a new port in an area that has the threat of piracy you must prepare the boat beforehand. When at sea the danger to the boat and crew is the weather, when you suspect that it will turn bad you clear the deck ensuring all is secure. As you, approach shore or an area in question, the concern shifts from weather to piracy with the precautions being similar. It is important that everything is put away before entering port, the less they see, the less the desire to steal *(Out of sight, Out of mind)*. Always remember that the attack starts when they observe something they want; so do not cause them to covet, or encourage the crime by having many items visible.

Another precaution you can take when entering an unknown port is to ask the women to stay below at first. This will limit the confusion caused in giving people multiple reasons to look in your direction. You need to evaluate your situation and safety first, and not be, confused, by those lusting after the women onboard.

You need to establish a watch schedule for the boat. It is always wise for the captain to watch the activity early before midnight. You should also plan for yourself taking the watch from 2:00 to 6:00 am when an attack will most likely occur. Please remember we are talking about places with a reputation for attacks, though it is good to maintain the practices of watches no matter where you are visiting. In addition, remember Pirate Attacks are on the rise and occurring more frequently in unsuspecting places, exercise on the side of caution, "Its better to be safe than sorry".

Should you happen to be at anchor, watch and track the location of other boats on the water, particularly the fisherman, in small boats? If you notice that they seem to be continually getting closer to you while setting their nets, consider this as a suspicious behavior and not acceptable. Most fishermen, will set their net and when they recover it move to another location a good distance from the prior set. Fishermen that continue to set a net without catching any fish are not fisherman now are they! They have decided to become pirates for a night by trying to ware you down, causing you to drop your guard. After a period, they figure you will get use to them being around and not consider them a threat.

It is my experience, that; they will fish in close before and after dark. This provides them with two of the things they need to attack you; one is they learn your attitude towards security and what security you have established. The other is that they are setting up the opportunity for their quick maneuver into a position to board your boat. Once on board they have to get to you before you can take action or pick up a weapon.

If you notice any vessel hanging close by, consider it a sign that they are watching you. If they continue to fish near you, be aware of their location at all times. Shine a spotlight in their direction showing that you see them, and take pictures if possible recording those you suspect. In any security situation, the standard measure utilized even by the military is to ensure the area is well lighted, and having a person visible and alert with a spotlight to shine at anything that draws your attention after dark. This alone will be enough to stop smalltime pirates.

The type of attack that is most worrisome is when they come to your boat while you are below with no concern for you being awake. These pirates are not troubled about confronting you. These attackers rely on intimidation and fear, and are not concerned about causing harm to others. You may try to stop them on their approach; if they do not scare easily and believe that you will cower if they persist, they will intimidate you into submission. If you are bold in the first seconds of this attack, you can gain the upper hand. Nevertheless, most people will restrain themselves for fear of harming someone, or the possibility of making the attackers more violent than they might have been if they did not act to protect themselves.

You hear people talk about how heroic they would be in a situation like this. But before you make your mind up, to do so; think about this. If you have studied the past attacks in the area then you have an idea based on what has been reported as to if anyone has been killed or injured by gunshot or knife wounds. You will make a determination as to the survivability of attacks in the area. If records show they have caused great harm to boaters once onboard, and you decide to pull out a firearm, you have made a decision that could be very good or absolutely, horrible.

If the pirate attacks have all been successful with out injury or death then it may be that they have never encountered an opposing force and will back down when confronted. If the opposite is true, your choice could turn it into a very bad situation which could be prevented if you knew your enemy better. Knowing of the past attacks and their attitude about taking life or injuring people will be one of your determining factors in planning. These are details that you need to think about, before visiting an area, where these possibilities exist.

My most important advice is first you need to know the meaning of DEADLY FORCE and, when you can use it. Then you need to practice with the weapons that you will have onboard to become proficient with them. Then study your vessel and learn how a pirate would approach and board your vessel and practice different scenarios in your mind, and with those onboard to be sure everyone knows what to do in the case of an attack. Make up your mind that you will not allow attackers onboard your vessel, and be prepared to fend off an attack by making the proper preparations.

You never really know when you are being watched, so; ensure everyone is visible and alert on security watch. In addition, you must prevent complacency form setting in onboard. Be aware of what is happening around you at all times. While at a dock or at anchor, be aware of those around your boat, especially when departing. It is very important that you observe the people at the dock and how much attention they give to your departure. Do not discuss your plans where others can hear or see. As we mentioned there are those who will pass your plans on to those who will be waiting on you, for the soul purpose of capturing you and your boat.

If you feel you may be, attacked, take precautions to prevent it. Leave late at night or very early in the morning, Head out to sea before adjusting to the proper course for your next destination.

Do not wait till you see the attack, take action when you feel or sense something bad is about to happen. Always be planning for the outcome you desire, when you quit strategizing you loose.

Captain Michael Pierce

Figure 19 Returning from South America

PIRACY AT SEA

When planning your trip you have already researched recent pirate attacks for the region. The information that you should have available is: the times the attacks have occurred, the area and distance from shore, the types of vessels used by the pirates, how the attack progressed from first sight providing the techniques used, and the weapons that were on hand. Below is a report let us now see what information we can glean from it that may help us plan a passage.

Pirate Attacks - Gulf of Aden 19, 20, and 21 August 2008

On our voyage from Dubrovnik, Croatia to Kantang, Thailand aboard our 36-foot sloop, we entered the Gulf of Aden from the Red Sea on 17 August 2008. Slight winds and a full moon, we chose to keep 50 miles off the Yemen coast in the company with many east and west, bound, commercial ships. At night, we showed no lights and saw close by a VLCC also, with no lights.

On 19 August at 1915 local time a Mayday was broadcast on channel 16 from chemical tanker Bunga Milati at 012°45´.1 North,

047°57′.7 East, 120 miles Southwest of our position and only 25 miles from our previous nights track. The Filipino radio officer sounded terrified and broadcast his Mayday constantly as pirates boarded his vessel, until radio silence prevailed.

From earlier radio traffic there were at least 2 coalition warships in the area, 1 United States and 1 Spanish, and from the time the Bunga Milati ceased broadcasting, her position, speed and heading was reported to the to USA warship from other ships nearby. The last we heard was she was heading at speed for the Horn of Africa.

On 20 August, we heard another Mayday pirate attack on channel 16 but were too far away to know the details.

On 22 August, we entered the Port of Salalah where a French coalition warship was visiting and from an Omani naval officer we learned first hand that an Iranian oil tanker, was also, and boarded by pirates the following night. He described how 2 pirate boats, usually Somali small fiberglass open boats, would be joined by a long rope across the path of the victim; as the ship's bow fouls the rope the 2 pirate boats are drawn alongside the victim and boarded.

On a lighter note, due to no wind and constant motoring, we had to put into Nishtun, Yemen for an emergency fuel stop. We found the local fishermen friendly, and who assisted us. Nishtun has no facilities for visiting yachtsmen, but we were able to buy 80 liters of diesel.

We know that the narrowest point of this passage is about 78 nm giving little opportunity to avoid the pirate vessels. They are like wolves traveling in groups laying traps for vessels. Attacks in this area can at any time and at any place in this area. To provide the most protection you should travel in an area about 50 nm off the coast of Yemen where you will find the shipping lanes and possible convoys that you can join up with for the passage.

You also know there are Military ships on duty to aid vessels from their related countries or those that have treaties with their country for this protection. Furthermore, that most vessels in the area travel with no running lights at night this adds danger of collision for those who travel across these waters. The pirates travel in open boats some fishing boats, and have been seen setting up traps for vessels like the one above. They stretch a line between two vessels and allow a ship to travel between them, the rope makes contact dragging the pirate vessels alongside then they are able to board her. This is an area in which you play Russian roulette by traveling; you need to take every precaution available to you for your protection.

The problem in this area is that most reports are of vessels hearing the broadcast of an attack with very little information from those who were, attacked. You can gather a lot of usable intelligence from the reports as they are. You will see that the same is true in these waters as in most other places; the pirates are for a good part fisherman, with the added danger of militants using this as a way to support their groups. In some cases they have travel close by a vessel, and radio this information to others who will attack you; or, return themselves to board your boat. They may fire weapons at you to slow you down or get you to stop. In this case what matters is how much risk you are willing to take with not only your vessel but the lives of those onboard with you.

It is not wise to travel this area and vessels that do so cost the tax payers hundreds of millions of dollars in vessels and manpower. Now with the added problems of Egypt and surrounding countries it is not a chance you should take with your life. On the other hand we need to try to force this route to be open by attempting to transit it in different vessels. So you should ask is this something you feel is worth your life.

When planning a passage by or near a dangerous area will have studied the charts, to prepare your passage. By looking for high ground and towers, you will be able to determine if they can see you before you have a chance to locate them from shore or with a string of vessels across the straight or channel. Be sure that you set your course to pass out of their range of sight, or plan to transit when visibility is limited. You will find the chart for use in determining visible range by height to eye for this purpose, but generally, it is roughly about a mile for every 5 meters in height, I would use a mile for every two meters in height when trying not to be, seen. Again your goals are to avoid the dangerous areas, see them before they see you and move away from the danger.

When attacks occur well offshore you will see two scenarios as you gather reports one is because of mariners normal transit time through the area the pirates have worked out a schedule that ensures they will find vessels during certain hours. The second scenario is that the information on boats traveling through an area is, passed from a marina or other vessels up the coast to the pirates, who now know that you departed a point and will be near their location at a particular time period.

If you have, several reports for an area you can start to make a determination on what the dangers are and how to avoid them. If you notice in the reports that someone is passing info to the pirates, you should avoid the normal stop made by mariners before entering the area. If you see that attacks are more or less during a specific time, period; you can avoid this time period, to avoid the pirates. This will not solve all the possibilities; some areas are just dangerous and un-predictable.

Another tactic is to travel at night with all lights turned off. This is a great way to make it more difficult on those trying to locate you but adds the danger of collision with other vessels. When using this as a tactic you must keep adequate watch to prevent such a possibility. It is always best to assign a person to each watch in a designated area, and they notify the helm to maneuver away from danger. When attempting this in an area where you must utilize radio silence causes you to consider every vessel to be a pirate vessel, unless you had communicated with others before entering the area of danger. Also use a directional red lenses light as a signal device to warn other vessels of your presents.

Radio direction finders have practically slipped from the memory of most people. But in recent times, they have become a necessity, and you should have one onboard your boat. When you hear a broad cast of an attack, you should locate the direction of the attack from your vessel. The strength of the signal can provide an estimate of the distance. Most marine radios have a range of just over twenty miles. You then can change your course to avoid this area. If you hear music playing on the emergency frequency, then you can assume that the pirates are blocking the channel to prevent communication or warning to other vessels. You need to avoid these areas as well. It is importance that you know the frequencies that the ships use for ship-to-ship communication for a back up. Contacting the military and civilian ships in the area, and establishing a protocol for this possibility would be a good idea before entering the area.

There is a established point of contact in this area for mariners to gather to plan passage in this region in convoys with military protection. You need to research these possibilities in what ever region you are planning your passage. For this region you can check http://www.noonsight.com where you will find the forms that need to be filled out and contact info for planning your passage.

When traveling in convoys make a Maneuver Board with the other vessels listed, their positions, and any special instructions for emergency situation. Every vessel in the convoy should have a copy on hand. This will help in identification of those with you during the passage, and make it easier to identify danger. Furthermore, pre-arrange a method of signaling and what the signals will be with a red light or other device that will not be visible over a great distance, to ensure others do not detect you. Should you be detected you will need to decide on what your maneuvers are for added protection. You may decide draw the vessels closer together to prevent a vessel from getting between you and the other members of the convoy.

You should be able to signal bring the vessels closer together in a tight group making it more difficult for the attackers. This must be established at the meeting as well as, how you will fend off attackers and utilize the added manpower of the convoy. Keep your signals very simple; you should only need a few. KISS (keep it simple stupid) should always be your guide in such planning, the more complicate you make something the greater the opportunity for something too go wrong. This is critical when you need everything to go right.

I want to give you ideas that you can use to work out your procedures for use in this type of emergency. Not everyone can or would want to take the same actions. Some do not believe in violence and would be happy with just running, others would be quite capable in fighting off an attack. This is your vessel, you are the captain, and you have to live with your decisions, so your plan is your decision and lives depend on it. I want to get your mind working on the subject with the information that you can use in creating your plan of action for such circumstances. In the latter chapter I also give ideas for devices that you can use to combat pirates and fight off their advances, these are in this book to prove that you have things available that can help. And many times they are at hand on your vessel.

Most pirates use open vessels with outboard motors for platforms to attack from, the basic coastal fishing boat that you see in travel magazines. Every boat has its strengths and weaknesses, especially when it comes to weather and the sea state. These can be used too your advantage as well, if you have to transit an area that offers little protection in other ways from pirates. You can delay your movement through the area until the weather is advantageous to allow a safe passage. The vessels that are used by the pirates must slow and be handled a specific way in these rough conditions, where as a sailboat handles much better and can travel faster. This is another tool, which you should keep in mind for use, when necessary.

When you are under way and see a vessel approaching you, it is always best to turn directly away from the approaching vessel to slow the closing speed and allow more time to evaluate the situation. Distance is time and time is a valuable commodity in these situations. In addition, in the same way a good set of binoculars allows you to see into the future. The further you are able to see the further into the future you are looking. If you can see an approaching vessel, a mile away you are looking at a vessel that will close with you several minutes in the future. You can see the vessel and make the decision as to friend, or foe; allowing you more time to prepare for what is to come.

When pirates are closing with you and trying to maneuver into a position that will allow them to board your vessel, your primary tool is maneuvering. They want to get along side you or forward to board you from the side, and you must keep them from that position. You can be in very close quarters with attackers and by turning your vessel too port or starboard can prevent a boarding long enough to allow help to arrive in some cases. In other cases, you must be willing to maneuver into position to ram and sink or disable their vessel. Again do not be timid; you must be aggressive in your efforts to find a solution that will allow your escape. Know how they have captured vessels in the past and how they intend to gain control of your boat. this will aid you in your moves to prevent the same from occurring to your and your vessel.

If and when you need to use the sea state to gain the advantage, you need to make maneuvering as uncomfortable and dangerous for the attackers as possible. The more difficult it is on the attackers to get near or along side your vessel, the better off you are and more likely you are too escape. Watch closely those onboard the opposing vessel watch for signs of indecisiveness or uncertainty in their vessel and its handling. If you can capitalize on this, do so; try to make it increasingly dangerous on those attacking you.

I have seen people make devices that they can tow behind their boat with hopes of fowling a propeller, crossbows with big firecrackers attached. I have even seen people take balloons filled with pepper of some type with a firecracker as a dispersing agent to toss at an attacker down wind. I do not know if they ever used their devices, but there are several things that you should carry onboard your vessel for such an emergency. I will discuss these in a later chapter. You should make every effort to ensure you have the materials, equipment and devices that could help you defeat this danger.

A big problem in vessels that are being fired on with weapons is the safety of those on board. I hope that you will take the time to look at the positions in and on your boat where people could be protected from projectiles, or devise a solution to this problem. You could purchase a movable barrier that can be stowed out of the way for this emergency; many vessels are low in the water and have areas that are protected. This deserves your attention and some thought to look at the possibilities and solutions.

Most captains that spend a lot of time away from land are like MacGyver's of the sea, and able to deal with almost any situation. This is just another item on your list that you need to plan for, remember; you must not miss the details in the available information, or you will leave an open opportunity for the pirates in the area you are visiting. Study the elevations and towers at coastal areas you plan to transit or visit, make modifications to your boat necessary for security. Carry parts and equipment that will allow you to make items for your protection.

You should also check the weather reports for the area, if there is weather that can be used to transit the area that would protect you from the pirates, you should wait for the conditions to develop and use the advantage that it provides. Look for others to travel with, Travel at the least likely time for an attack, and with as little signal from your boat as possible to prevent detection, (you do not want them to know you are out there). If the area has a bad problem do a little additional research for any local piracy reporting agencies, or military convoys, that you may utilize while in the area for your protection.

Figure 20 Myself at the helm, somewhere, sometime

PIRATE TACTICS & COUNTERMEASURES

It is difficult to plan a way to protect those on board if you have never been involved with such things as security or experienced it before. For this purpose, we will list a few possible encounters, after which we will list precautions that may be, taken; some you need before your trip starts such as modification you could make to your boat. Others are security measures and actions that could be taken by those on board during an attack. These are possibilities for you to look at and think about. You must decide your security.

These proposed procedures and actions will help you think and plan for actions that will protect your vessel and those aboard. If you devise a plan, and would like to share it with others, please visit our web site http://www.piracysurvivalguide.com as well as http://www.noonsite.com to share your thoughts.

Tactics utilized by pirates are few; after all there are only so many versions of climbing onboard a vessel and robbing it. You do need to know the methods of their success. A few scenarios, and understand the things that they (the Pirates) look for and how they set you up for the attack.

There are several things you need to do before you leave. Including a few modifications you can make to the boat and equipment that can assist you in security and safety. Below are just possibilities, you need make your own plans on procedures to be taken, by all on your boat. These are just ideas, which are to be used as a guide and not procedures required in any manual or regulation. You are the captain, plan for your needs and anticipated problems no matter how unlikely.

UNSEEN ROBBERS

When traveling to a strange new place the first thing any group of cruisers want to do is; get off the boat and have a little fun. I have in the past done the same. I would just shut the hatches and leave providing I was not going to be gone vary long. In many places, it is not safe to leave your boat unattended and necessary to making a few preparations before you do so. Therefore, the first type of attack is not really an attack at all; it is a robbery, you may have gone into town or possibly asleep below when this occurs. Most boats are not very secure and there are few places to hide valuables as well. If you make modifications for this purpose will give you greater peace of mind when traveling.

Precautions: A few of the precautions for leaving your boat must be taken, before the trip begins. They are structural in nature and should be accomplished while at home.

1. Ensure all items that can be of interest to pirates are out of view and locked in a secure location. Any weapons must be, hidden and locked, as well as, any valuables. This will require a location that is not detectable by those searching your vessel. Give this a lot of thought and when possible make the space look structural in nature.

2. Be sure that the hatches are locked and the locking system is strong enough to prevent someone from

being able to pry it open. Furthermore, ensure that the lock is of the type that is not easy to cut or remove. Most hatches are not made to protect from forced entry and need to be re-enforced. Check with a local yacht designer or builder if you do not feel you can solve this problem.

3. Install an alarm system on the boat. I prefer an alarm with not only sound but also lights. Lights cause more urgency in the thief's minds to leave or evacuate a location. If possible, an alarm that will notify you electronically while you are away from the boat.

UN-NOTICED OBSERVERS

Most pirates are not pirates full time, they are fishermen; or work in a trade that gives them access to a vessel and the ability to travel on the water. They use this as a cover while waiting for a chance to catch the occupants of a vessel off guard or away. They may fish in your area, or at least appear to do so, while never being very far off from your location. They return as soon as they fail to see anyone active on the boat. They may move closer, continuing to act as though they are fishing until they are next too your vessel. If you go below or plan to get some sleep, they simply climb aboard and steal what they want or wake you with a gun to your face.

This is one of the more common occurrences. The other possibility would be that you are awake below, and they have gained the advantage. You look up to find a stranger approaching you with a gun; which is a shock to the system in its self. Most often you would be dumbfounded for a few seconds, trying to decide whether you are dreaming or awake. No matter, they have gotten the jump on you, and now you must suffer the consequences.

Precautions: You can do a few things before the trip to modify your boat and precautions you can take during your travels will help prevent this danger. Insure you have a screen or bars for each hatch that you may want open that prevents intruders from entering. Your entry hatch must have the ability to be locked inside and strong enough to prevent entry should someone try to pry it out. The other precautions are standard and will be repeated, but very important steps in protecting you and your vessel.

1. Ensure everything, is put away, and; locked out of view.

2. Have not only the anchor light turned on, but also, any deck lights on too illuminate the deck as well as the area around the boat if possible. It is better to install lights that shine out and around the boat and not so much shining on the deck for some areas. This makes it easier for the person on watch to see anything approaching and makes it more difficult on those that are approaching to see you. On many boats energy storage is a problem, so you will have either solar flood lights or a person on watch with spot light to deal with your security.

3. Establish a security watch on deck in view of others. They must be visible and alert at all times. Do not allow the person on watch to leave the deck unless there is someone to take their place for the time they are below.

4. Have a spot light ready to light anything that looks or sounds suspicious.

5. Ensure that crewmembers have pepper spray and any non-lethal weapons near and ready.

6. Only open hatches that are near individuals or have screens that prevent entry from the exterior. These hatches must be ready and

easy to close and locked quickly. For this reason, the individuals near open hatches should have pepper spray, which can be used to repel an attacker and close the hatch.

YOU BLINKED FIRST

You may be aware of the situation developing and believe that you are being cautious; you keep the boat lighted and have someone on watch. The watch person on watch may be doing a good job, staying alert and watching the proximity of the other vessel. Then the "urge" comes, it does not matter what urge. Hunger, thirsty or maybe they need to go to the head to relieve themselves. In that moment, as soon as they go below for just a few seconds the boat that you thought was fishing moves in quickly.

Then they are aboard and move quietly until they are all at once "up close and personnel". You look up and see a man pointing a gun in your face, possibly slapping you with it to get your attention and insure you are stunned. Next, they continue to gather the people on board the vessel and demanding your cash and valuables.

Precautions: This is a problem of improper organization and watch keeping. When you have an established watch on the boat and a person on deck, you should always have one person off watch on standby, sleeping next to the entry hatch or on deck. To create the good defensive situation the person on deck would have pepper spray; the person on standby would also have pepper spray and a secondary repelling device.

Pepper spray and other devices should be at arms reach and out of eye site. You do not want the pirates finding them should you not have time or decide not to repel them an attack. Before you depart on your trip, go over the use of the weapons onboard. In addition, discus how to implement or use each item you have onboard for the purpose of defense. Act out situations and practice how to use them and what to do in each situation, so each person knows what is expected.

The person on watch must make the determination on whether to try to repel the attackers or not. As a captain, you may ask those on board to wake you when they become suspicious about the actions of vessels in and around your boat. You may also choose in some locations to "sound the alarm", then go below locking yourselves inside and wait for them to leave. This depends on your security policy and the modifications and the locks you have installed, as well as; type of attacks in the area you are visiting.

If there is an overwhelming force, a couple of boats or several attackers with weapons, locking everyone inside may be the best solution. This must be, discussed, and planned for, before hand. In each case the Captain when possible should relieve the person on watch and send them to another position. This would mean that you have set up a early warning for any suspicious activity long before a situation would develop, this would give you time to take charge and evaluate the situation. Possible countermeasures would be as follows:

1. Those inside grab their spray and shut the hatches.

2. Assign a person forward to Radio for help; do not be surprised if there is none offered.

3. Assign someone to grab the flare gun and find a location to fire it to signal help. (Be sure flare will clear rigging and sails)

4. Implement other measures that you may have in place for this emergency.

LOOSE LIPS

You have arrived in an area; and are docked at a marina. You have taken on fuel and ice, and picked up a few other items needed for the boat. You could be sitting on deck, on the dock or at a little café at the dock. You happen to be planning the next part of your trip. There are a few local people hanging around the area who can hear your discussion and your plans including your departure time.

After you have departed and traveled for several hours you notice a vessel approaching you. It looks as though it is a fishing boat but not fishing at the time. They just happen to be the group of pirate's that received information on your travel plans from a friend up the coast who overheard your plans while at the marina. They can look harmless, and wave as they approach; as soon as they are close enough that you do not have time to react they make a move to capture your vessel.

Precautions: All discussions of your vessel departure, route, times and security need to be made in private. Ensure, it is done without, anyone near by to, overhear or see what you plan.

1. Plan your trip inside so no one can hear and see.

2. Do not discuss your departure time, destination, or anything that could be used by others to ambush your vessel outside where others can hear.

3. When you leave do not share information with those at the marina, let them believe you are sailing out for a day trip, too some destination near by in the opposite direction of your intended route, and will return.

4. When you depart travel out to sea well out of sight before settling on your course to your next destination. Establish a look out at the highest point on your vessel. You must see them before they see you, as soon as you see danger turn away from it.

THE INVISIBLE

You are moving along at a nice 8 kts, it is dark; there is a moon but it is cloudy and no visibility besides what the running lights provide on deck. You do not notice the vessel approaching from the stern, they have no lights on, and you do not hear their engines. You have the autopilot on and the person on watch goes below to check the position on the chart. The next thing he knows is he's looking up from the deck into the barrel of a gun, and cannot make out what they are saying. Not a lot is getting pass the pounding he has in his brain bucket after being hit over the head.

Precautions: This again depends on the watch; in some situations such as those in the Gulf of Aden, you should have two or more people on watch. Assign each an area of responsibility. It may be a good idea to invest in night vision goggles for the boat. You can see ok with regular binoculars but only shadows, and nothing when there is no light available from the moon or stars. Make sure you have a good set of long range binoculars as well as a set of regular for short distances on your boat.

1. Tune our radar (if you have one) to the best for seeing the small craft at the greatest distance possible.

2. Set up watches with several of the crew on look out, at the highest point of your vessel.

3. The further you can see the more time you have, Try to stack things in your favor by using good long distance binoculars and night vision.

4. Turn off all lights visible from outside the boat. Block ports that have escaping light.

5   Radio silence and no talking on deck, if you are sailing you may hear something, in the distance.

6   If sailing it may be wise to lower the sails, Sails reflect light and can be, seen in some cases at night a good distance. During the day light, you can reduce your visible signature by running your motor and lowering your sails. Powerboats try to lower anything that may be, sighted over great distances.

7   Use the sea state and wind to your advantage in keeping ahead of possible boarders, making it difficult for them to access your vessel.

8. Use non-lethal weapons to buy time and slow down attackers.

SHOCK

You are cruising along and notice a vessel approaching you at a high rate of speed. Their course appears to be a little ahead of yours. Before you know it, they are almost along side you. All the sudden several other men appear and start firing their guns in the air and shouting at you. You have no time to react and throw up your hands try to not do anything that will give them reason to shoot at you.

Precautions: In most situations, do not allow your boat to continue in a direction that may put you at risk until you are sure there is no risk of attack. Furthermore, remember the distance is time and the further into the future you can see the more time you have to act, by using a good set of long distance wide-angle binoculars to evaluate the situation. Do not make a quick decision on their intent; change course that will take you most directly away from them. This will provide a little additional time to prepare.

1. Start evaluating the situation well in advance with as much

distance between you and the approaching vessel as possible. They want to look harmless until it is too late for you to react, so keep away from them.

2. Select a course that will put the most distance between you and the boat you are watching. Change course to a direction directly away from the approaching vessel. If you continue to travel at a right angle from a pursuer they will catch you more quickly than if you were on a course directly away from them. This also reduces your visible signature making it possible to slip from their sight more quickly.

3. Use the sea to cause your pursuers to slow, by setting a course into the seas if possible, at the best angle for your vessel and that hinder their progress.

4. Sound the alarm and have everyone report to his or her assigned positions with proper equipment to repel an attack.

5. When in danger sound the alarm calling for assistance over any communication equipment that you have access to. Ensure you have a person on board trained in the use of this equipment that can reduce your work load. This will make it possible for you to deal with the emergency in a more effective way. You may have heard the old saying: "When in danger or in doubt, jump and holler, scream and shout".

Remember if they start to fire weapons at you, you need to be very effective with what you have to defend yourself. Keep in mind that when you do fire a weapon, the situation could escalate very quickly to something you may not be able to deal with. For this reason you should fire to take out the propulsion (outboard motor) or only when you can effectively prevent someone from firing at you and your vessel. It is always best to hold this in reserve until you are sure of the possibilities and the outcome in your favor. If you can hit the engine knocking it out, this will stop the attack, if not you need to ensure all are below and out of site as well as the line of fire clear. If in a harbor be sure you know where your round will end up, you do not want to hit innocent bystanders while trying to defend yourself. This will cause the locals to side against you as well as land you in the local jail.

You must consider everything and select the best course of action by the second. You need to concentrate and use anything that will slow their boat and prevent them from closing with you. Try to cross these areas when the seas are in your favor using them as a tool to prevent a successful attack.

NEED ASSISTANCE

You are, making good time; and see a vessel on the horizon, which does not appear to be moving. You continue on your course, which brings you within a mile of the other vessel. As you start to pass them, they wave you down as though they are in trouble. Having read all the books on good seamanship you feel that you must render assistance, so you proceed to help them.

As you pull along side, someone on the other boat passes you a line to prevent the vessels from drifting apart. While you are securing it and all hands are close by trying to figure what to do in order to help these poor fellow mariners, you hear a gun shot and look up to see a couple of AK-47 and a pistol being waved at you. Now you wish you had remembered the horror stories about being fooled, by people doing this vary thing.

Precautions: Again, remember that distance is time and every minute of distance, you can use to your advantage you need. Try to evaluate these situation miles in advance. In some areas, you should ignore this situation all together and pass on the position to authorities when you are safe.

If you hear a radio call; and are assured, that they are not pirates, guess what? Unless they are on fire, you have no way of knowing for sure. Use extreme caution! They may have just captured this vessel, and forcing an individual onboard too call you in order to draw into this misery. It is best to let the Coast Guard or Military deal with it in many areas.

1. Do not approach a vessel that you are not sure of. When you sight them alter course to maintain your distance from these vessels.

2. Us the radio to communicate with the vessel, and pass their request to the information to authorities. Unless they are drowning do not approach these vessels in areas of danger.

3. Use your radio and Binoculars to judge the situation. Moreover, do not trust it as being safe to approach.

4. Plot the actual position of the vessel, as well as the time and the type of vessel, her name and home port. Pass this on to authorities as well as the piracy web sites to give other mariners a "heads up".

In other areas, (those that are relatively safe, and little risk) you will be forced to investigate further. Always go slow and force enough time that they may give themselves away. Keep a good distance from them while communicating, several miles if possible. Keep watch in all other directions from you vessel they could have another vessel closing with you while they distract you. Should the situation turn bad, use the tactics we have talked about in this book as well as the policies you have put in place? Radios for help fire flares and use the sea in your favor.

Hold any weapons at the ready and out of sight. Think of how you would react to the show of weapons in a situation that did not call for it.

BOAT IN TOW

There have been reports made concerning attacks that have taken place by two vessels using a line or rope stretched between them. They position themselves so that the vessel, they want to attack travels between them, and then they raise the rope to a level that catches the bow of the boat they are attacking, which swings the attacking boats into position, along side there prey. Making it possible to board quickly and gain control of the boat and crew. Fishing vessels can use there nets to trap boats as well as fish. Stay away from groups of vessels in areas of concern for piracy.

Precautions: Use distance for your protection and do not approach vessels or groups of vessels you do not know. Distance is time, so do not sacrifice it on uncertainty. Use the sea to your advantage and steer clear of what you may consider a threat. If you do not know the vessels or those on board, consider it is a threat. So you will consider that' all vessels are a threat until proven otherwise. Do not allow yourself to get into a position which will require you to pass near these vessels. You have time so turn around and leave the danger. Do not stop your vessel; your maneuvering is your protection.

1. The very second you locate vessels on the horizon, change course to at least forty-five degrees of the vessels you have sighted. You do not want to sacrifice anymore distance or time until you are sure of the threat.

2. If it appears that a vessel has set a course to intercept your vessel, alter course to one that is directly away from the threat. Do not waste time thinking about this. At first sight of the vessel heading in your direction react and change course quickly, maintaining your safety margin or distance while trying to loose your pursuers.

3. Again sound the alarm ensuring that your crew is at the stations for the emergency at hand.

4. Record the position, types of vessels and any other information describing the situation. Pass this to the authorities as well as the web sites that will warn other mariners.

5. Radio your position and the emergency that you are dealing with

in hope of locating any ships that can assist you and take the information that you have. Be sure to give your vessel name and home port. Also give all the information on those onboard your vessel in case it is needed by those searching for you to render assistance.

6. Utilize the tactics and techniques you have established to prevent a vessel from closing with you and boarding your boat.

7. If you become trapped inside the perimeter of a rope or net, do not get tangled in the device. You should utilize the tactic of ramming the vessel which will in most cases allow you to escape the situation. If you must ram the threatening vessel, do so at as near the center or a little aft, and; as much of a right angle as possible. The right angle can be achieved by turning your rudder hard over as you make contact behind the centerline or area you intend to hit on the pirate vessel, and at the opposite end of where the net or rope is secured. As soon as you make contact you need to turn your attention to keeping the stern of your vessel away from the obstacle, rope or net. This will cause the pirate vessel to swing to a right angel while you make contact and the greatest chance of causing the boat to flip or sink. Hit the boat and not the rope or net. This will disable one of the boats and slow the other for a several seconds while it picks up those on the other vessel and disconnect the rope or net so they can continue their pursuit. If you hit the rope or net you are in the trap and must cut it to escape, while have to deal with two boatloads of men trying to capture you. If on a sailing vessel, you should motor sail and <u>must not</u> ram the boat to windward of the trap if possible.

Should you do so (ram the windward vessel) and your boat stall, you will drift into the fray or threat. If you ram the leeward vessel, you will most likely drift faster than the other vessels, and away from the threat, allowing your escape. You need to act quickly and do not want to come to a stop. As soon as you believe the wreckage is clear get moving again. Weather you are on a sail or powerboat; you must keep the debris out of your propeller. You must know how your vessel is designed below the water line and how likely you are to get fouled, to make good and rapid decisions that can save your life.

8. Those at the back in the cockpit are ready to repel boarders with whatever are necessary as well as a team assigned to the foredeck in a location that is safe but ready to react. Ensure everyone remains in a position of protection and cover.

In some, recent attacks the pirates have, in order to isolate the victims and block any chance they have in calling for help or assistance; have started broadcasting music on the radio frequency that would be used for emergency communication. This is a serious problem for the vessels being attacked. Should this occur you should use switch from VHF too Single Sideband radio or, try different bridge to bridge frequencies on the VHF radio. These are normally channels: 13, 72 or any other channels that ships use for ship-to-ship communications in the region. I do not believe they have the equipment to block all the possibilities available.

When traveling to a new area, discuss the possibilities with those on your boat. Study past attacks and talk about how you will prevent the same from occurring to your boat. Devise a plan of action, assigning each person an area of responsibility. Set up practice drills along with man overboard and fire drills before you leave to ensure all are prepared and understand what actions to take for any given emergency. This will be your greatest defense, while it also creates confidence and rids everyone of confusion during emergencies.

Figure 21 Technology

TECHNOLOGY

Friend or foe

The tactics may vary a bit; but the technology that you depend on from day to day can be used by pirates to find you while transiting areas of danger. Recent reports have showed that the electronics designed to help make your travels safer and easier, requiring you to use less brainpower; has been used by pirate's for locating mariners, and too signal of a vessels approach in areas where they lay in wait for the arrival of unsuspecting vessels. Do not be lax in your education and use of the old techniques of navigation and signaling. Your ignorance and laziness could cost you, your boat as well as your life. Here are a few dangers that you need to consider and plan for when entering areas of danger, and risk of attack.

You are moving along a coast known for having problems with piracy. The reports stated that attacks have occurred as far as 25 miles offshore. While planning your course you decide to travel 30 miles off, figuring that this will be sufficient to prevent the attack. You are moving along fine not considering the distance the lights are visible plus the added distance pursuant to the height off the water. When out of the darkness you see visitors approaching with guns a blazing.

Vessel running lights are, made to be visible for a minimum distance according to the size of the vessel. Boats under 120 feet have lights that are visible for a minimum distance of three miles. This is the minimum and not the actual distance, they are visible. I would consider in situations where you do not wish to be seen, that this be a starting point in preparing for your vessels security. If they have line of sight, they can and will see you. Just as you do not want to draw any attention to your vessel in these areas, this is the principle that you should adopt in all areas from visible signature too electronic signature. You want to not be noticed or heard until you reach a position of safety.

Now you have to worry about how far you can actually be seen. Ships because of there height above the water can be seen at about 14 too 18 miles, as it starts to come over the horizon on a calm sea. At night you need to consider the distance your lights are visible. The luminous range charts claim that lights can be seen about 4 miles for every 10 feet. I believe that these are set up with a large safety margin and know that you can see lights from objects 10 feet above the water for 6 miles. My point is that you must consider all aspects involved when trying to safely, navigate, dangerous waters.

You have taken into consideration everything you can think of, when planning a passage through an area of concern. For instance; you feel you are far enough offshore, you have turned off the running lights and feel as though you are invisible. You are communicating with the ships in the area informing them that you are in the area, running with out lights. You are being very careful not to give your position over the radio, and are feeling good about your actions and secure. You have the boat on autopilot you decide to go below for a cup of coffee. Only to look up to see three men and a vessel along side, you have been boarded. How did they find you?

RADARS AND RADAR DETECTORS

They have radar detectors and a new system that lists on a computer screen, the location of the other vessels in the area it is, called, the AIS System. Do not get me wrong it is great for added information while traveling on the ocean. But, you should never depend on one thing for your safety and security. You may think that you are being clever and have everything turned off and only using this AIS System to ensure you are not on a collision course with other vessels.

However, two weeks before a group of pirates took a boat that had this system on board and are now using it to find unsuspecting victims like you. It is important you not take your safety for granted, or put too much trust in the technology used for safety and security. No matter how safe you are trying to be, there is always the chance that your precautions have been countered. And you will become a target while not knowing your guard is actually down.

Never allow yourself to become complacent with your security. Always maintain a watch, in all directions and when you must go below make sure someone takes your place on deck, if even for a few seconds. There is nothing on the market, which can take the place of your eyes, when it comes to your safety, and your security.

If there is a piece of equipment that can be used to locate a vessel, you can bet that those who make a living by robbing boats have it, and know how to utilize it for that purpose. When traveling through an area where the danger of piracy is present, you need to reduce your visible signature as well as your electronic signature to make your boat harder to locate. Even then, at night you will notice that sound travels very far; and can be used to locate vessel's miles away. As long as you are aware of these possibilities and plan for them, you can maintain the upper hand in these situations.

Radios

Radio communication is quick way to give away the fact that you are in the area. With a few parts and little equipment even a pirate can build a radio direction finder. Then once you know the basic direction a signal is coming from, the strength of the signal, will give you an idea of the distance in that direction too the vessel broadcasting the signal. If you wait for a few minutes, and check the signal direction again, you can learn, the direction of travel of the vessel you are hunting. For this reason radio silence is necessary when transiting some area where the risk is high, or a history of pirates using radio signals to locate vessels exist.

In some recent attacks, the pirates have figured out how to block the calls for help or warning broadcast from vessels that are being attacked, by playing music on the frequency. And they have had success at isolating the vessels that they attack. This tactic is used to prevent a vessel from being able to call for help and the warning to other vessels in the area, as well as; to prevent the rescue of the boats they wish to attack. It can also cause a vessel to give up more quickly after determining that they are alone.

If you are, attacked and find the emergency channel is blocked with music. You should at once, try a higher frequency and also, try other channels on the VHF. Ships have several frequencies that they monitor for communication between themselves and other vessels. You can check with the military and civilian vessels in the area to get this information but normally they monitor 13 or 72 for regular ship to ship communications. You should have this information in you radio manuals or must find it before entering the area.

RADIO DIRECTION FINDER

Radio direction finders, can be used by the pirates to locate vessels broadcasting near by. Utilizing radio silence will aid you in avoiding there detection. As long as you do not broadcast a signal they have no signal to follow. You can listen for traffic and warnings from other vessels but disconnect the mike to prevent an accidental transition of a signal. If you receive an emergency call for help from another vessel. Use the Single Sideband to relay the signal to authorities or ships that are in the area that can assist mariners in emergencies. After you broadcast it would be

PIRACY SURVIVAL GUIDE

wise to change course heading back to a position of safety or further out too sea.

If on the water you hear music on the marine radio emergency frequency, it is most likely from a pirate vessel trying to jam a signal from a vessel, during an attack. They have been using music to prevent skippers from broadcasting SOS during these attacks. It can also be used to your advantage, providing there is a radio direction finder on your vessel. If you hear music on the emergency channels, you should at once use a direction finder to locate the heading of the music, from your vessel. You now know the direction of the trouble spot or possible attack and should re-calculate your course to avoid this area. Again it would be wise to treat it as though you had sighted a vessel of unknown intent. Change course to forty-five degrees of the location and make a decision as to proceed or return to your last safe harbor. This depends on if you are approaching a channel, a choke point or at sea with plenty of room to avoid attacks. You can continue to listen to determine if the signal is getting stronger, and if so; turn your vessel to move directly away from the danger. The radio direction finder will aid you in avoiding this danger if used properly.

Most radios come with signal strength meters that can be used to determine if a signal is getting stronger. Know your equipment and how to use it. Be sure to teach those on your vessel what you know to free yourself from task that will distract you from maneuvering and protecting your vessel.

You should look at every piece of equipment you have on board your boat. Make a list of how it can help as well as how it can be utilized against you when trying to avoid pirate attacks. Next to each piece of equipment provide this information with the instructions for utilizing it so that anyone on board your vessel can use it properly in any emergency.

Figure 22 Unexpected sighting of another vessel at sea.

PLAYING THE GAME

Predator and Prey

When you decide to travel from your homeport to another country, for a trip, or to live your dream, you do not have to look at your departure as though you are in a Mad Max Movie. But you do need to be ready and able to make the switch from a relaxing trip, to one with security watches, and a reaction detail for your protection. For some it is difficult to switch this attitude for survival on, till something forces or scares them into doing so. Even then, some will give into the fear when a life-threatening situation develops causing the wrong choices to be made.

When you leave your home country, you need to shift your attitude and your defensive boundaries from one of your own individual spaces. To a defensive boundary that includes not only yourself but the people with you on your boat, and an ever-changing perimeter around your vessel. When someone tests your boundaries, you need to be protective and firm; and not foolish with your words and your actions. Displaying a manner that says to others, you will not be a pushover when challenged. This will become important in these societies outside of the United States where being a hard masculine male is still politically correct. To do otherwise is to be considered week and would say to others that you are someone of week mind and an easy person to target, that can be taken advantage of, as well as no danger too those who would steal from you.

When you depart you will be traveling to areas with little or no emergency services. There is little law enforcement in many places at sea, and security is your own concern. So in this environment if you look docile and timid you will become a target. You need to switch on the "I will deal with it", tough persona; this will help in establishing a boundary that people are not to cross. Use it in an intelligent way do not be foolish and insulting with others. Knowing when to exit a situation is a very important principle this is for you to decide. There is a point at which you will need to find a way to switch to a retreat mode, but you should not become timid when making this switch. Do not allow your boldness to trap you in a situation preventing your escape. You know what you are capable of, and you need to set your own boundaries according to this.

Your mannerisms are a very important tool that can be used for your protection; you must use boldness and be direct in your actions, being prepared to quickly challenge others who enter an area that could pose a threat to you and those on your vessel. How would you act should someone walk into the yard of your home and start for your house? Most would do nothing because in our society we have been trained, that we do not have the right to do anything.

What would you do if they opened your door and started to walk in? I hope that you would stop them or at least say something, but in our society, we are told, to go to a room, lock the door, and call for help. Well; you are not in Kansas any more and there are no police to call and no services that will be able to get to you quickly to help or prevent harm to you and your guest.

To protect your boat is your area of concern does not start on the deck, but with the area around your boat. You need to imagine a perimeter around your vessel at least several yards out from her, and this is dependent on the risk of the area. If at anchor you need to decide how close, is too near your vessel, this will increase at night, giving more time for action.

When you are anchored, there is no need for a fishing boat to hang near you when they have the whole coast too fish. This is the dangerous game that they play. They try to act as though they are busy fishing, while they check out your possessions; as well as your security. As soon as they believe they can get the jump on you, and board your boat, they win. Your part in this game or ordeal is that you need to confront them quickly, before they near your boat, do not wait to do so.

Just the fact that you have allowed them to work close to you for a short time is, perceived as you being unsure or timid, and you may be an easy target. This is how you develop your zone of safety and how they ware down your security. You must be firm in your resolve to protect your boat and crew. This has to be done as soon as you notice this behavior in the fisherman near your boat. You must confront them and ask them to leave, in a demanding way.

It is a game of cat and mouse, they want to catch you off guard and at a point where you cannot, and do not have time to get a weapon or react in a way that can harm them. You want to prevent this by denying them the chance to catch you unprepared. You are establishing a boundary that forces you to act before they can get close enough to create a circumstance that poses a danger to you.

You need to ensure that this safety perimeter is a distance that offers protection should you have to go inside for a few seconds. Therefore, they do not have enough time to cross this zone and board your boat before you have time to prepare. This is your first safety precaution. Keep in mind that a person can cover twenty feet, and board a vessel in less than several seconds. You need to understand this. Your safety depends on it.

Keep in mind that this situation can take place anywhere in the world. When ever possible you need to avoid high-risk anchorage area. Try to anchor with others and not alone. It is better to travel to a safe area before you anchor than to be in a place where you cannot enjoy yourselves. It is best in danger areas to use highly traveled anchorages where you can find other boats also traveling. Before you use an anchorage area, check with the latest reports on piracy. Check for the crimes in the area; speak with other cruisers that you see coming from the area you are traveling too. Should you not see any, check with the local marina owners while on your way to the area, to find the safest places or locations, and what the dangers are, as well as what to be on the lookout for?

You must use all of your safety and security precautions when in an area of risk. Ensure that you know how to contact the local emergency services, if any; and the radio channels that they monitor. Should other mariners be in the area select a frequency to monitor and stay in contact with each other? Should suspicious activity occur notify the others and keep them informed of the situation. If possible tie your boats along side each other to make your security watches more efficient and increase your numbers, and have a plan to assist each other in an emergency.

These areas require a twenty-four hour watch. The person on watch must stay on deck and be aware of any approaching boats or dangers. Should they hear anything they should use a good spot light. Do not use a flashlight; they do not have the range that you need or the intimidation power, when establishing a safety zone. You need to be able to shine any vessel within 300 hundred yards of your boat. This shows that you are aware of their presence and that you are alert and watching.

The person on watch should not go below deck without having someone take his or her place. It only takes a few seconds for someone to cover a good distance and board you. The importance of this must be, explained to anyone who is to stand watch. Have one person who is agile take the tender out a good distance and time them getting to and boarding your vessel. Then cut this time by 10 or 20 percent. This will give you as well as those on board an example of the danger. Remember; if they do not understand the reason for the policy, they will not abide by the policy.

Do not get too comfortable when not on watch; if the person gets comfortable they will disregard warnings and may fall asleep. Consider this as a passage situation when off watch sleep near by the hatch where you would sleep when under way in case the person on watch needs your assistance or to go below for some reason.

The person on watch should have pepper spray and not the small type for personal defense. They need the large bottle with a trigger that can spray twenty feet or more. The person off watch or on standby should have one close by as well. If you decide to do so you can purchase a paintball gun with pepperballs which are available on the market for defense. This will allow you to put a concentrated amount of the chemical on target a a range of a hundred feet or more. This will slow or stop an attack and possibly give you time to escape the threat.

Before you enter the area you should have everything stowed away on deck and any valuables should be placed in the secret place that you have set up to hide these things. Your passport and boat papers as well as money jewelry and other items should be placed in this secure location. Ensure there is nothing on the deck or in sight that could encourage someone to rob you and your vessel.

At night should you have to anchor in an area that has been known to have problems try to keep your tender on the deck, this is preferable to having it in the water with the outboard mounted on it. Should you have to leave the area because of the danger this would be the preferred location for it, making you quicker at getting out of a dangerous situation. If it is in the water, it is an easier target for a thief and can slow you down.

Discuss possible scenarios and then plan actions for each emergency ensuring everyone knows how to deal with them. Try to turn your cabin into a safe room installing good locks on all hatches. When all else fails you can retreat to the interior of the boat and have some measure of security. The deck lights should be on, and turn off all interior lights. If there is a loud sound alarm onboard, activate it. This could cause the intruders to leave if in a populated area. If not you need to ensure everyone proceeds to their station or post for that emergency, or to best place too repel the attackers should they gain entry...?

UNDERWAY

Now you are underway at day or night and have pirates approaching your vessel you are already in a tight spot. These pirates are in attack mode, you need to have a mindset for this possibility and not panic. There are things you can do to prevent their success if you think and have prepared yourself mentally and physically for this possibility.

You can prevent the pirates from boarding in some cases by showing yourself to be an organized and formidable opponent. This only works in areas where they are a few disorganized men where intimidation can successfully cause the pirates to break of the attack. You need to plan ahead, modifying your vessel and acquiring a few devices you can use in deterring the attack. When doing so plan for the area you are heading too; and do not go to an area that you are not prepared to deal with.

When under way the things to remember are, the radar must be tuned to a range which will enable you to identify small vessels. This is best accomplished at a shorter range of less that a couple of miles during the night. During the day you will have better detection by sight so ensure you have sufficient look outs. Have two or three people assigned as lookouts and give them an area of responsibility. This will help in sighting and giving you more time to escape or prevent them from closing with your vessel.

As soon as you can make out a vessel either on the radar or visually, do not wait to make a course change. A course should be too one that is directly away from the possible attackers. You need to put as much distance as you can between you and the attacking vessel, as fast as possible. In any case, you should head at least 150 % from the pirate vessel, and preferably out to sea. Do not get caught on the shore side of an attacking pirate. If sailing start your engine and motor sail on a course that offers the most speed while heading away from the potential threat.

Should they have a vessel that is capable of making the speed capable of catching you, utilize the sea state against them by making it too uncomfortable and dangerous for them to chase you on the course that you are heading? Moreover, just because they are chasing you does not mean that you have to run, charging them can be an effective tactic when you can no longer run, or if you are unable to out distance them. If you are able to disable or sink their vessel placing them in a survival situation, you have succeeded.

On modification you should make before departure is to rig your boat with a steering unit below deck for emergencies. At some point during an attack steering the boat from the deck will place you in danger. You will want to make this transition as early possibly when you see an attack start on your boat. Having the capability of not only steering the boat but also operating the engine in a position of safety and out of sight of any weapons that they may have will make it easier to defend the boat. This will also come in useful would you have to use the interior of the vessel as a safe room, giving you the capability to keep control of the boat while you head out to sea and to safety should the board the vessel.

If the wind is on your bow or the attackers are, downwind from the boat you can release a cloud of pepper spray or tear gas, which could possibly slow down your attackers and do some good. Should you have a good pump onboard with a tip that will send a solid stream of fluid you can spray gas in a high arch to soak the attackers. This will prevent them from using their fire arms and make it possible to prevent the attack from proceeding because of the threat of being set on fire.

They sell a shell that fits flare guns and shot guns that is called, a bird banger that are designed to fire into trees to chase off large groups of birds. They explode causing a loud bang these could be of some use in slowing someone down by intimidation, causing the attackers to believe they are some weapon that can kill them. This could cause enough confusion and fear to stop the pursuit.

If you are proficient enough with a good rifle you could disable their engine which would stop their pursuit and attack. You need to be well practiced and capable of making such a shot from a moving boat, this will of course causes the pirates to shoot at you if they have not done so already. So you must be successful at disabling the attacker's vessel and quick to escape there weapons fire.

You have everything onboard your boat to make a very effective weapon to defend yourselves. If you have a good pump, fuel and a torch with a spray nozzle and a shut off valve near the handle you can make a flamethrower. I will not go into detail on this, but if an attacking vessel gets close enough to board your boat and you feel you are in enough danger, this will stop the attack or at least prevent them from closing and boarding your vessel. You can make the device quickly, while being chased, in less than ten minutes.

You need to look for other possibilities that can be used for your defense, and please inform others by posting your ideas on Noonsite.com and on PiracySurvivalGuide.com so that others can benefit from your idea's. These sound silly or outright ridiculous till you are attacked and need to use them. At that point you are grabbing at straws trying to come up with something that can save you. There is a list of items you should carry on board your boat as well as things you can purchase for that purpose in the following chapters.

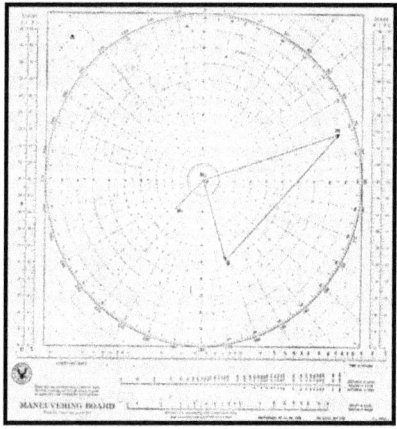

Figure 23 Devices

DEVICES FOR PROTECTION

Your research and planning is vital in ensuring that you are safe and secure in your travels. But the best of planning is no good if you do not have the needed hardware and equipment to follow through with your plans. When you plan start with your cabin security, insuring that you have the locks and items needed to prevent entry. This provides you with a fall back position or safe area for your crew and yourself. Then plan for securing the deck area and this followed with securing the area around your boat. You need to be sure you have what you need for each specific area of your security. Make a list of passive security items as well as your active equipment needed for the plans you have developed.

As you develop your security plans, make a list of items which can be purchased, and used directly for your protection and the items which can be used in making things for that purpose. Many items can be purchased off the shelf, which you can utilize in handling most any of the situations that manifest themselves. First, you must decide what the possibilities are involving attacks, and what you will do to solve or counter the problem should it occur. You make the decision on how active you will be in your own defense or security. And how much you are willing to do to when it comes too fighting off an attack. This will be not only your limits, but will also define how much risk you can accept, or which ports or areas you will be able too visit. In the recent months you have seen boat owners enter areas without any consideration for these facts placing themselves as well as their families in danger, and in come cases costing there lives. When you make the decision on how much risk you are capable of dealing with, do not waver or allow yourself to enter areas for which you are not prepared; or not willing to accept the cost in lives, should something go wrong.

If you are traveling by boat please make the decision to only visit areas where you and those on your boat will have safety and you will enjoy your adventure. Avoid areas of risk or danger. Some of what is mentioned sounds silly, but the intimidation factor can go a long way if you are prepared and have given it some thought.

The non-lethal as well as lethal weapons you could utilize:

Alarm-locks – These are similar to bicycle locks a length of chain or wire rope with a lock that has inside it an alarm. Should someone break or cut the wire or lock an alarm will sound warning you of the thief of your property.

Pepper Spray – Us the bear spray it has the distance and concentrated enough to be effective. Be sure that you do not use it inside the boat, unless necessary. They have a range of about fifteen feet or more.

Pepper Munitions - These are made to be fired by various guns and are effective over a long range which would be good for use on a boat. Primarily the paintball gun is most useful for the implementation of the chemical onto the target.

Taser – A taser is a defense weapon that looks like a flashlight. It fires two pins or small pointed projectiles with wire attached these are connected to the handle. Once they hit the intruder, an electric current incapacitates them. You may have seen this used on television by the Police. It is a very effective way for dealing with the pirate's once you have them on the ground to control them.

XREP – Is a new shell that you can fire from any shotgun, it is a self-contained taser round. When you fire it, the projectile contains the batteries and all the elements that make up the device, making it possible to move to the next target utilizing the same gun.

NLBHG Non-lethal Bursting Hand Grenade – This is a Hand Grenade that is non-lethal that will discourage attackers for a range of about 5 meters. You can use a 12-gauge launch system that has a range of about 100 meters to send a message. If you can get a hold of the device, I would recommend if for boat owners as a way to discourage vessels chasing or closing with you.

MCCM Non-lethal Claymore – I am sure that most of you know what a Claymore Mine is and how it is used. It is a curved mine that is mounted above ground with the curved side pointed towards those you are trying to discourage. This device could be hung below a lifeline between stanchions, ensuring you give a few inches to prevent blowing the lifeline apart. It has an effective range of about 10 meters, which is great for use against a boat full of pirates coming along side. It would scare and discourage a boarding. Should you have them be sure not to set them up in line with a hatch, be sure all hatches are closed and everyone is below deck before detonating this device. It would also be a good idea to have everyone keep there mouths open during the explosion to prevent ruptured ear drums.

Baseball Bats – Bats are a great tool for holding off attackers, offering control and the ability to threaten with a server physical penalty for who ever does not back down or head your warning. You should have several on your boat providing a number of individuals with them when needed.

Line Throwing Gun — A line-throwing gun is a great device to have onboard your boat. It can double as a weapon when needed, but has an added benefit as being a piece of maritime equipment that can be used for rescue.

Hand cuffs - You should have a way to handle an attacker should you end up having them onboard as a guest while waiting for the authorities. Plastic handcuffs are the bust because of the multiple use factors, and you can store several on your boat.

Duct Tape — When you do not have access to handcuffs, duct tape is a great substitute and most time quicker, easier, and better to use. It can be used in several ways to secure someone too anything you can wrap the tape around for that purpose. I recommend keeping several rolls handy for everything from patching a leak to securing a prisoner.

Tacks — Yes tacks the kind with long points. There have been single-handed sailors place these on the deck before trying to sleep. These would work great as long as you remember that you placed them there. If you are in the habit of wearing shoes then you will not have a problem. I have made mats that I on occasions place on the deck at locations on the deck where a person would have to step if they came onboard. These mats were rubber pads with small pointed nails placed not too far apart that would work very well should someone step on them. Again, remember that you place them on deck or be sure to ware your shoes.

Bird Bangers — These devices can be, purchased; that fit in the flare gun. They were, designed to be; fired, into trees and over buildings to chase off birds. They fly for a hundred feet or more and explode with a loud bang. This could cause confusion by convincing the pirates that you are better armed than they are.

Electric Fence Charger — They have now on the market a system that you can wire around the outside of your boat that works on the same principle as an electric fence. In areas this may aid in slowing would be pirates from climbing on your boat. In addition, could possibly provide a scream or yelp as a warning. This should, be used with cameras making an effective system.

Safe Room – This is a great idea for the home and boat. With some engineering skills, you could build a system on your boat using a cabin or best is to utilize the boat interior. If you can turn off the controls outside preventing the boat from being controlled by the attackers, you can steer in a direction towards help. Eventually, they will take whatever is on deck and depart before they have too far to go to get back. They do make a safe enclosure that folds down over the bed that is strong enough to protect the occupants from, gunfire.

Gun Powder – A couple of cans of gunpowder in camouflaged cans are always a good thing to have lying around. You can do many things with them, which I cannot discuss in this book, but you could think up ways to stop boarders with a little work. Keep these in a location where you can make use of them and away from areas that could cause you problems.

Security Cameras – On a boat there are usually several areas where you can install cameras that will give you a view of the deck area. This will be a great tool and can be used providing you with information on the location of the attackers while you develop a plan to rid yourself of them.

Air Cannon - Using PVC pipe you can build a gun that can fire a good size object, baby food jars filled with a gas and plastic combination with a gas soaked fuse. If you hit the other vessel, the jar would break releasing the contents and starting a fire that is not easy to extinguish especially with no extinguisher. By combining the gas and plastic from garbage bags makes a thick flammable slime, which is very sticky will not wash off with a bucket of water. This could cause panic, especially if far from land in a burning boat. You can find plans for different styles of guns on the internet; you will need to scale it for the size jars you would use in it. Test this before you use it, it is something that you can just leave in the boat. It can be, used; for fun if not for pirates.

Emergency Stun Gun - Stun guns are great little devices but the only down fall is that it requires that you are in close proximity to the attackers. There are occasions in which a stun gun could come in handy. Not for normal use but in preventing access to the interior is a possibility. If you have a disposable camera on your boat you can pry it apart, you will see a black round cylinder connected to the circuit board it is about an inch long. Two wires connect it, and this is all you need to make a device to stun someone. This when charged up can give a nice jolt.

Flame Thrower - A flamethrower, can be made if you have a fuel reservoir, a pump; some hose, a plumber's torch and a spray tip for the hose. You can find plans for them on the internet, they if nothing else would be a fun device to play with. It can be mounted on the stern and set up for operation from a lower position forward, and out of site; you may prevent any attacker from approaching you or at least getting close. You may also set a trap and actually hit their vessel with a stream of fuel, as they approach. You do not need a flaming stream of fluid, you can shoot the flammable liquid into there vessel as a deterrent. Only igniting it with a flare gun, should they not break off the attack? This could be made as a portable unit that can be stored in a compartment. This can be set up in a matter of seconds in an emergency.

High Pressure Fire Pump and Hose – This equipment could be installed as a piece of safety equipment for the purpose of repelling boarders. Could be designed and setup to also operate as pump system for a flamethrower. The secret is in the nozzle, which directs the pressure over the distance you wish to acquire. This could be as simple or as complicated as you wish, a pump with hard hose that can be placed into the water or fuel tank, with a flex hose and a nozzle that will provide the pressure over the distance you need. This system can be stored in a compartment and set up in a matter of seconds when needed.

Parts – You need to plan and collect the little parts that are not important by them selves but that can be turned into something amazing and useful when needed. You need to think of things like steel pipe with screw on cap, fuses, power spray tips with extensions, lighter fluid, and torch for soldering copper tubing; anything which can have multiple uses. These are things you need to plan to have in your equipment storage. If you have the parts, you have possibilities.

It is always a good idea to have the knowledge needed to build things which can be used for your defense or protection, when needed for your boat. Your first efforts should be to repel and discourage using non-lethal means, and only move to more lethal devices as a last resort when everything else has failed and your lives are threatened. This is providing you have the time for such action. If not you deal immediately with the force required to stop the advance.

Captain Michael Pierce

Figure 24 Alone setting in for a night at sea

VESSEL SECURITY MODIFICATIONS

ITEMS THAT YOU CAN INSTALL OR PURCHASE FOR SECURITY AND SAFETY

HIDDEN COMPARTMENTS

Regardless of your budget or the size vessel you own, there are things that you need to do that will increase the security of the items on your vessel. When trying to hide things on a boat you have two problems, the first is trying to install something that does not look as though it was added or modified, is very difficult. In addition, the second is when traveling between countries and dealing with customs this looks suspicious if they should find it? The best action is to install hidden compartments that are undetectable and is impossible to find, so you do not have to worry about its detection.

When designing a hidden compartment you want to utilize something that is installed, and then modifies it; such as the bunk, the cabinets, or piping/plumbing. Select areas that are not normally utilized or thought of because of there use, such as the anchor chain storage compartment or the toilet area is also a good place to modify. It must look unchanged when you finish with the modification. You can use PVC pipe as long as it looks as though it is being utilized by some internal system, this provides a great place to hiding items such as cash or ID's. You can take apart the bunk and install a false bottom creating a space below for storing items you do not want stolen. The list is not endless, the requirement is that you go through your boat and look for something that can be used for this purpose, which will look as though it belongs and is difficult to get at. It must also look as though it has not been modified.

LOCKS

It is important when you purchase a new or used vessel to inspect the locking system on the hatches and ports. If they do not meet a level of safety when it comes to someone breaking into the vessel, have them changed. They should be heavy duty, and you will not only need to check the locks on the hatches themselves but also the hatch frame to insure it is supported and will not fail should the lock and hatch be pried on.

SAFE ROOMS

In large vessels, some people decided to install a "safe room" for protection. I feel that you should make improvements to the vessel that would make the interior a safe room or secure area. If this is too difficult, you can modify one compartment improving the locks and hatch turning it into a safe area. If possible a hidden compartment would be best, which a couple of people could take refuge. And which cannot be opened by anyone from the outside.

This compartment is made of materials that cannot be penetrated by firearms and in best situations, has a security camera system installed making it possible for you to view locations throughout the vessel.

CAMERAS AND MONOTORS

One of the most useful items that you can install on your boat is a camera system that can be monitored from below. It is nice, but may not be for everyone. When designing a system you really need more than one camera to be effective. You can set up night vision cameras too also watch the perimeter around the boat. The systems also have alarms which sound when movement is detected, you could place one on the bow to watch the deck area. If a sailboat, you could mount one on the mast which would cover the whole boat. These are useful in situations that involve boarding's; the benefit of knowing where the pirates are on deck without revealing yourself is a great tactical advantage.

There are computer programs available on the internet for free that allows you to view up to 12 of these cameras on your computer screen at once. The program has a built in motion detector alarm. With this, should someone enter the field of view, of any of the cameras, a warning will flash on the monitor, and a sound alarm will activate. This is great when not giving all your attention watching the monitor or when in port without the number of people needed for a watch.

The cameras available have a wide range of capabilities; of particular interest for vessel security are the inferred or night vision cameras. These when utilized the programs that allow the multiple camera viewing with motion alarm creates a great security system. You can use these systems to develop a security setup that will allow you to handle most situations from the interior of the vessel, keeping you and your crew out of harms way.

SPOTLIGHTS AND LIGHTING

Lighting is one of the primary items that you can install that will stop many acts of piracy. The concern with lighting is the amount of power that you consume while using them. The payoff is so great that it would be worth the additional cost of upgrading your power supply. You need to pick out the lighting that you wish to use and then design the power supply system based on the amount of electricity that you would be using. The new lighting that is available utilizes LED low power high output bulbs making it possible to install a system that can run off batteries.

You already have lights installed for the deck, the thing that you want to do is add a dim switch for the deck area while lighting the area around the boat. Having lights mounted on the railing that directs their light out from the boat could add too your security, as long as it does not interfere with the navigation of other vessels. You can redirect the lights so that they do not shine directly into the wheelhouse of the other vessels navigating near by, creating a problem. The effect that you want to create is to make it possible to see others that are approaching your while interfering with their capability of seeing you or the deck of your vessel clearly.

Deck lighting does not take the place of having a good high power spotlight on the boat, this is vital to your vessel security in preventing pirate attack. It is best to have a deck mounted remote control spotlight as well as, a hand held spotlight. You can, and will need both. Using the mounted remote control spotlight with a camera system if very useful when short handed. This will make it possible to shine suspicious areas or persons without having to exit the interior of the vessel, or reveal your location. This could intimidate or discourage an attacker, creating uncertainty; in not being able to see you or know what you are doing.

RADIO DIRECTION FINDER

A radio Direction Finder has become an important piece of equipment once again. It is useful in locating the direction of and attack or emergency radio broadcast; enabling you to avoid the area of danger once you locate it using the equipment. You can estimate the distance by the strength of the broadcast giving you a plot able position to avoid. Using it properly can give you a good idea as too the location of the pirates and the attack when an emergency call is received. Then it is a simple matter of plotting a course to avoid contact and avoiding the area.

MOTION DETECTOR SPOTLIGHT

If you do not want the expense or will not be traveling to the higher risk areas that require a better system, you can purchase motion detector spotlights and mount them on the deck, permanent or with a temporary mount while at anchor or in port. You can store them below decks while underway, keeping the clutter down to a minimum. These are cheap and easy to install and provide a good return for the money in security. You can find them with other features' that may provide other options for you.

ELECTIRC FENCE & CHARGERS

A few companies are selling an electric fence device for boats. You can go to a farm store and purchase a battery or solar powered electric fence charger for yourself and design a system. Electric fence wire that is run on the outside of the stanchions is a deterrent to boarders. There are many ways to set this up; you can also use it in other ways to secure items. If you give it some thought you will come up with ideas for security utilizing this equipment. They have a few types of chargers, it would be best to purchase the most powerful jolt that they have for installing on your vessel.

SET UP FOR SMOKE

By injecting coolant into the exhaust of the engine, you can create smoke which can be used to confuse those pursuing you. This is simple, and plans can be found on the internet. If planning to utilize this technique, you need to design a system that is permanent, so that it can be put into use quickly at the turn of a switch. Furthermore, you need to test it to ensure you get the amount of smoke that you would need to be effective. If you decide to install this system, there are just a few parts which you need to added to the engine for a permanent installation. You will also need too add or increase the size of the coolant tank, install electronic activation to make it efficient.

HATCH SECURITY BARS

A few single-handed sailors have had some success with putting bars that can be locked in place allowing the screens to stay in place with the hatch open for circulation in hot climates. This prevents others from gaining entry into the vessel while allowing the skipper to sleep. These are simple to install make sure they are installed in such a way that in an emergency you can remove them from inside for quick exit. As long as everything on deck is locked up, you would be relatively safe. For added protection you can install a intruder alarm to warn you of a boarder. I would use a system such as this when alone or in areas with little or no danger.

BULLET PROOF MATERIALS

You may be interested in these materials if you are at sea and being fired upon, it is a nice addition too any vessel. You can utilize bullet proof material in one of three ways.

The first would be to purchase Kevlar material and with a little research on the layers needed for protection that you desire, apply it to the interior. Using a polyester resin you can build up points in selected areas for the desired protection.

Second would be to take the material too shop with a commercial sewing machine to help you build a layered blanket. This can be stored out of the way until needed but when you plan to use it you need to ensure that all four corners are firmly attached to create a protective wall.

Third, you can epoxy it up in layers to make a two foot by three or four foot rigid panel that can be stored until it is needed under the cushions' on the boat. It can be placed between you and the threat, providing protection for those on your vessel.

You can find many useful items that can be used in defending your vessel from pirates, and protecting those on board. Knowledge is always a good thing, especially when using it to extend your life. Remember to take proper safety precautions with items that warrant such caution.

HIGH PRESSURE WATER PUMP

A water pump that supplies a fire hose can be a great weapon when trying to repel boarders. This only requires the installation of a pump that can supply salt water at a pressure that can knock a man off his feet. I recommend this for more than just repelling boarders. This would also be useful in a makeshift flamethrower or method of soaking the attacking boat in fuel or gas as a deterrent. With a hard installed system you would have a greater range for preventing attacking boats from closing with you at sea.

Be sure you research and acquire the appropriate nozzle to obtain the desired range and pressure. These parts should be in your junk compartment with other supplies that can be utilized in constructing items that can protect your vessel.

Figure 25 Guns Onboard

GUNS ONBOARD

The thing that anyone who is considering the purchase of a gun for protection needs to learn for his or her own safety and peace of mind is; when the use of it is justified. Knowing the definition of "deadly Force" and going over scenarios in your mind will ensure that you will not utilize the weapon in a situation that could have been handled in another way. Making a bad choice with a firearm can result in problems that can last throughout a person's life, pursuant to the decision. Understanding this principle will not only help you in making the proper decision but save you from the harm that it can cause you by doing so, providing you obey this requirement. This is the definition of deadly force (when it is acceptable to use a weapon)

DEADLY FORCE

DEADLY FORCE IS THAT FORCE THAT WHEN USED CAN CAUSE DEATH

OR SERIOUS BODILY HARM

DEADLY FORCE IS THAT FORCE WHICH IS USED AS A LAST RESORT

WHEN ALL LESSER MEANS HAVE FAILED OR CAN NOT RESONABLY BE EMPLOYED.

DEADLY FORCE IS JUSTIFIED WHEN USED TO PROTECT YOUR LIFE OR THE LIFE OF SOMEONE ELSES FROM DEATH OR

SERIOUS BODIELY HARM

That is it, if you can remember it, and go over in your mind what it actually means; you can prevent permanently scaring yourself resulting from you causing harm too someone without justification or, when a lesser amount of force could have been used. If you can use a taser to deal with an attacker; that is what you should do. Only when no other method can be used, should you use deadly force to protect yourself and the others on your boat.

When using a weapon in a life-threatening situation, there are two things you need to be sure of before you pull the trigger. The first is your life in danger and deadly force justified? The second is. Where will the bullet go? You must know that the bullet will not hit an innocent bystander after it passes the one you are firing at. If you are not sure that you will not harm someone by accident or uncertain of the path of the bullet, you must move or change the angle of your shot. Only if you are certain of the two can you pull the trigger of the weapon.

I want to say this again! You have seen the news stories about small children who were killed by a stray gunshot. This is the result of someone firing a weapon without thinking about where the bullet will go, or end up. You must know where your round will not only travel but also where it will end up. This is one reason too use fragmentation rounds; to ensure the bullet does not travel past the point intended and breaks up so it can does no more harm. Think of all the possible outcomes to prevent something terrible from happening.

Now that this has been covered, we will cover some of the issues involved in carrying a gun on board a vessel. If you go out and purchase a gun just to place it on the boat and think that is all you need, you have made the greatest mistake a person can make. It is going to do you no good! You would have done better to invest in another type of protection. If you are going to have a gun, you have to know how to use it.

What does this mean? – Well you have to fire it, learned about things that affect it, the wind, the distance it travels and how to aim. You need to adjust the site for a distance of 100 yards. So that if you have to use it at that distances you will hit the target, as well as how to adjust for distance and conditions. This is true for every single weapon that you have on board the vessel. If you do not follow the proper procedures for becoming proficient with it, please leave the weapons at home. You will just get yourself in more trouble and place everyone on your boat in more danger, and possibly killed.

With each weapon you need to know how to judge distance and the effectiveness of that weapon. Shotguns included, you should fire each to learn the effects of the projectile over distance and how to make the best use of this effect. You should have each weapon sighted in for a specific distance and know when another weapon would be more effective.

Shotguns are known as a scattergun, this is because of the wide pattern of the shot or pellets after they leave the barrel. This weapon does not require precise aim but is only effective for use over a short range may be 100 feet. It is best utilized in dealing with multiple targets, at close range, or when trying to getting people out of a passage way or off the deck of the boat or when you are being over run.

A rifle preferably something of high power with a scope is a weapon for surgical strikes. It is a long-range weapon and not a good weapon for use in tight quarters because of the length of the barrel. It is best utilized when trying to demoralize the attackers as they approach. The use would include taking out the leader, which would result in the pirates breaking off the attack, or possibly in disabling the engine of the pirate's vessel. To accomplish either task you will need the proper ammunition for the intended target. You need to learn of the weapon, how to use it properly and what it is capable of before you plan to include this one of your boats choices for protection.

A pistol is a short-range weapon; it is for use in dealing with a target at close quarters when you have no choice but to protect your life or that of your crew. Preferably, a caliber that is large enough not too requires more than one round to put down an attacker. It is great in tight spaces, when dealing with a single target at a time. Again it will be of no use if you do not practice and follow the proper procedures for its use. And follow the Deadly Force rule.

Another weapon that I have grown fond of is the five rounds, short barrel revolver that fires 45 or 410 shells. It has a 4 inch barrel and would be great for use when trying to get people out of the hatchway and easy to handle as well as hide. This is a good weapon for use on a boat and easy to conceal near you while traveling. Since it is so small you can stick it behind a panel or under a cushion, and packs one heck of a punch. Before you add this too your boat, fire it on the range and practice with it. Get to know this as you would a shotgun, set up a sheet of plywood to learn the pattern that the shot follows. This will give you an idea of how best to implement the weapon, in knowing how the shot behaves over different distances.

I myself like to have the following weapons on board when traveling for protection should the need arise. In my younger years I preferred a 45 cal pistol for individual targets up to about fifty feet. A shotgun for targets up too 100 feet distance, such as a small boat with several attackers on board. And a good rifle, a 30/30 or 30/06 with scope for long range surgical strikes. Such as disabling a vessel or preventing the firing of an attacker's rifle at myself or the crew.

Now that I am getting a little older I find myself leaning toward the addition of a 410 pistol which fires four pellets or (ooo buck) each time you pull the trigger. Each pellet is about the size of a 38 cal round. This provides you a little flexibility in the aiming of the weapon, while still being able to hitting the target. This is for close range and perfect for use against attackers on your boat. This is also a good weapon to allow others to use when needed, a person who does not have much experience with weapons when necessary.

You had better carry other means of deterring pirates, such as pepper spray as well as other non-lethal weapons that you can utilize in emergencies having them placed by each hatch inside the vessel. You need to ensure you do not put yourself into a situation where your choice is limited to the deadly weapons and that you have tried (time permitting) all lesser means of stopping the attack first. You decide what you may need and/or would like to use should the need arise and situation permits.

When considering weapons you have other issues that you need to consider, such as problems with customs and immigration when entering another country, as well as the laws of your own countries concerning firearms. If you are a documented vessel in the U.S., you are considered United States territory, you have protection from being boarded by foreign governments to some degree, and US law applies onboard the vessel; SOMEWHAT! You still need to know the gun laws in your home country if not from America, as well as the laws of the countries that you plan to visit concerning weapons. Obey the law and you will have no problem.

The United States requires background checks and permits for many types of weapons, if you choose to carry an assault weapon you will need a license for that weapon and should you have more than one you will need multiple licenses. But if you get caught with it outside of the country it will not help you.

The UN has provisions for weapons in the **"Law of the Sea"**

Article 91 Nationality of ships

Every State shall fix the conditions for the grant of its nationality to ships, for the registration of ships in its territory, and for the right to fly its flag. Ships have the nationality of the State whose flag they are entitled to fly. There must exist, a genuine link between the State and the ship.

This simply states that the vessel must be "documented" or a vessel that has been, recognized as being protected by its laws.

2. Every State shall issue to ships to which it has granted the right to fly its flag documents to that effect.

You must have the documentation on board the vessel.

Article 92 Status of ships

Ships shall sail under the flag of one State only and, save in exceptional cases expressly provided for in international treaties or in this Convention, shall be **subject to its exclusive jurisdiction on the high seas**. *A ship may not change its flag during a voyage or while in a port of call, save in the case of a real transfer of ownership or change of registry.*

Only the state or nation where the vessel, is; documented can exercise jurisdiction over the vessel.

When entering another country the vessel may be the territory your home country but must abide by the laws of the host country. This requires that you check on the countries policy for weapons, that you plan to visit. Most countries allow you to have weapons on board but require that you to maintain the weapons in a secure location locked with a customs seal while in port. Some countries will require that you surrender your firearms, to be locked in a licensed and bonded location while in port. There are some countries, who will allow you to keep them on board your vessel under your supervision. However, there are countries who will not allow weapons at all. You need to know this before entering the waters of these countries.

When entering port provide a list of firearms to the authorities on arrival. The list must include the type of weapon, serial number and any other information that you have such as licenses permits, etc.

YOU'RE DECISION

The decision you must make is, if you do not want to deal with situations in which your life and the lives of those with you are in mortal danger; do not travel to areas where that risk exist. If you limit your travel to areas where you are safe from physical harm, you can enjoy yourself, your company as well as the environment. You may only need one weapon onboard for an emergency such as bringing a shark onto the deck. I you dare to travel to areas with problems; you will find problems and may not survive. If traveling the world you really do not know what may happen or where you may have to go in an emergency and should prepare for the un-expected.

You will hear those who are against guns justifying why not to have them on board, while they try to dictate your ability to protect yourself. If they should be the ones on the boat when it is being attacked, I guarantee that they would be barking a different tune. In addition, those who believe in the right to carry guns will justify their side. I believe that it is my life and my choice and does not involve them as individuals or governments. I will do what I need to do regardless of either influence.

I believe that if someone is going to make the decision to take my possessions, cause me physical harm or try too end my life; I am going to take every advantage I can to cause them to fail at their task. The thing that makes me angry is they always come off with these ridiculous, made up statistics and examples to justify their position for not allowing a person the right to defending themselves, and/or limiting us in doing so.

I will make this point and I hope that you will listen. If you travel to areas of danger with weapons for your protection, without preparing and becoming proficient with there use. If you are not fully prepared for this fight, you are endangering everyone's life to a higher degree than if you just had to worry about the pirates alone. If you do not learn how to use the firearms properly; you will not be able to correctly implement there use and will escalate the fight to a bloodlust situation and possibly cost all on board their lives.

If you encounter a situation in which you must fire a weapon at a supposed threat or pirate's; you must be, 100% sure that it is a pirate and you are in danger. A friend told me of this incident that occurred to him in the 1980's: He was traveling at night and it was a very dark moonless night. He could hear a vessel approaching him but could not see it. When all of the sudden it appeared directly behind him and turned its spotlights on him. He assumed that he was being attacked went below to place the call over the emergency frequency on the radio. As he started for the hatch with a rifle a call came over the loud speaker: "Don't shoot it is us, the Coast Guard". He was so shook up by the incident that the Coast Guard apologized for the scare. It was during a time when boats were being taken for use in the drug trades in the area, so his fear was warranted. But this goes to show that you must be sure of the situation before you take action.

It is best to wait till those attacking you fire the first shot, and then you are released from the responsibility of making the decision for the use of Deadly Force. If they are not firing at you, there are other possible ways that you could deter or escape the attack with less deadly means. Make use of every possible option that you have available to stop or escape the attack; this means that you have tried to change course, used the sea state to slow and loose the pirates; and have exhausted all the non-deadly options that you have available. Then only if you feel there is danger to your life should you choose to use your firearms, first to disable their craft, then too intimidate or slow your attackers. And only then if those have failed and you feel you have no choice, on the attackers. This is my process in taking action when attacked. I do not desire to cause harm to another individual, and take every option before I make the choice to do so.

As I stated previously, before you take a life you must attempt to disable their craft to stop the attack. If you have trained in the proper way with the weapons, and are sufficient with the operation and firing of it you can accomplish this. And it is a justifiable use of a weapon as well as the proper implementation of it. This is more for you than the legal implications or staying within the constraints of Deadly Force. Should you take a persons life and have any doubt as to the justification of your actions, or question as to weather you could have used another means to prevent the attack. You will be unsettled in your mind and this regret, or doubt of your actions can haunt you the rest of your life. A decision for use of Deadly Force that has any question as too its justification will echo in your mind and can ruin cruising for you; forever.

I cannot stress the importance of training with the firearms enough. You not only must train with them but also must practice on a regular basis. With practice, you will become confident in your capability to defend yourself should the situation arise. You must understand the proper use of deadly force in order to make the proper decision should the time come. You must also have other choices that you can make an effort at trying before you must use your last resort, giving every opportunity for not having to make the decision.

You have read and I hope memorized Deadly Force, here are a couple of examples that I hope will help you understand the concept of deadly force:

You are walking and see a man beating another man severely, he is a large man and you have you pistol with you. Is deadly force authorized? No, the man being beaten may be hurt but to use a gun would not be proper, when you may be able to stop it by other means. Only if you cannot stop the attack, and your life or his is threatened is additional force justified.

You hear a woman scream and go to investigate, you see a man with a knife holding her down and tearing at her clothing. Is deadly force ok here? If you warn the attacker telling them to drop the knife and move away from the woman first, then you have met the requirement providing he continues with the attack, but first must fire a warning shot.

Then yes, having a knife and threatening someone qualifies in the area of protecting another person from death of serious bodily harm. If you have a club and can strike him stopping the attack; that should be the course of action. And Deadly Force not an option until you make that effort and you feel that life is in danger. Only when all lesser means have failed is the rule.

When you are deciding on your course of action concerning "deadly force", you must analyze the situation in your head and must arrive at the conclusion that if you do not act that person or yourself will suffer serious harm or death. You cannot use deadly force to keep someone from fighting.

I know that these examples are different than defending yourself from pirates, but this is the one thing that you must grasp if you decide to own a weapon for self-defense.

I must also stress that you must remember or memorize the definition or rule of "Deadly Force" with out this knowledge, you cannot be sure that you will make the proper decision; as long as you obey this rule you will prevent the pain that can come from taking someone's life when it was not necessary.

If you can stop a situation by any other means, you should do so; only if you know there is no possible way that you can prevent seriously injured or death without using a firearm should you do so. That means that if you can stop a situation with pepper spray or other means that is the proper course of action to take. You will still have the weapon should it fail. The only thing that should force you to rush to the decision is if life is expiring quickly and there is no time to try other options.

In the case of piracy, you are considered to be in a dangerous situation, and are under attack. You are not required work your way up in weapons to satisfy the requirement of: "all lesser means have failed" in this circumstance. Once the crime of piracy is recognized to be in progress, it is automatically considered a life-threatening situation, and there fore whatever force you choose to use in order to defend yourself, your crew, and your vessel is justified. Only for yourself should you take the time to try other means as long as it does not place those on your boat in additional danger. I will tell you that the longer the attack continues the more danger those on your vessel are in, so protect those close too you first.

In the case of piracy you are officially in peril and are serious trouble and are under attack you need to monitor your opponent's weapons to ascertain the use or intent. Devices have never failed in this circumstance should the culprits be thought to be ruthless. If, after inquiry of a perceived life-threatening situation, and the vessel's master chooses to use in order to defend your crew, crew and your vessel, and decides if for yourself how you feel to him to try or offer floors for yourself does not have mercy on your boat in additional danger. I will tell you if you know he can do until he the more he asks those up until the he is so up that it can be done in order.

Figure 26 I am heading south (Sea Trial)

PASSAGE PLANNING

When planning a passage it is important to discuss with the passengers or crew the procedures for any emergency and how to carry them out. This includes your policy on dealing with attack by Pirate's. You must do a bit of information gathering before you sit to plan a course of action along with a course for travel. Now besides the light list, tide charts, sailing directions and pilots for the area you plan to travel. You also have to plan for the possibility of pirate attack. Piracy has become more of a concern in these recent times and deserves your attention in the planning stages of your passage. Do not take for granted that any port, harbor or country is safe and free from piracy.

When planning for travel near or too a country with a reputation for attacks, you must pay close attention to the type of attacks and the vessels that the pirates utilize. As you gather this information, record it on a note pad or on your chart. Pay close attention to these notes while planning your course and time schedule for the passage. When making notes or marking your charts with this information, record the location of the attacks, time of day or night, number of vessels and pirate's as well as the types of weapons used during the attacks. Also be sure to include with this on your chart any Navy, Coast Guard or local enforcement assistance that is available in the area for the protection of mariners transiting or visiting; and how to contact them.

When preparing you want to plan your passage according to your vessel capabilities, the number of people you have on board and the information you have gathered on previous attacks. You must consider not only the range that you vessel is visible by other vessels but also the distance you are visible from the shore line. Many coastlines have mountains or towers that can boost a person's visibility twenty or thirty miles which are easy to overlook but, can cause you to travel much further from shore than normal.

When calculating the distance you are visible you must start with what you know, and that would be the height to the highest point of your vessel, and the distance you can be seen over the water. You can find a chart for calculating the geographic range of visibility in your Light List. If the pirates are attacking 30 miles offshore and your vessel is visible to 10 miles then you need to plan a minimum of 40 miles. Knowing if the pirates are using any technology in order to find vessels to attack, (tracking vessels by radio or radar) is an added benefit. You also need to know if the pirates in the area you are dealing with are using weapons when attacking, and what type of weapons they are. This will tell you at what distance you will find safety when trying to get away from, or out run the threat.

You will use this information to plan your passage as well as the countermeasures that everyone should act upon, when attacked. It is always best to have at least a couple of options that can be used to handle each situation that could occur. Practice pirate drills while underway. Go over the different precautions you plan to take with passengers and crew. Assigning each person to a different task that must be completed during an attack.

Plan your actions by thinking fully through the details; from the first sight of a pirate vessel miles off your beam by radar and then by eye, while sailing. By planning ahead for this with something as simple as; turning your boat, placing the pirate vessel in line with your stern, or reduce the visibility of your vessel from a distance by angling the boom in the direction of the pirates, while you travel away from the danger; can prevent detection. By having this planned out in advance can save you life by using your plan and your quick action.

Planning well ahead for each possible scenario and outline your countermeasures for each circumstance, will help minimize the risk, prevent attack or allow escape from most situations. You need to think of possible dangers and circumstances, come up with solutions for them; and practice your plan. Working this out before hand will save you a lot of stress when a situation arises; by having establishing procedures to follow, you take the guess work out of the situation. This will also allow you time to think of your next action while enabling you to act quickly while moving to safety.

Decide on which equipment you will use for seeing, navigation and such; and which equipment will be turned off to help prevent your detection. You will also need to ensure that all port and windows are covered to prevent light from escaping. Establish the number of lookouts and the time of your transiting a dangerous area. Be sure everyone knows what to look for and what they are to do once possible danger is seen.

Pirates that attack at night are hoping to minimize danger by getting upon you, by catching you off guard; and also when possible to board your vessel before detection. Weather you are cruising, or at anchor; the goal is the same. By simply keeping a watch and maintaining it, you can prevent most attacks. The difference in being at anchor or underway is the distance you wish to notice approaching vessels is much greater when underway. If the pirate's are detected before they reach your vessel you may find yourself with the problem of preventing the attack, instead of avoiding detection. You should have plans for these possibilities, and discussed them with your passengers and crew for this stage of your protection.

There are varying degrees of security while underway dependent on the part of the world you are in. The difference will be sailing with a watch in place looking for suspicious vessels; and traveling in darkness without running lights to prevent being seen. Some parts of the world you will want to rest up before making the passage that may require all hands. In a circumstance such as this you should find a safe harbor to make preparations for the passage. Finding a well traveled secure port could be somewhat of a challenge. In any case you should try to anchor or tie up with other vessels for added protection. This is all dependent on the area you are traveling.

After you have rested and are preparing to make the most dangerous portion of your passage. You research the attacks that have occurred in the area most recently. If the attacks that have occurred in this area have been of various distances from shore with the furthest being 34 nautical miles. You have also found that most of the attacks have occurred during the day, but there have been a few at night. According to the reports, they used open cockpit speedboat about 20 feet in length, with outboard motors and capable of a speed of 20 knots, on calm or choppy water. The pirates were armed with rifles, and machetes and not much else is known. It has been reported, that information is being provided to the attackers on the vessels transiting the area, possibly from a previous port of call or by a fishing vessels close by the areas.

Knowing this before hand may encourage a decision to bypass ports that could be used by pirate's too pass info on your arrival and departure. But it can be used in your favor as well. You may decide to travel in the opposite direction, till out of site before setting the intended course for your passage, with hopes of throwing off those who may use this information. In addition, because there are fewer attacks at night, may make it a better time to travel. Night time is my favorite time to start a trip.

However, there are advantages of traveling during the day. With daylight, you can see all vessels on the water, much further; this makes it more difficult for vessels to slip upon you. This also is dependent on the area of the world you are traveling and the degree of danger involved in the attacks.

In the situation we are using for an example, because of the possible danger, and because there are fewer attacks; we will make passage at night. Considering the distance of the attacks from shore, we know that we want to avoid any chance of accidentally running into a threat. So we need a safety zone. If the furthest attack was 34 nm from the coast, the things to consider are visibility of your vessel over horizon. The height of eye, of the attacking vessels from the water must also be added to your vessels range of sight. This will give you the proper visible range for safety. If you have open sea, you can travel out as far as necessary to ensure your safety.

When planning one thing many mariners forget about is the height of any hills, mountains or towers, on the coast. You need to check for anything on the coast that can be used for sighting passing vessels. This information will be available on the charts for the area. In some cases this also will affect your passage. But as it is the areas with the most danger and more vicious forms of piracy at sea, are more often than not, in channels or choke points that cause vessels to travel in a known area. Because this example is in a choke point, we will use no light for the passage, but still need to try to establish a safe passage zone. You must keep a flashlight at the helm to shine ships that could collide with you and be prepared to turn on your running lights.

During times of darkness, with no moon you have a better chance of travel without detection so you may try to make dangerous passages by utilizing such times. You might use this if you can spare a day or so for the added safety. Traveling at night with a moon if on a sailboat, try to minimize the reflective nature of your sails by ensuring the angle is not giving away your position? If you choose to travel during the day, pay close attention to the visibility of your vessel and in some cases should motor to minimize the visible signature of your vessel.

Check the radios and ensure they are, tuned to the appropriate frequencies for vessel traffic and emergencies to limit confusion. You need to reduce your radar signature by removing radar reflectors. You should also maintain radio silence during the passage; this must be stressed when planning with those on board your vessel. It only takes a few seconds for a radio direction finder for locating the estimated direction of a vessel. REMEMBER! The pirates monitor the radio also.

Take every precaution should you need to contact someone on the radio for assistance. Do not give your location or direction of travel. Also do not mention where you are coming from or where you are heading. A pirate with knowledge of the region can make a quick calculation in their head and guess where you may be located. When calling for help in pirate areas you should not give your location on the radio. This could bring you more problems, ask for the location of the rescuer, and calculate your direction from them. Give them a barring and distance for your location. You must take precautions for all activities you are involved with in these areas.

You want to utilize anything that can give you the advantage. Check the weather, if by waiting for a change in the weather you can gain an added benefit, WAIT. If on a sailing vessel, you do not want to enter an area of danger with the wind on your nose. And by having weather that will make sailing a little rough will also be beneficial in preventing being seen and captured. Most small vessels do not want to be caught out at sea with a 10-foot swell. You may be a little uncomfortable but safety is a great trade off. A little rougher sea will make it more difficult for approaching vessels to catch you and if they do manage to do so, you can use it to prevent them from boarding your vessel. By taking advantage of such things for the toughest part of the passage, or the section at which it is most probable that something will happen, helps decrease the chances danger.

When making a crossing in a dangerous area, you want to position anything that you may want to utilize, in fighting off an attack at or near the position you would need it. You have a gun place it within reach; you have pepper spray have it at hand. Any equipment that will help you prevent a boarding by the pirates should be stowed at it point of use. And everyone should know where these items are located. For example, if your plan of action includes the use of a fire hose or some devices to prevent the boarding of your vessel. Ensure it is set up and ready at the location you will need it.

Drill the passengers on the task that they are assigned too. Show them where you want them and what their duties are. This helps in preventing confusion during the emergency. If you have them assigned to an area for a task, make sure you have an area assigned for them to take cover from any shooting also. Show them where to go and what position is best to prevent them from being, harmed. Make sure everyone knows what to do and when to act. All you want to do at this point is keep them from boarding your boat, and if you can prevent this for a period of time, they may give up the attack.

Your goal is to get through a danger area without being seen, by the pirates. How do you see on the water? By vision by day and lights by night, radio communication using a direction finder, by radar, these are what you are trying to limit. Think of how you would locate someone on the open sea, and with the knowledge that you have or have gained over the years you can figure your way through this situation. Minimizing the chance of being detected or seen by those who can mess your day up. Think of each problem and the precautions that you can take to minimize it. Analyzing every step of the passage, always lean toward the side of safety, and you will do well.

For our passage we have rested, analyzed the recent attacks. Checked the weather and studied the charts for the elevations along the coast. We have looked up the height of visibility for our vessel, and are prepared to make some decisions. But before we start lets check to see if there are any convoys transiting the area for added safety.

Traveling in groups can help prevent attack. But traveling in a small group may only make you more visible as well. You need to decide on if there is any protection or if you will just be seen faster and headed for problems. Larger vessels will travel quicker and you will be on your own. Not only on your own but your transit has been announced to everyone within 15 km. You may choose to travel in a group but should you do so be sure that everyone sticks together and you have planned for the possibility of fending off approaching vessels. If this is not possible you may be better off to wait for the weather and the optimum time to make the passage.

Now, take some time write down the information above and plan what you would do in the situation.

Figure 27 My team providing security for President

TAKING COMMAND

It is possible to fight off and defeat a much larger group if you work together. This is a tactic that is utilized by military units around the world. Small units of just a few men have defeated opposing forces in the hundreds. The secret is working together for a defined purpose which is survival. When you must physically oppose and attacking force, if you do not work together, you may not succeed. If you have several people in your group, divide into teams of two too four people, each group assigned a task. All tasks should be designed to accomplish the main goal of escape, or preventing capture.

I have been attacked with gun and knife and have had to deal with wrestling both away from individuals. In addition, have learned from experience that sometimes you do not have time to think about what is happening. And in others, you have to overcome the fear of acting, when you are not in immediate but growing danger. You must be able to overcome these obstacles, and become focused on a goal of nothing less than winning the action you are involved with. You must continue to look ahead and predict what is coming to ensure your actions have purpose.

Time is a tool; that you should use while planning your action. It can be used to run those pursuing you out of fuel or in wearing down the opponent causing them to become lax. At first the adrenaline will flow and everyone will stay focused, awake, and on guard. This process cannot continue, eventually they will crash and let their guard down and some will sleep.

This tactic can put the odds in your favor, if you have the patients; and foresight to utilize it. Watch for signs of the physical crash that occurs after the adrenaline and excitement of the event wares off. You may wait for a day or two for this to occur, but it will. Try not to do anything that will give captors reason to keep their guard up, allowing them to get comfortable with the situation.

When in a critical situation you must organize and work in small tactical groups of at least two. And develop a plan, which can be used for self-rescue. Do not "go at it alone" Believing you will be the one who saves the others. This only works in the movies, you need to work together. You will not lose a fight if you fight smart, two against one. Isolate individuals, the strongest person should act as the initiator in the fight, the others support and protecting them from being injured while assisting them in winning the confrontation.

You must plan for each detail and every possible action that you may have to deal with. If you are fending off pirates, and one of you are injured, do not break off the attack to render aid to the injured party, giving up on the battle. Win the battle first then you can provide all the assistance you need. Remember, Maneuver, Protect and Cover; you have someone maneuver, while protecting them and providing cover from attack in another direction. If you utilize this technique, you will win the small battles as well as the fight for your freedom.

This not only will assist you in winning the fight but in ensuring that each of you survives the ordeal. If you are the cover and protect element, you must prevent any blows that could injure the one you are protecting and prevent any flanking or side attacks from other individuals, doing this while you watch and assist in the fight from the rear or side of your team members.

Also you need to inform the one you are protecting of any developments that could cost you the fight if not dealt with by moving quickly or breaking off an attack and shifting to another point of contact in the fight. You must also be quick to obtaining any weapons that are available or dropped by the opponent for your use. But not at the risk of yourself being injured, or captured. You can win if you organize and work together.

When working together for overpowering an attacker who has a weapon remember the acronym R-CAT <u>redirect, control, attack, take away</u> the weapon. Remember, working with another you will divide up the different portions of the tactic, one will redirect the direction the weapon is pointing and control it while the other attacks the pirate and overpower them.

When the weapon is freed from the assailant use it to apprehend or remove other threats. When you have them under control by apprehending or rendering them unconscious be sure that they are secured or tied up to prevent having to deal with them again. Move to the next objective, or individuals that must be deal with. Utilize passage ways to channel attackers, this allows you to deal with one at a time when possible. Ensure every blow is of the strength to disable the attacker. You do not have time to wrestle when dealing with several individuals.

Another example: When having to combat a person with a rifle you should grab the barrel of the rifle at a position that gives you the most control. Whichever hand you grab it with is the hand and arm that is committed to that position, therefore, be sure to set yourself up to utilize your strength and balance for your advantage. You want to then, move as quickly as possible, maneuvering your body into position while directing the aim of the rifle in a direction that will not harm anyone in your group.

Your goal is to place yourself between the rifle and the person you are attacking. While you are controlling the rifle your team member is attacking the individual. You want to take the rifle away but while doing so you must control the direction of the barrel. Should you not be able to raise to a position between the individual and the weapon, using your free arm swing it in a circular motion as hard as your can aim for the forearm of the person holding the barrel hitting it from the top knocking it downward, freeing the area in front of the assailant. Then throw your body against them; grabbing the butt of the weapon, and push it away as hard as you can.

While you are pushing the weapon away from the individual your partner is attacking, the other crewmember grabs him from behind with a, chokehold, while placing the toe of your foot on his calf just below the knee. By pushing forward and down you lock his leg in place forcing him to his knees where you have total control of the individual. So stand on it as hard as you can, while you are pushing him to the ground you extend your body stretching him while chocking. This will do one of two things, break his neck, or render him unconscious.

I have found that it is much easier to take a weapon by having the one assigned to the chore of controlling it, too wedge their body between the weapon and the assailant. This while the other individual attacks the assailant, this gives total control of the weapon without a choice of counter action from the threat you are trying remove.

This method requires no training, and can be accomplished by anyone, when the need arises. It is much easier to push the weapon from the individual than pull and wrestle the weapon away in a rapid manner. This makes quick work of the situation and confuses the individual you are attacking by giving him two situations to deal with at once, making a take down quick and relatively easy. Be sure to keep the weapon pointed in a direction that will not injure anyone of your other crewmembers. And try not to allow the individual warn the others.

If you have to fight an individual with a pistol, remember that if it is a semi-auto pistol with a slide on the barrel. By shoving, the slide back slightly jams the weapon preventing it from being, fired. You can also block the hammer with your hand or the meat between your thumb and forefinger.

You should grab the weapon on the opposite side as the hand of the person holding it, trying to slide the barrel back slightly and raising the muzzle direction to prevent it from being, pointed at you. Grab it on the other side with the other hand, pushing the barrow in the direction of the hand side of the person holding the weapon. This will some times break the trigger finger freeing the pistol. All of this while the other crewmember attacks the individual from behind. I do not recommend trying this unless you have been trained or practiced it.

If the weapon be a revolver, use the same process as above but to stop the pistol from firing grab the drum to prevent it from turning or wedge your hand in front of the hammer preventing it from making contact. You must always be mindful of where the weapon is aimed, and prevent it from being pointed in the direction of any individual on your crew. Aiming it at their people is OK.

When you devise a plan or action against a group, you may utilize several smaller actions to accomplish your freedom. You must go over or practice each stage of your plan in your head completely. You must not stop short of the completion of each, no matter what should happen during the attack? If you get tired or quit short of completion, you will bring a more difficult situation on the group, with out the same opportunity of escape in the future. You must complete the attack, as you practiced in your mind, do not let up on the attack until the desired outcome is secured.

You have to plan your attack in stages, waiting until you have one or two of the attackers isolated and alone. Once you have completed the first portion of your plan; you can stage or prepare for the next attack on the other individuals that you must deal with. Utilize the weapons you acquire from the first group you overpower. As time progresses your captors will grow lax and they will trust that one or two can keep watch over you. This is the opportunity that will allow you to take them out, one or two at a time.

Separate, Isolate and remove the threat, you must keep them quiet while doing so to prevent them from warning the others, and then move to the next. In a situation where you must deal with several attackers you will do better if you only have to deal with one at a time. In a passage way where only one at a time can advance on you is also a good tactic to utilize. This also works well when you have boarders on your boat. A hatchway, door or passageways are great place to make a stand. Utilize these tactics when necessary.

If dealing with many on your vessel, and having isolated one or two. You must have one or two people assigned to securing the hatch or door. Do not hold a fiberglass or wood door shut from directly inside it. Stand off to the side while holding is shut. If the door or hatch is locked do not hold the handle. This is where the attackers will first try to shoot. Hold the door about chest high until the others are ready for it to be opened. Think not only about what you need to do too secure your freedom, but about the actions of the attackers that could cause you harm. You must plan for their actions to prevent harm to yourself and crew.

Figure 28 Uninvited Guest

SLEEP OVER WITH UNINVITED GUEST

Surviving as a hostage

You are traveling and have some unexpected guest stop over for some un-translated conversation, your belongings and a little ransom; if they can get it. What do you do then? Well, after some thought and remembering those who have died at the hands of their rescuers I felt that some instruction is needed, with the hopes of providing a little information that might save these un-necessary causalities. In addition, to explain that just because you have guest does not mean you can let your guard down. So here we go from here?

You had tried to prevent and attack by using tactics to prevent you being noticed or detected, and attacked. Regardless, they found you. You have tried to prevent their boarding your vessel, but now have some unwelcome guests that you must deal with. You now switch to a different survival mode, and must regain or maintain your composure, must deal with the situation. I have in the past been blindfolded, with weapons pointed at my head for hours. I can tell you that if you know what to expect you can handle the situation more efficiently than if you do not. For this reason, you should know what things you might have to deal with should you become a hostage.

You will have not only your feelings to deal with but also those of your friends and crew; if you are aware of these, you can counter them. You are terrified, and everything is bright in color and you have tunnel vision, and your hearing is focused; but after a bit you start to crash. This is not a situation that you have to blindly stumble through hoping for the best. There are many books on the topic of surviving a hostage situation that you can read. However, most people will not study this topic. This is not a subject, which is appealing too most when you are leaving on vacation.

However, your chance of survival increases if you understand the process of your mental state during a hostage situation as well as the psychiatry of the attackers. You also need to know how to deal with rescue attempts, which can be the most dangerous part of the whole affair.

After the attackers or pirates calm down the first thing you need to do is check and see if any one was injured and needs medical attention. You can offer this to the attackers as well, if an attacker is injured. You can score points with them if you care for their wounds. This is a great opportunity to get them to think of you as a person instead of a thing. You must try to become friendly with them, which will make them less willing to harm you.

You also need to gather information on things that may help you, such as how well prepared or trained they are, are they afraid or timid, how many of them are there, their age and physical shape; etc. All of this will help you make decisions on how you behave during the capture.

Try to establish a dialogue with them, talking and listening to them when they speak. While doing so ask questions about their, purpose and what they, plan to do, with you? This effort at communicating will be the most important thing that you can do while you are being, held, captive. The closer you become to the pirates, the better chance you have of surviving the ordeal. Remember; you may have been just as they if you were born in the same part of the world.

Keep track of time; date and things said as well as things that happen during the ordeal, this would help you stay mentally active. Ask them for small favors, and if on your boat ask if you can cook a meal for everyone. The more you make them feel as guest, the less likely they will allow you to be, harmed.

If rescuers are close by and are not prepared for your escape attempt, you will just waste the opportunity making it more difficult, if possible in the future. You should watch for signals that those in the area are prepared to provide assistance when you attempt any self-rescue or escape.

Watch and listen for any signals or attempts of communication from those trying to free you. You will be surprised at what you can learn by listening to the types of messages near by. You can provide information by hand signals when you are visible providing information on the number of captors and there location to the rescuers.

You will have to deal with the traumatic emotional stress when taken hostage, you have just fought off pirates who have been able to board your vessel and capture you and your boat. Many people with out a positive mental attitude will suffer while captive; depression will cause some to sleep and others to anguish over their circumstance. It will be up to the captain to deal with these and create a positive outlook by planning for the possibilities of their capture.

These behaviors can diminish your chance of survival.

The understanding of what it is to be, held captive will aid in circumstances where you are held in isolation where you could be deprived of your sense of time and companionship. If you are forced to remain quiet for hours and days at a time, increasing the sense of, fear especially if the hostage takers cannot or refuse to have any dialogue with you.

Latter you will deal with boredom and extreme terror, creating a feeling of exhaustion. Dealing with your emotions and the emotions of the others, being, held with you will be important in creating a positive environment for all involved. It will be easier to survive with everyone working together and not having to drag and plead with someone to go along with your plans and routines while being held captive, during escape attempts or rescue. You must keep everyone involved in looking for possibilities or things that will shift the circumstance in your favor.

Discuss the situation and talk of possibilities that will result in your freedom and continue to look for signs from the hostage takers revealing their plans and your future situation. You must be prepared for the possibility that escape will be your only option, and should be continually formulating a plan for this purpose. If you are at sea, escape is only part of the problem the rest being preventing recapture.

While being held captive listen to your captors, do not argue with them. If you can start conversations with them do not discus topics that could lead to disagreements or make them angry at you and those with you. Should you believe at any time that they plan to kill all captives you must enact your escape plan. If you out number, the hostage takers you may plan to over power them and take back control of your vessel. You may plan to dive into the water at night and take your chances. What ever you do must be calculated and weighed against the alternative. Only if you have no choice will you take such a drastic chance.

Try to organize and overpower the pirates is a possibility wait till they let there guard down and are separated from each other, a couple below with you, and the others on the deck. If you try to overpower them, you must take control of the weapon and ensure that it does not fire into the group while you wrestle with them. You must think of each detail of the attack and discuss it with everyone involved so that there are no mistakes. Work in groups at least two people when attempting to retake control of your boat.

The pirates want to detain you and receive a reward for your freedom or kill you. If you allow them to transport you to there, area or home your chances of escape and rescue decrease to almost nothing. You must be rescued or attempt self rescue before you get to a point where they will bring others on board to help them as they move you closer to there home base.

You have to calculate this in your head by knowing the direction you are heading and the distance to shore in that direction. Then deduct what distance you figure they will find others that will assist them in getting you to shore. This is the amount of time you have for rescuers to reach you or for you to overpower the hostage takers or escape from them. You will work against this time schedule in your head with out panicking the others being, held, with you. I well thought out plan will succeed providing everyone work together when the time comes.

After you are, taken, hostage, you must begin to understand your situation, which will aid you in planning your escape. There are several types of hostage takers identifying them will provide information on your situation. They types are Military action, terrorist, criminals; and emotional distraught persons. By identifying, which type of person or group is holding you will describe your situation somewhat? This information is important when planning your escape; you defiantly want different plans that are more, detailed, for captors that have military training than a thug off the street.

The manner in which they hold you is also an identifier for you, like a <u>Barricade</u> where you are, held with the hostage takers in the same area, a room or on a boat. <u>Containment</u> where you are held in your boat or vehicle, at a position like a dock or harbor and refused the ability to leave or depart usually by a large force acting to prevent your departure. As a <u>Human Shield</u> by individuals in desperation, this can be a stage of a pirate attack, which started as a barricade then turns to a human shield when rescuers arrive. Alternatively, a <u>Kidnapping</u> in which people are, captured, for a ransom, a pirate attacks often include many or all of these as the circumstance changes and others become involved in your circumstance.

If you are isolated, the actions of the captors can reveal to you the situation outside and if rescuers are nearby.

The hostage takers also follow stages which if you can interrupt in the first stage can stop the ordeal from occurring, which was discussed in earlier chapters. The steps they follow are planning and Surveillance, Attack, Movement, Captivity, and Release.

You should know that the behavior of the captors towards the captives could include any or all of the following, which you must be aware of and mentally prepared to endure. They are Physical Restraint and Sensory Deprivation, Mental Cruelty, Interrogation, Indoctrination and Brainwashing, Verbal Abuse and Humiliation, Threats of Injury and Death and Physical and Sexual Abuse. Being aware of the possibility will lessen the shock of the situation should it occur.

After you become a captive, being aware of the stages of adaptation to captivity in those with you will become important as you deal with them and plan for your escape. Making them aware of this mental process will ease the problem and make it easier to counter the emotions that follow. They are as follows: <u>Startled or Panic</u> because of the abrupt change in your freedom. <u>Disbelief</u> in this happening to them, which can come before the feeling of <u>Hypervigilence and Anxiety</u> as they become wary and alert to minute details in the surroundings.

The feeling of <u>Resistance and compliance</u> in some as they resist the terms of their captivity, and are not able to deal with the pressure of the situation; the feeling of <u>Depression and Despair</u> sets in on some people. Gradual Acceptance of the situation follows this where a decision is made to gain some control of their life and make use of limited resources.

The stress reaction of individuals in captive situation must be dealt with because of this first hour of captivity is the most dangerous and could cause serious problems if not handled, as you communicate with each other to ensure everyone can function when the time comes to make the decision to escape. The reactions you need to be aware of and must discuss with those with you are:

<u>Initial phase</u> is the shock, disbelief, denial, confusion, and a sense of unreality and fear. The <u>intermediate phase</u> is emotional numbness, apathy, social withdrawal, scapegoating, complaining, bickering, irritability, hysteria, crying, generalized anxiety, anger, protective behaviors towards females and children, extreme talkativeness and reflection on ones life are common in the first few hours and days of capture.

<u>Long-term phase</u> of more than a week are depression, fatalistic thinking, deliberate self-injury, sleep disturbance, vivid dreams, mental confusion, ritualistic behaviors and loss of emotional control and ill-health which can be partly stress induced examples are asthma, diarrhea, skin disorders, stomach complaints, aches and pains.

Everyone is aware of the <u>Stockholm syndrome</u> this is always a possibility especially when trying to build some type of relationship with the hostage takers to prevent them from being able to consider you an object instead of a person. This is an important step in surviving a hostage situation but there are factors that you need to keep in mind while involved in surviving this and trying to minimize any harm that could occur.

By managing certain things, you can minimize any harm and maximize your chance of survival during the ordeal: You must ensure that everyone regains and maintains their composure as soon after capture as possible. Keep your head and calm the others down is important for the safety of everyone in the first few minutes. Hysteria can cause a situation to fall apart quickly resulting in a hostage taker reacting by shooting someone if not careful. Do not cause the hostage takers to feel that they must take extreme measures in securing you, which could make escape more difficult.

Maintain a low-key un-provocative posture will make the hostage takers feel that they do not need to pay a lot of attention to you and that you are going to not give them any problems. This is very beneficial and could save your life when the time comes, by acting as though you are agreeable they put their guard down and when you need to overpower or escape you will find it easier when you do not have so many things to overcome. You are also less likely to be, killed by projecting this type of behavior.

Getting the captors to recognize you as a human, the more they know about you the less likely they will do you harm. You should offer to treat them as guest if on your boat, engage them in conversation about various things as you would someone you meet and befriend. I do not mean you must be friendly just try to become more than an object that they feel nothing for could cause them to think for a few seconds before pulling the trigger and saving your life.

Follow the rules set by the captors; this will over time, earn you more rights. In addition, with this comes more opportunity to escape. In a situation like this when you are trying to save your family or friends any resistance is counterproductive and reduces your chance of survival.

Say, as little as possible if questioned, talking and meaningless conversation is one thing but when they are trying to get information out of you it could be something that could cause your chances to decrease. If you must answer, make it short and sweet, no long detailed answers.

Earn your captors respect, people in most parts of the world respect values rather than talk. They also respect those of faith, praying and reading are a couple of things that will give them cause to think better of you. Learn what the captor's value and utilize those principles in your talk and actions. To act as though you have no faith and manners makes you regarded as an infidel, as and of no more value than a dog.

Set goals for the future after you are, released, or freed this gives you things to look forward too and affects your attitude when going through hard times. This is very important, do your goal setting and planning of the future with the ones that are with you, your children and friends. If captive for a long time you may have to change the dates, but do not give up on the plans.

Keep your mind active; write a book in your head if they will not let you have paper. Invent things go over figures; plan your route to a new destination. Keeps your mind working on things to maintain your sharpness and good reactive timing?

Attempt to understand your captors, be courteous and caring about them and their situation. When they talk of a problem, be concerned and helpful, do not assume anything about their intelligence or knowledge, and be willing to play games and cards with them anything to be more an associate than a captive is. It may be wise to let them win shuttle.

Inject humor when ever possible with out being sarcastic, being funny is good for lightening up a situation. Only after several, hours when things have settled down to do so in the early stages of captivity would be arrogant and cause problems. Use common sense when attempting this it could do as much harm as good if the timing is not correct.

Ensure that everyone eats; some people will avoid eating in a stressful situation like being a hostage. They must keep their strength up and maintain some level of activity, you must exercise even is you cannot stand up you can do some type of exercise to help keep the blood circulating. This is important especially for the older ones to prevent blood clotting in the legs and such.

You must maintain HOPE, if you loose hope you loose everything. As long as you hope for the future for safety for help there is always something to hope for, without hope life has no meaning. You must instill hope in the others, by planning and talking about what could be happening outside in order to free them; by doing this you provide a little bit of the hope that they need to keep moving towards the future. Keeping their minds active looking for things and planning an escape that you may use in the near future all helps provide hope in the individuals with you.

Practice stress management techniques with the others, this will help calm them down and in doing it together can be part of a group activity that you can use when you see someone having a hard time. This instills the techniques in the individuals giving them the tools to use when they need them.

Accept your feeling, and do not dwell on them, you can suck the hope out of the situation if you dwell on your feelings. Instead, accept the way you feel then as my father uses to say, "Go have another cup of coffee". Not that you can have, coffee but you get what I mean, get on with, the, business of, survival. Pay attention to the others, when you see they have that lost expression on their face get them thinking of something that is productive for the group. You need to look out for each other and protect the hope you have, try not to allow yourself to make statements you will regret latter.

You must be tolerant of each other, especially in this situation. Each person has there own limitations and each will need to help the other through the times that come. Not everyone will feel the same thing at the same time this allows those who are feeling OK now to help those who are in despair. Pay attention and care for each other's feelings, by doing so you may be able to ensure that everyone is ready when the time comes to act together for an escape.

Everyone copes with things differently; in this situation, you can suggest additional tools and actions that can aid the individuals during this time of captivity. Do not forget that you are all each of you have at the time and count on each other for the assistance each can give to lift moral.

Release or Rescue is the most dangerous aspect of being a hostage. Keep the children close to you, so you do not have to rush to them for protection should a rescue attempt begin. Most of those that are, killed in trying to reach a loved one and while trying to do so move into the path of a bullet. Remember when a rescue attempt starts to move the highest part of your body vertically straight down to the ground, any movement laterally could result in you moving into the path of gunfire.

After you are as low as you can get only then can you move left, right, forward or backward. Remember keep your hands visible and do not appear to be a threat or you will be, treated as a threat. Be sure to teach the young ones how to get low without moving in any direction but down. This could save their lives, and do not try to reach someone to provide protection when a rescue starts, that action could cost your life. For this, reason I recommend that you keep the children by your side to prevent a rush to get to them; and the possible injury or death that could result.

The same goes for the men who try to reach their wives, you must be on the ground before you can try to reach anyone but it is best to maintain your position for everyone's sake. This will ensure that all of you live through the rescue attempt.

Captain Michael Pierce

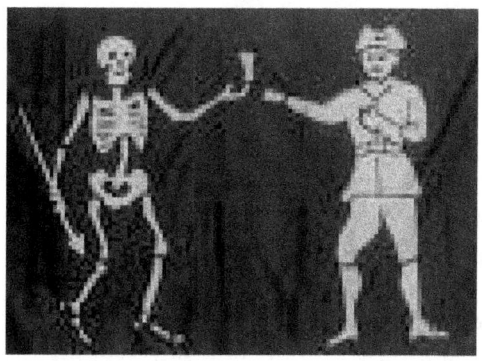

Figure 29 Ransom or Escape

RANSOM OR ESCAPE AND EVASION

For those who can or believe it to be wise they offer hostage and terrorism insurance for the purpose these situations. I do recommend checking on these as well as SOS membership, which provides you with a number that you can call to get help when in a strange land. Those that do not have this protection will have to deal with the situation themselves while waiting on government agencies to resolve the situation.

Should you be captive and transported to the camp or mainland of those who captured you keeps your head and continues to use the principles and tactics we have discussed. Even though you are in the territory of the pirates, you can still escape and make it to safety. You must utilize the tactics that the military uses to evade capture once you escape from your captors.

You will continue to use time as a tool, while allowing those holding you to believe you have accepted your situation. Continue to look for opportunities and individuals that are sympathetic to your situation. Like Christians that you may come in contact or farmers who do not participate in the behaving of the groups that are holding you. Do not give any signal that you are planning an escape.

Eventually you will be given some freedom; they may untie you and allow you to move about a room freely. This is a good sign and you must use it toward your advantage.

While you were being moved to this new location, you should have at least recognized your direction of travel. By the location of the suns warmth on your body or by seeing the position of stars and moon; these are things you should watch for and remember while being moved. Pay close attention to all the signals and try to estimate your direction and speed of travel to your new location. You will need to get to the coast to escape; unless you know the country and any location of a safety nearby that you can try to reach.

You look for the opportune time to escape and a direction to travel while doing so. When you escape, try to do so when you will have the most time before they know you are missing. This will allow you to put a little distance between you and them before they start to hunt for you.

When you are trying to hide; and prevent your discovery, you need to stay off roads and trails. Do not travel on regular routes used by the locals. You need to stick to the roughest area to avoid contact. In well-populated areas you should travel at night, in some areas this could be dangerous because of the local wildlife but you will have no choice. You will need to be aware and avoid them as well, watch where you walk and place your hands. Some areas have many poisonous creatures that you must watch for; snakes that look like branches, scorpions and crocodiles as well as large cats.

You must be watchful as you move through these rough areas, you may avoid being shot or hacked to death, but what these creatures have to offer is just as deadly. Use caution and your hearing, move a few paces and listen and look. As you get further away from your captors, you can move to less difficult path to travel, but continue to travel at night. Find a good place to rest by day, which is out of sight, and where no one will cross your path.

Look for local dress as soon as possible, by looking as a local at a great distance you will not draw attention. Move to a location where you can find aid or transportation to leave the country. You may have to steal a boat at night, if you do be sure that have as much darkness as possible to try to get over the horizon before you can be seen.

Distance is your security in this situation. You must be unseen until you are in an area where you can be picked up by rescuers. Maintain your energy by eating anything you can find. You can live for three days without water but you must maintain your energy, to be successful at your escape. Do not go without eating in hopes that you will be rescued soon, and eat then.

You may travel for as long as ten days before you are rescued or possibly longer. If you are too weak to move, you will die. Maintain your moral and the moral of those with you during the escape. When you have lost your pursuers, you can set traps during the daytime while you rest. In addition, look for food and water while you travel. Do not start fires at night unless you are in a location where the light and smoke cannot be seen, or the fire smelt by those who may be close by.

Remember these principles when trying to avoid contact with individuals chasing you.

Watch were you step- do not to leave tracks

Avoid silhouetting yourself – stick to dark shaded areas if possible

Sound Discipline – sound travels farther at night

Smell – you can smell others when in close proximity

Sudden movement – you may not see someone unless they move

Camouflage – use camouflage when moving and hiding

Exposed areas – do not move through clearings but around them

Use hand signals – do not speak to each other unless necessary

To escape you must not be seen; or heard; by those chasing you; leave no signs that show you were at a location that can give you away.

For survival, remember this acronym.

Size up the situation

Undue haste makes waste

Remember where you are

Vanquish fear and panic

Improvise

Value living

Act like the natives

Learn basic skills

If you can maintain your energy lever, prevent coming in contact with the locals and know where you need to go to reach safety you will survive this situation and make it home.

VESSEL SAFETY MANAGEMENT

Vessel Safety Management Plan

The vessel safety management and contingency plan provides procedures for handling emergencies that may occur while at sea.

You may encounter medical emergencies, fires, grounding, collisions, and criminal acts including terrorism. Each emergency may require a different response involving different segments of those onboard the vessel.

During an emergency, it is important that everyone be aware of their environment, be informed of the vessel's design to handle emergencies; be informed that they are in safe and competent hands; and be prepared to follow directions.

Management Plan's Outline

The plan should include:

Provide information to assist those onboard in preparing to handle an emergency, and to take the necessary actions to stop or minimize the damage and to mitigate the effects of and emergency.

Establish procedures to get everyone from various spaces on the vessel to an assembly station; direct them on to the embarkation; and evacuate them to points of safety in an emergency.

Describe the different training that will be scheduled to prepare those on board to handle emergency situations. The training should include theoretical instruction and practical training through simulation of incidents so that they can rehearse and practice their roles.

Be reviewed, evaluated, exercised, and updated regularly.

Be readily available on board, located throughout the vessel so those onboard are aware of their responsibilities during and emergency situation.

Prevention and Emergency Preparedness

Safety Management Policies

The objective of the plan must always be to deal with the situation onboard and get everyone to safety in an emergency.

Onboard Training

Determine the training required for each person of the crew.

Have specific responsibilities during and emergency that each person should be familiar with the position they are assigned and their role in an emergency.

If they do not have a specific responsibility during an emergency they should know where they should go and do during it.

You should conduct drills and give instruction as necessary to ensure that all are familiar with their duties during emergencies.

Responsibilities

Prepare instructions for each person for each emergency that may occur.

List the responsibilities for each person in it, a person duties should not vary with different emergencies.

List the duties and responsibilities of all that are tasked to ensure that the emergency equipment such as fire extinguishing equipment, first aid kits, communication equipment and lifesaving devices are operational.

PIRACY SURVIVAL GUIDE

SAFETY INSTRUCTIONS

Each person should be familiar with following information

How the signal for emergency will be given

How each person is to proceed after hearing the emergency signal.

How and what instructions will be given during the emergency.

How abandon ship procedures will be carried out including moving to the life raft. What additional equipment and provisions should be ready for and emergency. Where to gather on the boat to ensure everyone is ok.

How to don a life jacket.

How evacuation will proceed.

How the boarding and launching procedures will work.

Discuss the purpose of an abandon ship bag I always prepare one that has food, water first aid kit, sun screen, radio; and anything that I believe will be needed for survival. I keep it next to my life jacket in case an emergency should occur. Give each person a bag the size that would be easy to carry and discuss what each person should be concerned with and need in their bag in case they must leave the vessel and board the life raft, just items that would aid in their survival.

Emergency Action or Contingency Plans.

This emergency action or contingency plans should list actions to take in responding to specific emergencies.

In responding to a injury, you should ensure the safety of personnel and the vessel, and take precautions to prevent the escalation of the incident.

Develop a plan of action for each emergency that you might encounter. The steps for each emergency should be similar if possible.

You should have plans made for:

Fire Fighting

Injury at Sea

Piracy at Sea

Vessel Sinking

These are a few, you need to develop plans for every thing that could go wrong with your particular vessel and ensure each person knows their duty during such.

PIRACY SURVIVAL GUIDE

INTERNATIONAL DISTRESS SIGNALS

The following signals used or exhibited either together or separately, indicate distress and need of assistance.

A gun or other explosive signal fired at intervals of about a minute;

A continuous sounding with any fog-signaling apparatus;

Rockets or shells, throwing red stars fired one at a time at short intervals;

A signal sent by radiotelephony or by any other signaling method consisting of the group

···---··· (SOS) in the Morse code;

A signal sent by radiotelephony consisting of the spoken word "Mayday";

The International Code Signal of distress indicated by N.C.;

A signal consisting of a square flag having above or below it a ball or anything resembling a ball;

Flames on the vessel (as from a burning tar barrel, oil barrel, etc.);

A rocket parachute flare or a hand flare showing a red light;

A smoke signal giving off orange-colored smoke;

Slowly and repeatedly raising and lowering arms outstretched to each side;

The radiotelegraph alarm signal;

The radiotelephone alarm signal;

Signals transmitted by emergency position-indicating radio beacons;

Approved signals transmitted by radio communication systems, including survival craft radar transponders.

The use of exhibition of any of the foregoing signals except for the purpose of indicating distress and need of assistance and the use of other signals which may be confused with any of the above signals is prohibited.

Attention is drawn to the relevant sections of the International Code of Signals, the Ship Search and Rescue Manual and the following signals:

(a) a piece of orange-colored canvas with either a black square and circle or other appropriate symbol (for identification from the air);
(b) A dye marker.

OPEN WATER SURVIVAL

When traveling in a vessel at sea it is important that you prepare for any situation that could occur. One of the situations that require planning is should your vessel sink or you be required to evacuate it for some reason. There are issues that you need to be prepared and knowledge that you need in order to survive in this situation.

When being stranded at sea

The first challenge is the sea state. You will need to deal with waves and wind. This can cause a problem for those who are not prepared mentally for dealing with it. It could be that the water is extremely cold, to prevent this from becoming a serious situation take precautions immediately. Evaluate your situation and inventory the items that you have in order to protect yourselves from the wind and waves.

You must also be able to find food and water; you can improvise and make the equipment that you need to make water and to get food, should you not have any onboard the raft. You must include this in your evaluation and take immediate action to resolve the problem, and not wait till hunger and thirst set in.

Providing for these three things the wind food and water, will help in creating a positive attitude in all involved

Surviving depends on the survival equipment you have available, your skill and ability to handle the situation you are involved in; and most important your will to live. You should have studied the possible situation and learned to make water stills and how to collect food at sea, these are very important skills for the offshore mariner.

Should you find yourself in the water in a survival situation, conserve your energy and your body heat. If you have to swim utilize the Dog paddle for swimming on the surface, or the side stroke and the back stroke are good relief stroke, the breaststroke is a stroke for swimming underwater through an area with oil or fuel on the surface of the water.

You need to cover the possibilities with those on the vessel, be sure they know the proper method for dealing with the obstacles that may involve their survival in any situation.

Cold Weather Survival

Instruct everyone on how to use the survival suit should the situation arise. Instruct them to keep their clothing loose and comfortable. When evacuating the vessel be sure they know to be careful not to snag the life raft with things that could puncher it sharp objects or even their shoes.

Protect yourselves from spray and the wind if the raft does not have a canopy rig a wind break to shield you and those with you. Keep the floor of the raft dry to protect you from the cold, this is difficult when boarding it but work on drying yourselves and the floor of the raft. This will not only improve your survival situation by increasing the probability but also the attitude of those with you.

Huddle together to share warmth this is a method for survival on land as well as at sea, try to keep the blood circulating by moving you're arms and legs. You greatest danger is Hypothermia in colder latitudes as well as cool water. You loose heat around 25 times faster in the water than on land this must be keep in your mind encourage everyone to move to circulate their blood and huddle to keep warm.

In the back you will find a chart that list the survival time in cold water for individuals this will vary according to the body size keep this in mind for those small individuals onboard with you. They could loose body heat quicker than normal and will require attention, so be mindful of the others and the situation they are in at the time while trying to survive.

Hot Weather Survival

A hot climate the challenge will be during the day time, the sunshine will dehydrate a person quickly, and you will need to construct a canopy to block the sunshine. Keep your skin covered to protect them from sun burn you can also burn your eyelids, back of your ears and chin; try to cover these if possible.

Water will be the biggest challenge, remember the 3 of survival which means you can live for three minutes with out air, for three days with out water and for three weeks with out food. You know your priorities now be sure that you start to work on the water problem as soon as you find yourself in this situation.

Do not consume any food or water for the first 24 hours if your supplies are limited, work on the problem of water and food in that order. When you drink moisten your lips, mouth and throat before you do so.

Replace your water with chemical or a mechanical water purifier if available. If not construct a solar still to make it, this method is slow so start at once and be sure to protect your water from salt.

During the hottest part of the day wet your cloths with water to help you cool down try to ensure they are dry by night because it will be cool and miserable should you not do so.

Food

In the open sea there are some poisonous and dangerous fish, be sure you know what you can eat and what to stay away from. In most cases out at sea the fish are safe and near land there are boat safe and dangerous fish.

Look around for thread from something to use as fishing line should you not have any on the raft. Use several threads together to give it strength you can test it to insure you make it correctly. Fish hook can be made from plastic or wire if none on the raft look for something in the general shape or that is strong enough to hold its shape. You can use anything shiny as bait as long as it can be swallowed by the fish allowing the hook to acquire the position needed to prevent escape.

Sea weed is a good source of food; you can also find crabs as well as other small sea dwellers that are eatable. Once you have caught a small fish you can use it as bait to catch something larger.

Physical Problems Associated with Survival at Sea

You may suffer from dehydration, headaches, and exhaustion to name a few. Knowledge of these problems will help to dispel fear when they start to occur.

Sea sickness could pose a problem on the raft, when a person becomes sea sick the results could be: extreme fluid loss, loss of the will to survive, others can become sick as a result and unclean problem are created. This will attract sharks and needs to be taken care of to create an atmosphere of hope.

When someone becomes sick wash both the individual and the raft to remove the site and odor of the vomit, Keep the person from eating until it subsides. Have the individual lay down and give seasickness pills if possible if not able to take the pill orally, insert them rectally for absorption by the body.

Salt water Sores

If at sea for an extended period of time several days your skin will become irritated by the salt in the water. The skin exposed to the salt water will break and scab which will form pus. Do not open or drain them, flush the skin with fresh water if possible and let dry. If a first aid kit is available use antiseptic on the wound if possible.

Blindness and eye irritation

Just as in the arctic you can become blind because of the glare of the sun. Your eyes will become bloodshot and sore you can make protection from cloth or plastic by cutting a small slit in it to see through to protect your eyes from the glare. If this occurs bandage lightly the eyes of the person when this occurs.

Bodily Functions

When in a raft do not take laxative as it will cause dehydration, try to exercise and drink water if possible

Urination may become a problem due to the dehydration; it is a sign that you are not getting enough water. You need to try to increase the water production and drink more.

Abandon Ship Bag

I will mention this again I always prepare a small bag; with the supplies that I feel we would need should we have to abandon the vessel for our survival. I include some food, water, first aid equipment, sun screen; light, portable marine radio; navigation equipment and a few other items that I feel are important and would make the ordeal easier. I keep this next to my life jacket where it would be easy to grab in case of an emergency. It would be a good practice to make a policy to do the same and teach the others on board the vessel to do the same, each individual has specific needs which may be medication that is needed for survival they should make sure they have this and anything else that is needed in their abandon ship bag. Make sure they place it in a place that they will be able to grab it in case of such an emergency.

Captain Michael Pierce

MARINERS RESOURCES

PIRACY INFORMATION

Websites that provide a source of information to the cruiser and yacht owner on piracy as well as many other things are included in this chapter. These sites are supported by contributions and offer their information free of charge to those who visit it making it important that we support them. If you want to keep this information accessible and like having an organization that is interested in piracy against the boat owner and not just commercial vessels then it is up to us to help maintain these sites. Please send in a contribution once a year and use these sites often. The more we support them the more they will be able to offer us, Should you have an idea for the site they would be happy to hear them. They are also a good source for all the information that you need when planning to visit an area including info on clearing customs and immigration, weather reports, local organizations that can help as well as message boards and more.

There are only a few of these sites, and I am impressed with what I

have seen they are easy to navigate you should learn what all they have by spending time at the site on a regular schedule. They should be part of your routine when you sit down to plan a trip. I will give you the addresses of these sites and as much information on what you can find there but I will not be able to cover everything so log on and check them out. They are as follows:

HTTP://WWW.NOONSITE.COM

Noonsite.com aims to provide a one-stop website featuring essential information on all matters of interest to sailors planning an offshore voyage anywhere in the world, whether already underway or still in the preparatory stages.

PIRACY SURVIVAL GUIDE

<u>Countries</u> : All cruising destinations are covered (currently 193 countries and 1798 ports) with information on clearance formalities, visa requirements, fees, weather, special events and other facts needed by visiting sailors. Also featured are details of repair facilities as well as marine and shore services for every major port visited by cruising boats.

<u>Text version</u> : A low bandwidth version for access over slow links. All material on noonsite.com can also be retrieved by email. Send a blank message to <u>text-help@noonsite.com</u> for instructions on how to use this service.

<u>Sponsors</u> All reputable companies providing services to yachts are listed on Noonsite.com for free. Companies that would like a more prominent entry on Noonsite.com, with the chance to provide more detail about their services, even their own Noonsite.com webpage, can take out an annual sponsorship.

Noonsite's main objective is to provide cruising sailors with comprehensive information regarding essential marine facilities in any port visited by yachts. Basic details of specialist companies are listed so that sailors may contact those that they are interested in. Companies listed are not necessarily recommended by noonsite and noonsite declines any responsibility for unsatisfactory services provided by any company listed on this website. Unfavorable reports on such companies may result in their removal from the site.

Contributions: Visitors are urged to bring any news or changes to the attention of the site manager. All contributions will be personally acknowledged.

<u>http://www.noonsite.com</u> – information for the cruisers including piracy

<u>http://www.yachtpiracy.com</u> – a piracy site with some good info

<u>http://www.safetyandsecuritynet.com</u>

http://www.icc-ccs.org – information that deals mostly with commercial shipping

The CSSN is a Short Wave SSB Net for cruisers in the Caribbean. This net operates on frequency 8104 at 8:15 Monday through Saturday

The IMB Piracy Reporting Centre is located at: ICC International Maritime Bureau, PO Box 12559, 50782 Kuala Lumpur, Malaysia

Tel ++ 60 3 2078 5763, Fax ++ 60 3 2078 5769, Telex MA 31880 IMBPCI

24 hour Anti Piracy HELPLINE Tel: ++ 60 3 2031 0014

E-mail IMBKL@icc-ccs.org

INDIAN OCEAN

The French Navy has a program of surveillance in the Indian Ocean called CNVOI (stands for "Control Naval Voluntaries en Ocean Indian"). Email contact: Alindien@free.fr (Include in subject: Pour cellule control naval et opem) Phone in France: 00 33 4 94 02 84 67, Immarsat Mini M : 00 870 762 698 930.

ADEN

Aden Port Authority, PO Box 1316, Tawahi, Aden - Republic of Yemen

Tel Exchange 202666/8 - Fax +967-2-205805 or 203521, Channel 16 or 2182 kHz. e-mail: ypa@y.net.ye

info@portofaden.com

Yemeni Coastguard 24h Ops Center Tel 967 1562 402 English speaking. The Yemeni government has provided the coastguard with modern equipment and boats as well as setting up surveillance systems in an effort to prevent piracy in its territorial waters.

DJIBOUTI

Djibouti Port Authority (Port Autonome International de Djibouti)

Tel: (253) 35 23 31, Tel: (253) 35 61 87, Email: port@intnet.dj

OMAN

Salalah: listening watch on 2182 kHz and Ch 16. Harbormaster Capt. Ahmed Burham Ba'Omar, Tel. +968 219500 ext 420, fax (+968) 219253, email AhmedB@Salalahport.com.

BAHRAIN

Headquarters of the US 5th Fleet in Bahrain CUSNC.FWO@me.navy.mil

+973 1785 3283 (CUSNF in Bahrain) this is Security duty-officer.

US flagged vessels may also try the RCC Alameda (+1 510 437 3701). The contact is Ltcdr Tomas Stuhlreyer.

British flagged vessels should try UK Coastguard on +44 1326 317575

It must be stressed that even if the authorities are prepared to respond, it could take several hours for help to reach a yacht in distress.

THE NORTHWEST CARIBBEAN RADIO

VENEZUELLA ON SA A.C. (The Venezuelan National Rescue and Maritime Safety Organization) is a national voluntary and civil organization which publishes a Boater's Risk Zone Map of dangerous areas. Visit http://www.onsa.org.ve/enindex.shtml# for the link.

ICC COMMERCIAL CRIME SERVICES

Captain Michael Pierce

IMB/ICC-CCS 24 Hours Anti Piracy HELPLINE
Tel: + 60 3 2031 0014

Services

The information is shared with the industry, law enforcement, and governments in a transparent and open manner.

The services provided free by the PRC are as follows:
- Issuing daily status reports on piracy and armed robbery to ships in the IOR and AOR via broadcasts on the Inmarsat-C SafetyNET service

- Reporting piracy and armed robbery at sea incidents to law enforcement

- helping local law enforcement catch pirates and assisting in bringing them to justice

- Assisting and advising ship-owners whose vessels have been attacked or hijacked

- Assisting and advising masters and crew members whose vessels have been attacked

- Collating and disseminating information on piracy in all parts of the world

- providing updates on pirate / armed robbery activity via the Internet

- providing access to the Live Piracy Map

- publishing comprehensive quarterly and annual reports detailing piracy statistics

The above services of the Piracy Reporting Centre are provided free of charge to all ships irrespective of their ownership or flag.

On a chargeable basis the IMB – PRC:
- Investigates / locates vessels, which have illegally deviated for insurance purposes or for illegally selling cargo

Should you have more information that could be helpful for mariner please pass by going to noonsite.com, onpassage.com, and yachtpiracy.com websites?

In Closing:

Safety and security should be your top priority. You must keep things prioritized in the back of your mind. Always remember that the protection of those onboard your vessel is most important. Should you not take the precautions or do the preparation needed for this purpose would be neglect. Should the unthinkable happen pursuant to not doing what you can to prevent it, will result in carrying that regret for the rest of your life.

Your boat can be, repaired or, replaced, but the lives and health of your friends and family cannot. Every precaution you take must have this as a root, and no plan that puts them at risk is acceptable unless the option is worse for everyone. You will live with the decisions you make and for this reason, you should think twice about traveling to areas where you may put their lives at risk. Gods speed, and safe sailing hope, I will see you on the water

Capt Michael Pierce

A

Abrolhos, islands	69
ACTS OF PIRACY	6
ADMIRAL OF THE NAVY	43
admiralty law	7
Adriatic Sea	3
Aegean	1
Air Cannon	212
aircraft	9, 98, 100, 133, 136
Al Mukalla	115, 164
Alarm	209
Alatou	123
Al-Qaida	117
American	i, ii, 3, 43, 57, 98, 100, 117, 118
Anatolian	2
Angola	137
Antigua	138
Anxiety	257
Arabian Sea	86, 142
Archipelago	125
Armorica	2
Article	4, 8, 229, 230
Aruba	33, 138
ARUBANS	43
Asia	4, 94, 123, 139
asleep	11, 21, 57, 157, 177
attackers	11, 12, 53, 62, 65, 87, 88, 93, 150, 156, 162, 163, 166, 167, 172, 174, 181, 184, 204, 205, 206, 210, 211, 212, 227, 240, 250, 253
attacks	i, 5, 6, 7, 10, 11, 12, 13, 21, 50, 59, 61, 64, 84, 85, 87, 94, 95, 110, 111, 116, 118, 131, 134, 135, 136, 137, 138, 139, 140, 142, 145, 146, 147, 148, 150, 156, 157, 158, 160, 162, 163, 164, 165, 166, 167, 168, 171, 181, 188, 190, 193, 196, 237, 240, 241, 247, 249, 256
Australian	29, 83, 123, 126
Ayerabu Island	121

B

Bahia Guayraca	33
bandits	33, 34, 40, 42
Bangka Strait	140
Bangkor Bar	140
Bangladesh	142
Baran	92
Barbados	138
Barbary	4
Barbuda	138
Baseball Bats	210
beaten	21, 25, 36, 91, 127, 233
behaviors	254, 258
Belem	67, 68
Belgium	85, 142
Bird Bangers	211
Black Sea	2
boarding	5, 9, 18, 24, 49, 50, 51, 53, 56, 57, 58, 64, 79, 84, 96, 127, 132, 138, 140, 174, 204, 210, 218, 243, 252
Bonaire	138
BONAIRE	37
Brazil	67, 68, 69, 138
Britannica	2
British human rights	8
British Navy	86
British Virgin Islands	138
broadcast	60, 74, 82, 86, 116, 169, 170
Brunei	85, 123
BULLIT PROOF MATERIALS	221

C

cabin   20, 25, 28, 29, 32, 33, 34, 38, 50, 52, 56, 75, 99, 109, 129, 204, 211
Caesar   2
Cairns   123
CAMERAS   218
Cameroon   137
Canadian   107
Cape Comorin   111, 112
Cape Gerhard   123
captain   43, 50, 62, 65, 72, 78, 91, 98, 100, 112, 121, 122, 145, 165, 173, 177, 181, 254
captive   76, 127, 253, 254, 255, 257, 260, 264
Caraballeda   76, 77
Carausius   2
Careano   45
Caribbean   4, 17, 21, 26, 35, 50, 69, 137, 138, 139
CARRIACOU   37
Cartagena   33, 34, 35, 36, 41, 42
causalities   252
CGM   75, 76
chased   28, 69, 105, 126, 129, 207
Chennai Anchorage   140
China   141
Chinese   4
Chittagong Roads   140
choke point   241
Cilician   2
circumnavigation   37, 55
circumstances   3, 12, 77, 85, 90, 173, 254
Classis   2
Closing   285
CMA   75, 76
coalition forces   86
Coast Guard   14, 18, 20, 25, 34, 35, 36, 38, 45, 48, 50, 58, 72, 78, 86, 114, 116, 187
Coastal   2, 128

Cochin   112
Colombian   32, 35, 36, 37, 38
Combined Task Force   94
commercial ships   74, 132, 169
communication   7, 63, 87, 155, 172, 190, 195, 243, 254
compartment   213, 217, 218, 222
Congo   137
Containment   256
Corsica   72, 78
Cossacks   4
Costa Rica   23, 24
credit cards   20, 34, 47
Crete   2
crew   9, 12, 19, 24, 29, 32, 45, 61, 71, 72, 75, 78, 84, 88, 110, 111, 123, 133, 140, 141, 161, 164, 184, 188, 201, 219, 227, 234, 249, 252
Crewmember   128
crime   7, 9, 14, 15, 71, 73, 132, 138, 153, 165, 234
Curacao   19, 138
Customs   111, 113, 114

D

Danger Zone   105
DEADLY FORCE   167, 225
defending   222, 234
Depression   257
disarm   25
Djibouti   76, 87, 96, 98
Dodecanese   2
dollars   26, 80, 121
Dominica   19, 20, 21, 138
drifting   116, 141
Duct Tape   211

E

Eastern Europe	3, 4
Egypt	137
El Estor	25
ELECTIRC FENCE	220
Electric Fence Charger	211
Emergency Stun Gun	212
enslaved	2

equipment 12, 15, 17, 29, 40, 53, 76, 80, 113, 155, 156, 157, 162, 163, 174, 177, 185, 190, 195, 196, 210, 213, 239, 243

Escape	264
EUROPE	71
evacuation	37
Evasion	264
explosive	114
extra territorium	8

F

Far East	141
felony	8

firearms 12, 58, 218, 229, 230, 231, 233
fired 18, 52, 54, 57, 58, 63, 65, 72, 78, 83, 88, 104, 110, 113, 174, 206, 209, 211, 221, 226, 249
fishermen 40, 51, 75, 84, 106, 113, 140, 165, 169, 178
fishing boat 18, 29, 40, 41, 51, 52, 53, 54, 62, 69, 79, 96, 103, 104, 112, 121, 123, 173, 201

Flame Thrower	213
flank	99

flare 52, 65, 76, 124, 127, 182, 211, 213

Food	96
Frankish	2

French 21, 50, 57, 72, 74, 75, 76, 77, 78, 84, 86, 87, 91, 96, 98, 107, 108, 109, 169

FRENCH, GUIANA	37

frequencies 48, 86, 87, 97, 116, 172, 190, 196, 242

G

Galapagos	27, 28, 29
Gaul	2
Gelasa Strait	140
German	57, 72, 78, 86, 90, 91, 98
Ghana	137
glance	149

government 2, 4, 5, 86, 89, 131, 138, 141, 264

Greece	3, 103
Greeks	1
Grenada	50, 138
Grenadines	22, 138
Guadeloupe	138
Guanaja	19

guard 24, 41, 42, 43, 109, 161, 163, 165, 178, 195, 201, 246, 252, 255, 259

Guatemala	25, 26, 27
Guayraca	33
guerrilla tactic	2

Gulf of Aden 5, 73, 74, 84, 85, 86, 89, 90, 93, 94, 95, 97, 110, 137, 168, 169, 183

Gulf of Thailand	140
Gulf States	77, 93

gun 15, 19, 42, 45, 47, 56, 58, 60, 63, 64, 68, 107, 121, 122, 124, 125, 126, 127, 179, 180, 182, 183, 186, 209, 210, 211, 212, 213, 224, 226, 229, 233, 243, 246, 252

Gun Powder	212
gunmen	57, 60, 65, 77, 93
gunpoint	103, 126
Gunpoint	60

H

Haida	3
Hand cuffs	210
hand-grenades	93
harbor	35, 55, 62, 103, 104, 113, 123, 126, 129, 130, 256
Henry VIII	8
HIDDEN COMPARTMENTS	216
High Pressure Fire Pump and Hose	213
HIGH PRESSURE WATER PUMP	222
high seas	7, 8, 9, 133, 230
Honduras	19, 25, 36, 138
Hong Kong	141
HOPE	260
hostage	6, 60, 75, 85, 90, 252, 253, 254, 255, 256, 257, 258, 259, 260, 262, 264
Human Shield	256

I

ICC Commercial Crime Services	140, 141, 142
icc-ccs.org	11, 111
illegal immigration	112
IMB Piracy Reporting Centre	110, 111, 164
India	111, 112, 142
Indian Coast	4
INDIAN SUB CONTINENT	141
India's	111
Indonesia	120, 121, 128, 140
information	i, 5, 6, 7, 10, 11, 12, 13, 14, 15, 27, 35, 58, 59, 60, 62, 69, 85, 87, 91, 103, 109, 111, 118, 131, 132, 134, 135, 139, 140, 141, 142, 145, 147, 154, 160, 163, 164, 168, 170, 171, 173, 187, 195, 196, 212, 230, 237, 238, 240, 252, 253, 254, 256, 259
Initial phase	258
intermediate phase	258
international	5, 7, 86, 89, 95, 96, 97, 98, 136, 230
International law	7
International Maritime Bureau	9, 61
Iran	142
Iraq	100, 142
Island	1, 64, 109, 120, 121, 140
Italians	86

J

Jamaica	18, 19, 138
Japan	4
Johannesburg	137

K

kalashnikov	79
Kama	3
Kandla	140
Kanniyakumari	111, 112, 113
Kantang	74, 169
Kenya	92, 137
ketch	89, 93
kidnapped	1, 6, 77, 140
Kidnapping	6, 256
knives	29, 38, 65, 68, 80, 84, 108, 124, 125, 129
Kota Kinabalu	120
Kourou	37

L

Lae Papua	123
Lake Izabal	25
Las Qoray	92
Law of the Sea	8, 133, 229
Lemnos	1
Liberia	137

lighted	11, 161, 166, 180	Mobile Maritime Net	114
LIGHTING	219	**MODIFICATIONS**	216
Line Throwing Gun	210	**Mongla Anchorage**	140
llanchita	51, 52, 54	**MONOTORS**	218
locks	129, 181, 204, 209, 217	MONSERRAT,	37
Long-term phase	258	Montego Bay	19
Lord High Admiral	8	**Morocco**	137
		Moskito Coast	24
		MOTION DETECTOR	220
		Mozambique	85, 136, 137
		MSPA,	95, *See* Marine Security Patrol

M

machete	25, 58, 126, 129, 130
machetes	12, 26, 64, 129, 240
Madagascar	106, 107, 110, 136, 137
Madang	123, 124, 125, 129, 130
Malaita	125
Malaysia	98, 111, 120, 128, 140, 164
Malgash	108
Manila Bay	140
Maniots	3
Margarita	46, 49, 58, 60, 61, 64
Marina	26, 57, 58, 68, 76, 77
Marine Association	139
Maritime Security Patrol	94
Marmara	2
Martinique	50, 138
MARTINIQUE	37
master	88
Mayday	48, 74, 82, 86, 98, 116, 124, 169
MCCM Non-lethal Claymore	210
men	4, 18, 19, 21, 24, 25, 26, 27, 29, 38, 41, 45, 46, 47, 49, 51, 52, 53, 54, 58, 60, 61, 63, 67, 68, 69, 72, 78, 79, 80, 81, 84, 91, 96, 103, 104, 115, 124, 126, 128, 129, 147, 184, 190, 194, 245, 262
Messina	102, 103, 104
methods	5, 7, 23, 177
middle ages	2
militant	17
militants	91, 141
mines	93

N

Narentines	3
naval	2, 74, 84, 87, 96, 169
Neretva	3
Nevis	138
New Caledonia	125
New Caledonian	124
New Guinea	123, 125, 129, 130, 141
Nicaragua	24, 25
Nigeria	136, 137
nightstick	25
Nishtun	75, 169
NLBHG Non-lethal Bursting Hand Grenade	209
noonsite	i, 10, 13, 69, 92, 94, 132, 142, 177
North Africa	4
Novgorodian	3

O

Occupation	4
Ocean Cruising	29
Oman	80, 85, 86, 114, 117, 142, 164
open water	12, 147
outboard	18, 25, 45, 47, 51, 57, 62, 63, 80, 115, 121, 122, 156, 173, 204, 240

P

Panama	25, 27, 28, 29, 31, 138
Parts	213
Passage	128
PASSAGE PLANNING	237
Pepper Munitions	209
Pepper Spray	209
PETIT	37
PFDs	34
Philippines	140
Phillip Channel	140
Phoenicians	1

piracy   i, 1, 2, 3, 4, 5, 7, 8, 9, 11, 14, 17, 19, 31, 35, 49, 71, 73, 81, 83, 89, 90, 95, 97, 106, 110, 111, 112, 114, 115, 116, 117, 131, 133, 135, 138, 139, 140, 141, 142, 153, 154, 155, 157, 158, 160, 161, 164, 175, 193, 195, 202, 219, 234, 237, 241

Piracy Reports   18, 19, 21, 23, 24, 25, 26, 27, 28, 29, 49, 50, 55, 58, 59, 60, 61, 62, 63, 64, 67, 68, 72, 74, 81, 85, 88, 89, 90, 92, 94, 96, 102, 104, 107, 111, 114, 120, 123, 125, 128, 129, 159

Pirates   iii, 2, 3, 4, 5, 6, 8, 23, 45, 62, 90, 92, 94, 96, 97, 111, 125, 145, 146, 148, 164, 177, 239

pirogue	46, 47, 62, 63, 76
pistol	25, 45, 47, 103, 186, 227, 233, 249
police	5, 14, 19, 24, 25, 35, 40, 41, 42, 43, 58, 68, 71, 76, 80, 92, 104, 111, 112, 113, 114, 117, 126, 127, 128, 130, 149, 201
policemen	40, 41
Porlamar	55, 57, 58, 59, 61, 64
Port Antonio	19
Port Bintulu	120, 123
Port Moresby	127, 128
Port of Salalah	74, 169
ports	77, 93, 111, 132, 140, 154, 164, 217
poverty	15, 17, 73, 109, 131, 137, 140, 155
PREDATOR	199
PREY	199
Puerto la Cruz	45
Puerto Santos	51, 55, 63
Pulau Ungar	128, 129
Punta Hermosa	32, 33, 36
Punta Mejillones	51
Punta Pargo	50, 51, 53, 54
Puntland authorities	92

R

radar   7, 25, 28, 30, 63, 80, 82, 83, 95, 105, 183, 194, 195, 205, 238, 239, 242, 243

radar reflectors	242

radio 7, 26, 27, 30, 47, 48, 57, 63, 74, 79, 83, 86, 87, 88, 89, 97, 99, 100, 105, 116, 128, 136, 169, 170, 171, 187, 190, 194, 197, 238, 242, 243

raiding	2, 3
Ransom	90, 264

Red Sea   74, 84, 87, 89, 100, 104, 110, 117, 169

Reggio di Calabria	103, 104
rifle	18, 62, 65, 99, 116, 206, 227, 248
Rio de Janeiro	69
Rio Dulce	25, 26
Rivers	3
Robbed	19, 79
Rocella Ionica	103
rocket propelled grenade	93
ROYAL PASCADERAS	98, 99, 100

S

Safe Room	211
safetyandsecuritynet	11, 50

Sailing Yachts	85
Sailmail	85, 107, 109
sailors	i, 61, 76, 90, 106, 164, 211, 221
Salalah	80, 85, 96, 114, 117, 164
Saline Joniche	103, 104
Santa Cruz	81
Sao Luis	68
Saxon	2
Scandinavian	3, 29
Scots	3
security	11, 14, 50, 59, 60, 64, 71, 72, 77, 78, 88, 92, 96, 109, 117, 118, 124, 130, 139, 140, 145, 153, 154, 155, 156, 160, 161, 162, 163, 165, 166, 175, 177, 179, 182, 195, 200, 201, 202, 204, 216, 218, 219, 220, 266, 285
SECURITY BARS	221
Security Cameras	212
Security Corridor	94
Security protocol level one	155
Security protocol level three	155
Seychelles	75, 110, 136, 142
ship	6, 9, 30, 68, 74, 75, 76, 81, 89, 98, 105, 110, 116, 132, 133, 134, 140, 141, 169, 170, 172, 190, 196, 229, 230
shot	42, 49, 50, 52, 53, 54, 57, 58, 59, 61, 65, 76, 98, 99, 107, 115, 124, 127, 186, 206, 226, 227, 266
Sierra Leone	137
Simonstown	37
Singapore Strait	140
skipper	45, 49, 76, 125, 126, 221
SMOKE	221
Solomon Islands	124, 125
Somali Press	90, 91
Somalia	73, 75, 79, 81, 88, 90, 91, 92, 93, 94, 95, 96, 110, 111, 125, 136, 137
SOUTH AFRICA	37
South China Sea	141

Spanish	4, 17, 19, 24, 34, 40, 46, 51, 54, 58, 59, 63, 84, 169
special forces	75
SPOTLIGHTS	219
Sri Lanka	104, 106, 141
St Kitts	138
St Lucia	21, 138
St Vincent	18, 138
ST VINCENT	37
St. Marten	138
St. Thomas	18
State Department	114, 118, 142
Stockholm syndrome	258
Strait of Malacca	5
stress	10, 151, 233, 234, 239, 254, 257, 258, 261
Sunda Strait	140
survival	114, 135, 146, 150, 199, 246, 252, 253, 254, 258, 259, 261, 267
Suspicious activity	12

T

Tacks	211
Tanimbar Islands	128, 129
Tanzania, Togo	137
target	5, 99, 117, 149, 163, 195, 200, 201, 204, 209, 226, 227
Taser	209
techniques	168, 261
terrified	74, 97, 127, 169, 252
Thailand	74, 104, 105, 140, 164, 169
The Venezuelan National Rescue and Maritime Safety Organization	139
thousand yard stare	148
Thracian	1
threat	2, 12, 81, 96, 100, 133, 145, 146, 148, 164, 165, 188, 200, 205, 241, 262
threatening	12, 35, 65, 136, 199, 225, 233, 234

Tlingit	3
TOBAGO CAYS	37
tolerant	261
travel.state.gov	10, 118
Trinidad	36, 37, 46, 48, 49, 50, 51, 53, 55, 63, 138, 139
TRINIDAD	37
Tuticorin	112, 140
twenty talents	2

U

UAE	142
UNCLOS	8, 133
UNDERWAY	204
United Kingdom	142
United Nations	8, 133, 136
United States	14, 15, 26, 27, 71, 161, 169, 229
universal jurisdiction	7, 8
US Citizens	117
US Embassy	114, 117
US Navy	86, 89, 96, 98, 110
US Virgin Islands	138
Ushkuiniks	3
Uskoks	4
USS Gonzalez	88, 89, 96

V

valuables	50, 65, 72, 78, 84, 103, 125, 146, 156, 178, 180, 203
Venezuela	36, 45, 46, 48, 49, 50, 54, 55, 58, 59, 60, 61, 62, 63, 64, 69, 76, 138
VENEZUELA	45
vessel	8, 9, 11, 13, 18, 21, 26, 27, 28, 29, 30, 32, 33, 38, 41, 43, 48, 49, 51, 59, 62, 71, 74, 75, 77, 81, 82, 83, 84, 86, 87, 88, 89, 92, 93, 96, 103, 104, 105, 106, 141, 145, 146, 147, 148, 154, 155, 156, 161, 162, 163, 166, 167, 169, 171, 172, 173, 174, 177, 178, 179, 180, 182, 183, 184, 186, 187, 188, 190, 194, 195, 197, 200, 201, 202, 203, 204, 205, 206, 212, 213, 216, 217, 218, 219, 221, 222, 226, 228, 229, 230, 231, 234, 238, 239, 240, 241, 242, 252, 254, 255, 285
vessels	5, 7, 13, 15, 29, 30, 46, 49, 85, 86, 87, 93, 94, 95, 96, 100, 103, 105, 106, 110, 111, 117, 118, 124, 131, 135, 136, 140, 145, 146, 148, 152, 156, 161, 163, 168, 170, 171, 172, 173, 174, 181, 188, 190, 195, 196, 205, 210, 217, 219, 238, 240, 241, 242
VHF	18, 25, 26, 29, 34, 38, 47, 50, 52, 57, 59, 63, 68, 77, 81, 82, 83, 84, 86, 96, 97, 98, 116, 190, 196
victim	74, 88, 110, 158, 169
Vikings	2, 3
violence	8, 49, 76, 108, 133, 146, 147, 151, 173
Volga	3

W

watch	17, 29, 87, 95, 105, 108, 126, 147, 148, 149, 151, 152, 154, 155, 156, 157, 160, 161, 165, 167, 171, 174, 179, 180, 181, 183, 187, 195, 203, 218, 247, 254, 265
Waypoint	93, 94
Welsh	3
Wewak	125, 127
*William Mauri*ce	3
Wokou	4
wounds	55, 68, 109, 166, 253

X

XREP 209

Y

yacht i, 21, 27, 28, 29, 31, 45, 49, 50, 51, 59, 60, 61, 62, 63, 65, 67, 68, 71, 72, 76, 77, 78, 79, 82, 84, 89, 90, 93, 98, 99, 100, 103, 106, 107, 124, 127, 128, 164

Yarngurral 129

Yemen 73, 74, 75, 81, 84, 85, 86, 89, 92, 94, 97, 99, 114, 115, 116, 117, 118, 164, 169, 170

Yemen Navy 114

Yemeni Coast 86

ABOUT THE AUTHOR

Capt Pierce, at a young age fell in love with the ocean, as a result started sailing and scuba. After school he entered the Marine Corp. While in the Marines was trained in many skills including security and anti-terrorism assault along with many other specialties. He also assisted in the development and training of one of the first anti-terrorism assault teams on the west coast. During this time was asked to volunteer for a special operation with Naval Intelligence which resulted in his records being sealed and his transfer home for his protection. After a brief break in his service and at the start of operations in Beirut. He requested the too be reassigned at which time he was sent to 2nd Marine Division where he requested assignment to the 8th Marines.

After the Marine Corp he joined the Merchant Marines becoming a captain where he worked in cargo transport operations. During this time he also continued working with recreational vessels, he owned a vessel delivery company which allowed him to make trips too and from the Bahamas, Caribbean, Central and south America on a regular basis. Making an attempt at the "Single-Handed Around the World Sailboat Race" in the mid 1990's, he loved being out on the ocean traveling. Over the years, has had several close calls with both drug runners, and pirates, in both commercial as well as private owned vessels.

When encountering these situations he would apply his training and knowledge gained from his training as well as previous experiences. While working under contract with a major oil company in another country, and seeing the devastating results of attacks: a commercial vessel attacked its crew beaten and tied up. And the vessel stripped of practically everything. And a husband and wife sailing on vacation, their bodies never found and vessel stripped. During this time his vessel dealing with several attacks and confrontations with the local pirates, including one very serious encounter.

The company noticed his success in repelling attacks in the area and asked him to write the company policy too deal with pirate attacks on vessels under contract in the area. Capt Pierce established the policies for the company which drastically reduced losses and danger too the crews by prevent the success of the pirates.

With the increase in piracy around the world and the loss of life of unsuspecting mariners Capt Pierce has decided to share his knowledge of vessel security involving piracy. With the hopes of aiding other boat captains in preventing the escalation and successes of these violent attacks. By introducing a procedure that others can build on in research of attacks and policies that can be established onboard your vessel, you can reduce the danger to your boat as well as those onboard.

PIRACY SURVIVAL GUIDE

www.ingramcontent.com/pod-product-compliance
Lightning Source LLC
Chambersburg PA
CBHW071659160426
43195CB00012B/1515